TEXTBOOKS AND THE AMERICAN INDIAN

by the

American Indian Historical Society

RUPERT COSTO, editor

JEANNETTE HENRY, writer

Library of Congress Catalog Card Number: 75-119022
Printed in the United States of America

THE INDIAN HISTORIAN PRESS, INC.

AMERICAN INDIAN EDUCATIONAL PUBLISHERS

"HOW BIG A DOSE OF TRUTH CAN MAN ENDURE?"

Nietzsche

Contents

I

The Background

Following European colonization, American Indians were engaged for more than three hundred years in a life and death struggle to protect their lives, their homes, and their lands. When the long struggle had finally ended, and the Tribes had withdrawn into a special insularity of their own in order to preserve the remnants of their culture, the federal government began to send the Indian youth away to school. The idea was to "assimilate" the Native into American life, to destroy Indian culture and lifeways, to fashion him in the likeness of the white man. To some extent this was successful, and some Natives blended into the white homogenized society.

However, this victory, like the victory on the battlefield, served only to subdue the Native, not to vanquish him. Indian traditions and customs still exist. The Native still lives on his own land, however poorly. One day the Indian awoke to the fact that the youth of this country, including his own sons and daughters, were learning some strange things about the First Americans. Searching the record, he read some horrifying distortions about himself, his history, and his culture. The distortions appeared in books which young people were made to study as part of their education. However, hemmed in as they were into reservations, held in the vise of federal autocracy, the people could do nothing to correct this.

Early in the present century many groups of Indian people began to pay heed to this process of falsification, which affected their children as well as those of the white man. It was then that an Indian organization known as the Grand Council Fire of American Indians addressed a

1

Memorial to the Mayor of the City of Chicago. Their historic words
are an inspiration to the Native peoples of America. Here is the full
text of their Memorial:

> *Memorial and Recommendations of the Grand Council Fire*
> *of American Indians presented to the Hon. William Hale*
> *Thompson, mayor of Chicago, December 1, 1927.*

TO THE MAYOR OF CHICAGO:—

You tell all white men "America First." We believe in that. We are
the only ones, truly, that are 100 percent. We therefore ask you while
you are teaching school children about America First, teach them truth
about the First Americans.

We do not know if school histories are pro-British, but we do know
that they are unjust to the life of our people—the American Indian.
They call all white victories, battles, and all Indian victories, massacres.
The battle with Custer has been taught to school children as a fearful
massacre on our part. We ask that this, as well as other incidents, be told
fairly. If the Custer battle was a massacre, what was Wounded Knee?

History books teach that Indians were murderers—is it murder to
fight in self-defense? Indians killed white men because white men took
their lands, ruined their hunting grounds, burned their forests, destroyed their buffalo. White men penned our people on reservations,
then took away the reservations. White men who rise to protect their
property are called patriots—Indians who do the same are called murderers.

White men call Indians treacherous—but no mention is made of
broken treaties on the part of the white man. White men say that Indians were always fighting. It was only our lack of skill in white man's
warfare that led to our defeat. An Indian mother prayed that her boy
be a great medicine man rather than a great warrior. It is true that we
had our own small battles, but in the main we were peace-loving and
home-loving.

White men called Indians thieves—and yet we lived in frail skin
lodges and needed no locks or iron bars. White men call Indians savages. What is civilization? Its marks are a noble religion and philosophy,
original arts, stirring music, rich story and legend. We had these. Then
we were not savages, but a civilized race.

We made blankets that were beautiful that the white man with all
his machinery has never been able to duplicate. We made baskets that

were beautiful. We wove in beads and colored quills, designs that were not just decorative motifs, but were the outward expression of our very thoughts. We made pottery—pottery that was useful and beautiful as well. Why not make school children acquainted with the beautiful handicrafts in which we were skilled? Put in every school Indian blankets, baskets, pottery.

We sang songs that carried in their melodies all the sounds of nature —the running of waters, the sighing of winds, and the calls of the animals. Teach these to your children that they may come to love nature as we love it.

We had our statesmen—and their oratory has never been equalled. Teach the children some of these speeches of our people, remarkable for their brilliant oratory.

We played games—games that brought good health and sound bodies. Why not put these in your schools? We told stories. Why not teach school children more of the wholesome proverbs and legends of our people? Tell them how we loved all that was beautiful. That we killed game only for food, not for fun. Indians think white men who kill for fun are murderers.

Tell your children of the friendly acts of Indians to the white people who first settled here. Tell them of our leaders and heroes and their deeds. Tell them of Indians such as Black Partridge, Shabbona, and others who many times saved the people of Chicago at great danger to themselves. Put in your history books the Indian's part in the World War. Tell how the Indian fought for a country of which he was not a citizen, for a flag to which he had no claim, and for a people that have treated him unjustly.

The Indian has long been hurt by these unfair books. We ask only that our story be told in fairness. We do not ask you to overlook what we did, but we do ask you to understand it. A true program of America First will give a generous place to the culture and history of the American Indian.

We ask this, Chief, to keep sacred the memory of our people.

GRAND COUNCIL FIRE OF AMERICAN INDIANS

By Scott H. Peters, President
DELEGATES: George Peake *(Little Moose)*, Chippewa; Albert Lowe *(Little Eagle)*, Winnebago; Daniel St. Cyr. *(Flaming Arrow)*, Winnebago; A. Warren Cash *(Spotted Elk)*, Sioux; A. Roi *(Clear-*

water), Ottawa; Babe Begay, Navajo; Maimie Wiggins *(O-me-me),*
Chippewa.

Attached to the Memorial, was the following list in evidence
of the truth about the American Indian:

HISTORY BOOKS DO NOT TELL:—
    That tobacco, potatoes, corn, squash, pumpkins, melons, and beans
were raised by the Indians, who showed the colonists how to cultivate
them. That the Indians gave food to the suffering Virginia colonists,
and then were forced by Capt. John Smith, who marched upon their
village with armed forces, to give up more.
    That the Indians who attacked the Virginia colonists did so because
they were so anxious to establish huge plantations that they took more
and more land from the Indians without paying for it or asking permission.
    That the Indians helped the Pilgrims in many ways during the first
winter. That Squanto, an Indian, who was lured with four others upon
a trading vessel and carried off to England, upon his return was a true
friend to the Pilgrims, and showed them how to live in their new home,
and brought about friendly relations between them and the neighboring tribes. That King Philip tried his best to remain at peace with the
Pilgrims, and it was only after many acts of injustice that he took up
arms. That King Philip's tribe was completely exterminated, and his
wife and child sold as slaves in the Bermuda Islands, while he was
quartered and his head carried about on a pike.
    That until 1637 scalping was unknown among the New England In-
dians. The Puritans began by offering cash for the heads of their enemies, and later accepting scalps if both ears were attached. The French
were the first to offer bounties for the scalps of white people, with the
English quickly following suit, and such vast sums were expended that
scores of white men took up the lucrative business of hunting scalps.
    That the Indian was first of all a hunter, instead of a warrior, as his-
tory books state, for upon his ability in this direction depended his
living, and his early training and games were all designed to teach him
skill in hunting. That the Indian was skilled in arts, song, story telling
and oratory. That Pontiac fought because the English laid claim to all
the land belonging to his people, without regard or consideration for
them.
    That during the Revolutionary War the Oneidas steadfastly refused

to side with the British or join with the other Indians who were fighting for the English, but many times helped and protected the colonists, although they were attacked by both British and Indian forces for doing this. That during the Revolutionary War many so-called Indian massacres were committed by English soldiers dressed as Indians.

That the true reason for Tecumseh's uprising was that he protested against the unjust act (together with other injustices) of General Harrison, who called a council of a few tribes and by way of treaty got from them three million acres of land which they did not own, but which belonged to Tecumseh's tribe. Tecumseh's speech in reply to General Harrison presents his case clearly and fairly and should be taught to the children. That the Fort Dearborn massacre was a fair fight, and brought about because of broken promises on the part of the whites.

That Black Partridge demonstrated his friendship for the whites many times, and during the actual battle saved several of their lives— one in particular, Mrs. Helm. That Shabbona, through sheer oratory alone, prevented his tribe, the Potawatomies, from joining the Winnebagoes in their war, and also from helping Black Hawk, endangering his own life by his work. That Shabbona in 1832 rode throughout the State of Illinois warning settlers of the approach of Black Hawk and thus saving thousands of lives.

That the Black Hawk war was brought about because of the forcible removal of Black Hawk and his people from their lands and of the attack upon him and a small party of white soldiers when they were going peacefully to their homes. That the direct cause of the Sioux outbreak in the Dakotas, with the resultant Custer battle, was the broken treaties on the part of the United States government. That the Custer battle was a fair fight, with Custer marching upon the Indians, surprising them in their village, and striking the first blow. That at Wounded Knee Indian men, women and children were lined up, all weapons removed from them, and then slain by white soldiers—even fleeing mothers with their babies were pursued and bayoneted to death.

That the war with Chief Joseph was brought about because he refused to sell the lands that he and his tribe had owned for centuries and that had been given to him by treaty with the United States government. Upon his refusal to sell, he was set upon and was to be forcibly removed. That Chief Joseph led his band of 300 warriors, together with women and children, sick and aged, on a remarkable retreat that lasted 75 days and that covered 1,300 miles—through Rocky Mountain country, and with fighting all the way, attacked in turn by Generals Howard,

Gibbon, and Sturgis, and finally General Miles.

That Joseph's people took no scalps in this memorable fight and waged no war on the white soldiers whom they encountered. His speeches made upon various occasions are some of the most remarkable ever made and should be read in every public school. When the Government violated its promise to Joseph to return him to his own country when he had ceased fighting, he then made his impassioned plea for justice, which through its sheer oratory earned for him the victory—it aroused the American people, and Joseph and his tribe were returned to their homes. Joseph is pronounced by military authorities to be one of the finest natural military leaders America has ever produced.

That Osceola arose against the whites because of the impending removal of his tribes from their home in Florida simply because the whites desired the land. That Sacajawea, the young Shoshone girl, with her baby on her back, guided the Lewis and Clark expedition through wild and mountainous country and among enemy tribes, acting as interpreter, and everywhere establishing friendly relations between the whites and hostile Indians. Without her aid undoubtedly the exploring of this vast territory would have been held back many years.

. That many Indians, such as Sitting Bull, Logan, Red Cloud, Geronimo, Crazy Horse, Gall, and others, who have always been presented as treacherous and warlike men, if their true stories were told, were patriots and fully justified in their actions. That many Indians, such as Hole-in-the-Day, Seattle, Pushmataha, Spotted Tail, Quanah Parker, and others, were always friends to the whites and helped them many times. Could not one chapter be devoted to mentioning the names of those who were friends to the palefaces?

On May 11, 1928, the Memorial was printed in the Congressional Record, upon motion by Senator Frazier.

Nearly forty years after this first official action of the Indian people protesting the distortions and inaccuracies of the school books, Indian efforts to correct them were continuing. On August 19, 1965, the American Indian Historical Society, an All-Indian organization of scholars and Native historians, appeared before the California State Curriculum Commission to present its views on books then being submitted for adoption by the State. The Society's representatives at that time were: Rupert Costo, a Cahuilla Indian, president of the Society; Al Hicks, a Navajo; Jeannette Henry, a Cherokee, editor of The Indian Historian; and Martina Costo, Cahuilla, a fourth grade schoolteacher. The representatives stated in part:

We have studied many textbooks now in use, as well as those being submitted today. Our examination discloses that not one book is free from error as to the role of the Indian in state and national history. We Indians believe everyone has the right to his opinion. A person also has the right to be wrong. But a textbook has no right to be wrong, or to lie, hide the truth, or falsify history, or insult and malign a whole race of people. That is what these textbooks do. At best, these books are extremely superficial in their treatment of the American Indian, over-simplifying and generalizing the explanation of our culture and history, to the extent where the physical outlines of the Indian as a human being are lost. Misinformation, misinterpretation, and misconception—all are found in most of the textbooks. A true picture of the American Indian is entirely lacking.

The textbooks say that life at the Spanish missions was like a school for the Indians, that they were well treated and had their rights. But Hubert Howe Bancroft, the historian, says: "The Indians were set to work on the plantations; not severely, for friar rule was tempered by religion; but without any incentive or hopes beyond that of a slave, and maintained in a political condition of ignorance and abjection." According to Robert Glass Cleland, historian, "The habits of the priests, and the avarice of the military rulers of the territory, soon converted these missions into instruments of oppression and slavery of the Indian people." Who is lying? We Indians know too well that it is the textbooks that are lying.

The textbooks describe the gold rush as a progressive and adventurous period in American history. But Bancroft the historian says, "California was overrun by the dregs of the world's society." And Cleland adds, "Deserters, desperadoes, professional gamblers, undesirables from the States, men who deliberately shed their moral standards as they left civilization behind, criminals and outlaws from Mexico and other Hispanic American countries, the riff-raff of Europe and Asia—all those helped to make up the later mining population." These facts do not appear in the textbooks. Instead, the Indian is made to appear as a subhuman being, whose lands were taken in the name of progress. This, most clearly, is a falsification of history.

Following this presentation before the Curriculum Commission, there arose an outcry in the State of California. On the one hand, certain descendants of gold miners protested because the Indian Historical Society stated that the miners criminally stole Indian lands, attempted extermination of the Natives, destroyed vast amounts of Indian food stores as well as the homes of the people, and in general blackened the record of humanity as a whole and that of America in particular. Another protest arose from a few of the Catholic clergy, who resented having the Spanish missions described as forced labor camps. Nevertheless, the demand mounted that the books be cleaned up.

The Indian Historical Society presented a Criteria for the adoption of books in history and social sciences as they deal with the American Indian. The Criteria were tabled by the State Curriculum Commission, and were then assigned to the Statewide Social Sciences Study Committee for "further consideration." Fully a year later, the Committee made its report, stating, ". . . informational support of the kind that the American Indian Historical Society has provided to the Committee is much appreciated by the Committee . . ." To this date, the Criteria had not been adopted; the books continue to contain the same errors of fact, and to commit the same distortions of history as heretofore.

However, the textbook correction program opened up the whole tragic state of affairs concerning education ABOUT the Native people of this country. It also brought to light certain hard facts concerning the education OF the Indian youth. A new movement began to take shape nationwide. The California Indian Education Association was formed shortly thereafter, the first in the country. In Minnesota, a group of Indian people protested the use of a state history book which degraded the Native people, and succeeded in having it removed. Incredibly, the American Civil Liberties Union resisted the removal of the book on grounds of "freedom of speech."

Slowly, the falsification of Indian history by way of the textbooks is becoming a national issue. Classroom teachers all over this country have written to the Indian Historical Society calling attention to books which distort American history. Average Americans ask for books which either could replace or supplement existing textbooks. At this writing, not less than one hundred such letters come to the offices of the American Indian Historical Society every week.

Despite the growing clamor demanding that the textbooks be corrected, it is utterly disheartening to note that very little change has come about. The new books still contain gross inaccuracies, distortions of history, and misconceptions as to the role of the Indian in the story of our country. New and more sophisticated methods of teaching have been introduced, that is true. But despite these new approaches (conceptual, multi-ethnic, discovery, inquiry, etc.) the basic content of instructional materials about the American Indian continues to be inaccurate and distorted. The situation has not changed.

In testimony given before the Senate Committee on Indian Education (January 4, 1969, San Francisco Hearings), the Society stated: "There is not one Indian in this country who does not cringe in anguish and frustration because of these textbooks. There is not one Indian child who has not come home in shame and tears after one of those sessions in which he is taught that his people were dirty, animal-like, something less than human beings. We Indians are not just one more complaining minority. We are the proud and only true Natives of this land."

As a direct result of the failure of the publishers, educational writers, and school administrators to provide accurate classroom instructional materials, an independent Indian publishing house has been formed. The Indian Historian Press, Inc. (American Indian Educational Publishers) has begun to publish books about the Native Americans, written by Indian scholars, and offered to the educational community as well as to the general public.

TEXTBOOKS AND THE AMERICAN INDIAN is a preliminary statement in this publishing program. The American Indian, as scholar and historian, is confronted with the task of correcting written history. Books used in the schools, television, as well as newspapers, magazines, and radio, have so misinterpreted American history as to the role of the Indian that nothing short of a complete re-write will correct the record. Oddly enough, there is an enormous quantity of authentic source material. No people have been so researched, investigated, and examined from every aspect of their culture and lifeways, as have the Indians. Yet, few if any textbook writers take advantage of these sources; nor is there any evidence that they have studied them or are even familiar with them.

Four years ago, the Indian Historical Society stated in a report on education: "What is needed, and quickly, is a massive program to provide new materials of instruction, new curricula, a whole set of new values which take into consideration the original owners and the First Americans of this land, as an integral part of our history.

In Minnesota, a group of Indians have prepared instructional materials kits, including written documents, films, and examples of Indian crafts and material culture. In Santa Fe, New Mexico, Mr. Louis Ballard, distinguished Indian composer and educator, has formed an All-Indian film company, to produce motion pictures by and about Native Americans. In many parts of this nation, Indian students and scholars are meeting and planning to correct the situation whereby history is falsified so that the Native receives still another type of injustice.

The textbook correction program is a fight for truth. The struggle for historic justice cannot help but be victorious. All young Americans will benefit, learning to become men and women with a broad understanding of Man, in his progress towards the Good Society. This is an ideal which holds more promise for life's values than has been the case with the so-called "Great Society."

II

Let the People In

These evaluations are the work of thirty-two Indian scholars, native historians, and Indian students. More than three hundred books were examined in the course of this Study. Not one could be approved as a dependable source of knowledge about the history and culture of the Indian people in America. Most of the books were, in one way or another, derogatory to the Native Americans. Most contained misinformation, distortions, or omissions of important history.

All these books are currently being used in the schools of this country. Some of the older ones have given way to others which are just as bad. All of those listed as texts of the Bureau of Indian Affairs were in use for teaching Indian students at the date of this printing. None have been retired by the publishers. A textbook is an instrument of learning, which may be compared to an automobile as an instrument of transportation. An automobile which has defective brakes or is otherwise not dependable, is recalled by the manufacturer, so that lives may not be endangered. But a textbook which is defective, inaccurate, and unreliable, is not retired despite the possibility that minds may be endangered.

There is a difference between a book for general readership, and one accepted for classroom use. In the first case, the individual has a choice, and this choice we must protect. It is part of our freedom. The student, on the other hand, has no choice; he is compelled to study from an approved book. In this case, we have a right to insist upon truth, accuracy, and objectivity.

Someone, or some agency, finally makes the choice on the basis of which textbooks are placed in the classroom for the use of students. How and by what standards should such choices be made? As to the role of the American Indian in the story of our country, the Indian Historical Society submits Criteria for approval or disapproval of the books, as part of this Study. The mechanics for evaluating and adopting the books is another vital matter. It is most essential that informed Indian people be brought into the process of evaluating and helping to decide upon textbooks, as they relate their history and culture. Indeed if this is done, the quality and amount of instructional source material will vastly improve. Indian scholars and students, parents and teachers, have been too long ignored in the educational process.

This Study has been limited to books utilized in primary grades through high school. The study of college texts is for a later time. But the same Criteria may be applied in this field as well. Methods of evaluation have included written critiques, replies to prepared questionnaires, discussions in small groups on various questions of tribal history, consultations with scholars both Indian and nonIndian who have certain expertise, together with a careful reading of each textbook and an evaluation of each one by at least two readers.

TEXTBOOKS AND THE AMERICAN INDIAN is the collective work of many Indian people; some are scholars in professional and academic life; some are Native Indian historians who know their history and speak their languages; others are experts in some aspect of Indian culture and history. Basic source materials which have stood the test of time and the approval of the Natives on the basis of whose information the materials were gathered in the first place, have been utilized. More recent theories, research, and data have been examined, critically studied, and made available in the course of evaluation.

The work which has resulted in this study was begun four years ago with a committee established by the American Indian Historical Society, comprised of these Indian people: Rupert Costo, Edmund Jackson, Richard Fuller, Bertha Stewart, Wallace Newman, Jane Penn, Marie Potts, Jeannette Henry, John Porter, Viola Fuller Wessell, Henry Azbill and Robert Kaniatobi. Shortly thereafter, the preliminary work having been accomplished, a permanent committee was established composed of these Indian people: Rupert Costo, Edmund Jackson, Rosalie Nichols, Jeannette Henry, Philip Galvan, P. Michael Galvan, Leatrice Mikkelsen, and Henry Azbill. This committee from time to time had the support of such Indian people as Lottie Beck, John Stands in Timber and Martina Costo. A young Indian student, Andy Galvan, then aged eleven, was an active participant. One member of the committee is 18 years of age, a college Junior; another is 32, a postgraduate student in history at a university. Meetings were held with tribes and tribal representatives, and eleven resolutions of endorsement in the textbook correction program were received in this way. There was no time to pursue this part of the program further. There seemed no possible doubt but that the entire Indian population was behind it. NonIndian teachers, students and interested experts participated as readers and consultants. Altogether, eleven schoolteachers in primary and high school levels participated.

No program of this type can be successful without the Indian people themselves being an active part of the whole. Let the people in, and they will provide the enthusiasm which is needed in order to make a program of Native studies the success that it deserves to be. Let the people in, and they will dig into their distant past and come up with knowledge, sources, and information which will bring to brilliant life the whole story of our country, from its Native beginnings. Eliminate the stark and stony phrase "Resource Person," as well as its frigid and uncreative type of participation, and make the People a basic part of the process of planning, organization, evaluation and approval. Education as a whole will benefit. Most particularly will the young student benefit. Recognize the authority and the expertise of the Indian leader, the Indian scholar. Let him help. The textbooks must be cleaned up, and if we let the people in, it can be done.

III

The General Criteria

In order to judge a particular text, these general Criteria must be adapted to the specific curriculum in which the book is to be used. The general standards of judgment here described are valid for elementary through high school instructional materials, particularly in American history.

Textbooks and instructional materials utilizing advanced methodology are just as much subject to these Criteria as are the more conservative types, which utilize the narrative approach. Books utilizing the "Discovery, Inquiry, Multi-Ethnic, Multi-Media, Conceptual" approaches have been evaluated, and have been found wanting in practically the same way as the more conservative books. The precise manner of their failure is perhaps more sophisticated. But, so far as the role of the American Indian in the history of this country is concerned, they are failures just the same. However, with these newer methods, the teacher has a better opportunity to correct the failures. All that is needed, is a completely qualified teacher with an open mind, a high intellect, a capacity to absorb and impart knowledge, and accurate sources of information.

1. Is the history of the American Indian presented as an integral part of the history of America, at every point of this nation's development?

If the history and culture of the American Indian is not treated as an integral part of the story of America, the developmental aspects of the nation's culture, economy, technology, and history itself are lost. Certainly the development of this society cannot be studied or understood, if the environment in which the European newcomers found themselves is ignored. By environment, is meant not merely the geography of the land and its climate—but the Native peoples, their culture and social order.

The Indian was a crucial factor in early American history. Through the end of the 19th century, his status and problems, his relationship with the federal government, were of major concern in every aspect of the life of this country. The books should deal with these factors, not in a fragmented way, but as a living part of the American story.

The fact is, furthermore, that this land was the Land of the American Indian. The Indian is the only Native of this country. Politically, his relationship with this government is still a matter of special concern. To ignore the development of such a living part of America, the ORIGINAL part of America, is to falsify our National history. American history must be treated as a whole, a fully integrated subject, considering origins, participants, and contributors, including all the myriad peoples who added to the growth of this country.

2. Does the text explain that the first discoverers of America were those Native peoples whom Columbus described improperly as "Indians?"

Most textbooks begin American history with European immigration, colonization, and culture, opening the panorama of American discovery with Columbus. All these approaches are incorrect. America was already a land in possession of a well developed race of men, at the time of European contact. These people occupied the continents of North and South America and the islands along the coasts. The book should state this clearly, as a fact and not a supposition. The discovery of this continent was one of the most exciting and important steps in man's development upon the earth, and first credit should go to those who accomplished this. As a further fact, it is not necessarily true that the discovery of this continent by the Native was an accident. Native discovery was the result of man's slow and painful rise from a lower stage of society to a higher, from simple technology to more complex ways of living, and because of an increasing contact between continents. Scientists are learning more about this event all the time, and it is a safe prediction that when the whole story is known, it will be recognized that early man on this continent was a true explorer who found a New World in which he could have peace and a good life.

Exploration was one of the great achievements of the Native once he had settled upon the land. The Indian trailblazers and pathfinders explored and knew every river, stream, mountain, canyon, grove and meadow in the land by the time the Europeans came. They knew the ocean shores, its currents as well as its smooth passages. This knowledge they gladly gave to the Europeans. No evidence exists of European exploration of America without the exploring party being accompanied by a so-called "Indian guide" who showed the way, protected the members of the party, made friends with the tribes they encountered so that they might proceed safely without danger of being accused of trespass, and brought them safely home. There are no monuments to THESE men, nor does history know their names or credit them with discovery.

3. Is the data contained in the text accurate?

A considerable amount of inaccurate data exists in the textbooks. Population figures before white contact vary from 800,000 to one million for the country as a whole. Recent scientific findings have increased population estimates measurably. Population estimates for California vary from 50,000 to 200,000. Recent figures give the population figure in California as at least 150,000, and as high as 250,000.

Such subjects as tribal entities and cultures, listings of current tribes and reservations, descriptions of languages and areas of occupation, foods, attire, dates of historical importance—are too often inaccurate.

In place of facts, generalizations are given. Such generalizations result in stereotypes, one of the most insidious and vicious forms of racial prejudice. Certainly the young student should be given the advantage of most recent scholarly findings. For example, the question of origin of the Indians upon this continent is handled without consideration of recent research. All books without exception "play it safe" and get the Native into this continent by way of the Bering Sea. Descriptions given of the first comers are almost ludicrous. The student receives a picture of primitive, subhuman beings trudging across "the bridge," low-browed, heavy-handed, stooped over like animals, dangling hair, dark and grimy faces, and usually with a spear in his hand.

Many recent findings indicate that Man first came to this continent in at least several ways, and from several directions—and not necessarily always on foot. The stage of human development in which man lived when he first arrived, must have been (according to descriptions in the textbooks), when Cro-Magnon man first emerged. This is, of course, false. According to Dr. Harold Driver *(Indians of North America,* p. 2), our present knowledge is "that man evolved from brute ancestry to Homo sapiens IN THE OLD WORLD and migrated to the New World only after he was a fully modern man." (Our emphasis.) Indeed Man was fully developed, with a social system and a distinct technology, by the time he discovered this continent.

4. Does the textbook faithfully describe the culture and lifeways of the American Indian at that time in history when the Europeans first came in contact with him?

Such terms as "primitive, degraded, filthy, warlike, savage" as used in the context of these books, are derogatory statements which demean the Native. They are taken from the diaries and imaginative stories told by white Europeans who had no knowledge of Indian manners and customs; by Jesuits who found no mention of the Native in the Bible and hence assumed him to be subhuman. Some books even mock the Indian with such descriptions as "why did they need water; they didn't wash much anyway." This is the semantics of racism. Describing the culture of the Iroquois, for example, modern writers still list atrocities which supposedly took place as ritual practices of these highly developed people. Torture, human sacrifice, and delight in war, are descriptions given of Iroquois customs by some historians and anthropologists, as well as by textbook writers. Not to understand the differences in culture and standards of conduct, displays the lack of an objective, scholarly mind. Describing Roman history, for example, few if any historians and textbook writers give blow by blow accounts of the many atrocities committed by this society. The Spanish Inquisition is not dealt with as a "delight in torture," but the thought and philosophy, the contributions of these people are indeed described with considerable detail. It would appear that the contributions of the Iroquois would far outweigh any "strange" accounts of their religious customs (which are usually not understood and highly exaggerated).

In this respect, it is apropos to quote a noted writer, who expressed this thought: "Unnatural affection, child-murder, father-murder, incest, a great deal of hereditary cursing, a double fratricide, and a violation of the sanctity of dead bodies—when one reads such a list of charges against any tribe or nation, either ancient or in modern times, one can hardly help concluding that somebody wanted to annex their land." (Gilbert Murray, "Greek Epic" in John Adams, "The Founding of New England," 1927, p. 8, 14, 15).

An accurate description of the Native upon white contact would avoid the uses of such words as "primitive," or "stone age people." If an era in the cultural and technological history of man is being described, then the new and more accurate scientific nomenclature should be utilized. The word "primitive" implies a society with little or no technology, whereas the American Indian made tools such as drills; he developed irrigation and sophisticated farming methods; he knew navigation through thousands of years of observation of the waters and their currents, the climate and the terrain. He knew botany, biology, the uses of medicinal herbs and plants. Because he had no writing, does not mean that he did not have knowledge. Painstakingly, with utmost care, this knowledge was given from one generation to the other, and became part of the vast knowledge of the land and its ways, a knowledge which was owned by the Native, and used with great efficiency.

5. Is the culture of the Indian described as a dynamic process, so that his social system and lifeways are seen as a developmental process, rather than a static one?

An error made by textbook writers, is the failure to consider the Indian American in a process of continuing change—a dynamic process in which the European with his different and more advanced technology played a great part. The fact that the Natives quickly adopted many of the manners, customs and technology of the white man are a part of history. These are facts which constitute a part of the great body of literature about the Natives. One need only mention the Cherokees, who had grist mills and other manufacturing enterprises, newspapers, published books including novels, established governments modeled after the United States but with far more democratic elements; all this was accomplished not too long after European colonization. Mention of the Choctaws, the Delawares, the Iroquois, should be made, among many others who were advancing at great speed toward sophisticated technology and a truly remarkable society in which the best of two cultures was retained and further developed.

6. Are the Contributions of the Indians to the Nation and the world described?

Generalizations describing Native culture include such descriptions as "simple economy, seed gatherers and hunters, collectors and teepee dwellers." By itself, this description is accurate, but it is inaccurate unless given in its full connotation. Such generalizations when describing the complete culture, lead to distortion, implying that the people were without technology, had no knowledge of tools, and lived in a primitive world in which man huddled in a cave. Dr. Harold Driver states, however: "In all of North America, a complete list of all species of fish, animals and plants utilized by the Indian total more than two thousand species; only an intelligence educated and trained through centuries of intense effort could have accomplished this . . ." That the Indian had domesticated plants is proved by the fact that he grew at least four varieties of corn, beans, squash, tapioca, potatoes. Beans are grown from seeds; tapioca and potatoes from cuttings.

A partial list of foods utilized by Indians of the west alone includes acorns, mushrooms (some 20 varieties), wild onions, celery, clover greens, mustard greens, wild plums and cherries, watercress, manzanita berries, elderberry, and many bulbs. Other foods included mountain lion, squirrel, deer, rabbit, quail, wildcat, coyote, bullsnake, striped watersnake, a variety of grasshoppers which are now an expensive delicacy, lizards, frogs, river mussels, turtles, salmon and other fish, and caviar. Dried foods included deer meat, mountain and valley quail, whitefish, salmon, trout, and vegetable greens. At least 17 varieties of seeds were utilized. Nuts were harvested and used, in many ways. A variety of oats, balsam seed, grass and flower seeds, and hundreds of other plants of which the seeds were found to be edible or made edible by Indian technological methods. Tomatoes, corn, sweet potatoes, were Indian contributions. The income from world use of corn and tomatoes alone would account for the fortunes of many millionaires. They furnish at least half the world's food supply. The lowly potato saved the Irish from starvation at one point in their history.

The Indian method of girdling trees was adopted by the Americans. It cleared the forests, and the westward movement of the white man was made possible by "an advancing fringe of 'deadenings' " (as the eminent geographer Dr. Carl Sauer stated). The Indian method of tree girdling was done with care for the environment, with love for nature. But the white man was heedless of the future and had no respect for the land. He denuded the forests and will have deprived humanity of its livelihood in the end.

The hammock, invented by the Indians, made life more bearable for sailors. The snowshoe, invented by Indians, made it easier to negotiate heavy snows in the mountains. If this is not an ingenious and inventive method of transportation, what is! In its time in the history of man, it was quite as important as the invention of the steam engine at a later time. The use of hundreds of medicinal plants is one contribution of the Indian to mankind. Ways of treating fractures, blood clots, fevers, have been taken over by Europeans without thought as to who originated them—the Native Americans. The so-called "Finnish bath" in which steam is used, is both cleansing and healthful. The textbook writers do not credit the Indian with this invention either. The ancestors of the North American Indians, such as the Maya and Inca civilizations, gave many inventions of scientific importance to the world. The Maya invented the zero in mathematical computation before anyone else did. The architecture and arts of the Indians of South America were such works of infinite beauty that it caused the Spanish to describe them as "palaces of kings," when in fact there was no royalty in South America. The Native people of America utilized cotton, harvested wild rice, invented weathertight homes and shelters which could be easily dismantled and discarded in favor of new and better ones. Indians all over the continent had excellent watercraft, which varied from place to place according to the materials available and the waterways upon which they were to be used. The harpoon was invented by the Indians, with which they successfully fished the huge whales. To describe this type of culture as "savage, primitive, lazy, filthy, and unkempt," is not only to degrade and vilify a whole people, but to display ignorance of the nature of man's history and his immense achievements on this continent. The eminent anthropologist, Dr. Harold Driver, sums it up correctly when he states: "The American Indian takes his place among the major contributors to the current composite civilizations of the world today." (Indians of North America, p. 612.)

7. Does the textbook accurately describe the special position of the American Indian in the history of the United States of America— socially, economically, and politically?

The American Indian has had in the past and has today, a unique position in the life and history of the United States. Federal-Indian relations began with treaty making, which did not end until 1871. Consummation of Indian treaty-making was accomplished through the device of the Indian Appropriations Act of 1871. Many treaties are still in force today. Most of them, however, have been distinguished by their violation rather than their observance by the United States government. No other section of America's population has this position. The Native American tribal member lives not only under the Constitution of the United States, but by a set of regulations of an entirely different nature, known as *Title 25—Indians*. The tribal Indian is instructed, through Title 25, to whom and in what way and for how long he can lease his land; the constitution and laws of his tribe are governed by these regulations and by the Secretary of the Interior directly through the Bureau of Indian Affairs. His funds are kept for him in the United States Treasury, and it takes an Act of Congress to dislodge any of it for even normal tribal pursuits. The Bureau of Indian Affairs, which operates under the Department of the Interior, directs tribal life and particularly its economy—openly and brazenly in the past, covertly in the present day. The American Indian does not receive a monthly check from Uncle Sam, as so many misinformed persons believe. If he receives a "per capita payment," it is for his own land which was taken from him by the United States, or for land leased for him by the BIA, and such amounts vary from $1.24 a year to $200 per annum. Any excess of this amount is the exception.

It is quite true that some tribes have natural resources which they managed to retain. The Osages are examples. Many of them have a better economic position. Other tribes, such as the Blackfeet, have been purchasing land through the years. They are now competing with the white man in the cattle raising business. The Native, if left to his own ingenuity and talents, is usually successful in his endeavors. But these instances are the exceptions. That it has occurred rarely, is due only to the bureaucratic control which is imposed on the people by governmental agencies.

Perhaps the most important aspect of past and present Indian affairs, is his relationship to his land, the relationship of the Indian and the federal government to lands claimed by the Indians, and the determination of Indian legal ownership of the land. The relationship of the Indian to his land was not merely a physical relationship. It was a social relationship in which he participated as a member of his tribe, in which land boundaries were known and respected, whereby use of the land was not merely one of "occupying" it or "roaming" in it, but utilizing it and possessing it. Textbooks, without a single exception found to this date, express this relationship as though the Native merely roamed in it, hunted and fished, and was just "there," like the scenery. Such descriptions support the racist theories that the Indian really did not lose anything when the white Europeans took his land. Felix S. Cohen, the distinguished attorney, and author of "Handbook of Indian Law" wrote in 1954 that:

When, for example, a court begins an opinion in an Indian property case by referring to Indians moving from one place to another as "roaming, wandering, or roving," we can be pretty sure that it will end up by denying the claimed property rights of the Indians. For these words are words that are commonly applied to buffalo, wolves, or other subhuman animals. They suggest that the relation of an Indian to land was a purely physical relation and not a social relation. These are plainly "outgrouping" or "they" words to describe movements which most of us, thinking of ourselves, would describe by means of such words as "traveling, vacationing, or commuting," words that we would not apply to animals, words that are distinctively human. These latter words connote purpose in movement. Only when we regard a person as strange or perhaps subhuman do we customarily impute aimless motion to him. Thus, if I or a friend should move from one place to another, this physical motion will ordinarily either be described in "we" terms or be assimilated into a more highly descriptive term. We might speak of ourselves as transporting merchandise, or surveying, or berry picking, or selling life insurance, or settling the West, depending on the occasion and purpose of the physical motion. An unfriendly Indian might disregard all these nuances and describe our action in "they" terms as "trespassing or invading the Indian country." And conversely, white judges, or white settlers who do not consider Indians quite human will be apt to disregard the purposes and occasions of Indian travel and refer to any moving Indian as a "nomad," thereby implicitly justifying the taking of Indian lands and homes by more civilized "settler" or "corporation." (Quoted by Lowell Bean, in his article, "The Language of Stereotype and Distortion," in The Indian Historian v. 2, #3)

Finally, the treatment of the Indian in the textbooks should be handled factually. The truth should be told, not a dilute solution of it. One noted historian of Los Angeles stated in an official document that there is danger, if the historic truth is told, the white children in the schools will develop certain unhappy "complexes" of insecurity. Such a philosophy of teaching history will serve only to develop a country of ignoramuses, ill equipped to deal with the problems of life and ill prepared to understand the uses of history.

8: Does the textbook describe the religions, philosophies, and contributions to thought, of the American Indian?

It is a great mistake to consider the history, culture and contributions of the American Indian entirely from the viewpoint of the material culture. The religions of the Native should be described, for in itself it provides the best insight into his history and development. While the Indian has largely adopted Christian beliefs and religion, the traditional beliefs and religions still exist and still hold sway over large numbers of Native people. Just as in considering material culture, however, so it is with the religions of the people. There was great variety, and one description will not be applicable to all. Generalization will cause misconception. Many Indians believed in one God, whom they called variously "Great Man," or "The One Above," or "The Big One Above." In some parts of the west, the Supreme Being was not personified.

The philosophy of many Indian peoples is considered by scholars as part of a system of thought well deserving of special study. Here too, variety is the key. The Pueblo people were peace-loving people. Even so, we know the story of the great leader Popé, who led a successful revolt against the Spanish in the seventeenth century, and held them off for twelve years. Indian philosophy and thought has to do with hospitality, family and tribal ties, respect for the land, which they called MOTHER EARTH, speaking the words reverently in hundreds of different languages. The body of thought and philosophy spoken by Indian leaders through the years following white contact, is contained in their speeches, their replies to governing bodies and representatives, their words in times of stress and pain.

It is also contained in the beliefs and personal conduct of many Indian people. What the white man designates as a "shy, bashful, hesitant student" may well be the demeanor of a child who is respectful and thoughtful. Again, it is wrong to generalize, and one such generalization is particularly wrong: some scholars have come up with the determination that the Indian in general is not competitive. This is inaccurate, and an improper generalization. But first, one must ask: in what context are you talking about competition? For, the Indian in many tribes is highly competitive, glorying in accomplishment.

9: Does the textbook adequately and accurately describe the life and situation of the American Indian in the world of today?

At best, the books have a short and highly generalized paragraph concerning the Native American today. The Indian is wholly a part of modern America. Whether on reservations or in the urban centers, he makes his contributions, he works and has his problems. Many of the Native's problems are different from those of other citizens. At least the present situation of the Indian should be known and his current various opinions studied. Social life and culture in the United States today would be incomplete without the Native. Certainly knowledge of the country's history is incomplete and inadequate without knowledge of Native history and culture.

The special political and economic status of many Indian tribes continues as a special part of the governmental structure of this nation. Understanding how this came about, and how and why it continues, is absolutely essential for an understanding of the current history of our country.

In the evaluations that follow, distinction is made between those books which are approved texts for Bureau of Indian Affairs schools, those which are utilized in the Public Schools alone, and those used in both public and BIA schools.

In order to identify such use, the following devices have been placed at the beginning of each title:

    Bureau of Indian Affairs School texts . . . . †

    Public School texts . . . . *

    Both BIA and Public School texts . . . . *†

If certain of the evaluations that follow appear to be repetitious, blame the textbooks. Their weary telling and re-telling of inaccurate information, misconceptions and distortions of Indian life are repeated in all the books. We have tried to develop as many varied approaches and as much variety of thought as it is possible to do under these circumstances.

If the continued use of the words "white men" or "white settlers" disturbs the reader, blame the textbooks. These are direct quotes. We don't like it either.

IV

American History and Geography

*†THE MAKING OF MODERN AMERICA. By Canfield & Wilder. Houghton Mifflin, 1964, 792 pp. Bureau of Indian Affairs, Fort Sill Indian School. Public School Text.

Approach is one of European contact as the beginning of American history: "America owes much to Europe. Europeans brought to the new world their religion, their institutions of Government, and their way of living." The beginnings of America should deal with those basic necessities of life and certain cultural modes which were borrowed from the Natives: Food, clothing, medicines, sports, new methods of transportation (canoes, travois); used their roads and trails, imitated their rhythms, and named towns after Native places and personalities.

There are maps, photographs, illustrations, but the usual innuendoes of a "superior" culture continuously pushes forward. William Penn secured "peace with the Indians, whom he treated fairly, even (!) paying them for their land." (P. 52)

An effort to be "fair" is prominent in the text. This would be praise-worthy, if such fairness were justified. After all, one could present both sides of the Hitler crimes too. This ideology is evidenced on page 353: "The retreat of the Indians may be looked at from two points of view: That of the Pioneer and that of the Indian himself." This position is analogous to presenting the equal but opposite points of view of a hold-up man and his victim.

The statement concerning Indian education and governmental domi-nation on page 353 is a generalization of conditions.

A misrepresentation of Indian life exists by innuendo on page 87: "The Indians there (in the Ohio Valley) grew restless under the threat of losing their hunting grounds." Although this paragraph is a fair generalization, the term "hunting grounds" does not convey permanent occupation of the land.

The use of ambiguous terminology is also evident in the text. Page 188: "Spain had agreed to keep Florida Indians from attacking American citizens and property, but she was powerless to control these lawless bands." The word "lawless" is ambiguous. It does not denote *whose* laws.

Another misconception is bred in the mind of the student with these words from page 352: "Whites and Indians are rivals for the West." According to Webster's New Collegiate Dictionary, "rival" means "one of two or more striving to reach or obtain that which one only can possess." The Indians were already in possession of their lands and had been for more than 20,000 years. They were not in the relationship of a "rival" to the white man, but rather in the position of attempting to defend their homes. Another objection: Indians in the gold rush are ignored.

This text is marred by inconsistencies, distortions of the rights of man, and misinterpretations of the true situation in early America.

NEW LAND, NEW LIVES, OUR COUNTRY'S BEGINNING. By Gilstrap & Patrick. Steck-Vaughn Co., 1967, 310 pp. Public School text.

This text admits that the history of America begins with the Natives. It is explained in the preface this way: "The story of America began thousands of years ago. At that time tribes of people roamed the plains and forests and prairies of our great continent." The word "roam" implies a people without a complex culture, without technology of any sort, nomads who had no land rights nor occupancy privileges. It is wrong.

Quoting from the earliest letters and diaries kept by Europeans, the text continues, on page 32, to make these erroneous statements: "The manner of their (the Indians) living is barbarous. They do not eat at certain hours. They eat as often as they want to and at all hours. They eat upon the ground without a tablecloth or any covering. They keep their meats either in earthen basins which they make themselves or in the halves of pumpkins." This is an improper comparison with European niceties and "culture," principally the property of 15th century aristocracy of Spain, Italy, and other countries. Such a comparison is derogatory.

A type of prejudice is shown on page 150, when, in the storytelling narrative style, the authors write, "It was a beautiful summer Sunday in the Virginia colony. In one section of the colony, however, a veil of gloom had fallen. While on their way to church, the people of Stafford County had discovered a dying neighbor. The man, who owned a small plantation, had been brutally attacked by Indians. In his dying breath, he gasped the name of his killers, the Doegs, the most hostile Indian tribe, had broken their treaty of peace. They were again on the warpath." And so, the narrative continues, the Colonists were "enraged," and any Indian that came in sight was fired upon. It is a fact that treaties of peace made by the Indians were violated by the Europeans, who took more land than had been permitted, who proceeded to consider the land as property, which never had been intended by the Indians, and who consistently infringed further and further upon the Indian homelands. This conflict of civilizations took place in 1675, the time of this narrative, and continued throughout America's history.

The burden of this textbook, so far as the beginnings of the American nation in the conflict of the White-Native civilizations, is that the Indians were brutal, savage, fierce, uncivilized, and had to be removed from the land before "progress" could be made. It does not matter that the Native Peoples were in another stage of culture. What matters is that they owned the land, had adopted definite boundaries among themselves, were utilizing the land, and that the Europeans were trespassers.

*THE STORY OF AMERICAN FREEDOM. *By Edna McGuire.* Macmillan, 1965, 390 pp. Fifth grade basic text public schools.

European "discovery," colonization, development and growth is the approach.

Indians appear towards the end of the book, pages 253-254. Before then, the Spaniards, through the missions, are said to have taught the Indians, provided food and shelter for them, and civilized them. No mention is made of the Indian peoples during the gold rush.

Treatment of the American Indian is entirely from this viewpoint: that because white men *wanted* things the Indians had; explorers *wanted* food and gold; the traders *wanted* furs, and settlers *wanted* land—the Native peoples had to surrender.

From this point of view, the textbook is at least honest. However, an excuse for this inhuman treatment and philosophy is soon found. On page 254, it is stated, "The Indians wanted to keep their land. They wanted to keep their old ways of living too. So they fought the whites. The Indians were making their last stand for their lands and the right to live in the old way." In this and other statements, the reader is made to feel that the usurpation of Indian land and property was justified, because "they wanted to live in the old way." There is no treatment of the American Indian today, his relationship with the government, his way of life, or his problems.

*OUR NATION FROM ITS CREATION. *By Platt & Drummond.* Prentice Hall, 1964, 905 pp. Public school text.

The approach is European, and begins with the English colonies. The Natives as well as Negroes are diminished in this statement, page 2: "Except for the Indians already here and the Negroes brought here from Africa, practically all the colonists were of European origin." Considering that the majority of the population at this time was Indian, this is a statement for a book written by whites for whites.

No effort is made to analyze the conflict of cultures and economies. Indians are described as "hostile" when they are defending their lands. The massacre of the Indians at Fallen Timbers by Wayne is termed a "victory." On page 251, the Seminoles are said to have "massacred" 100 American soldiers. The fact is, that the soldiers attacked the Seminoles. On page 459, the "wild west" is said to have been "tamed" and made more progressive by settlers. But nothing is said about the tragedy of attempted genocide against the Indian people in the process. Page 337, the Spanish missions are said to have helped train the Indians, giving them a better life. The gold rush is described as a great pioneering adventure, without mentioning the dispossessed Indian population.

The Indian today is described in extremely general terms; the government is said to be "helping" their situation. According to these authors most Indians prefer to live on reservations. Inaccuracy exists in discussing the results of the Dawes Act, page 464, in which it is stated that the Indians lacked the incentive to cultivate the land allowed them as allotments, and "Many soon gave up and returned to their tribes on the reservation." These allotments were ON THE RESERVATIONS. Besides, allotted land was incapable of cultivation. Spliced in at intervals, some effort is made to show a certain limited sympathy for the Native peoples. In the content of the book itself, there is shown a definite white-dominant ideology. Inaccuracies and misconceptions exist throughout the book.

*†OUR COUNTRY'S HISTORY. *By David Saville Muzzey.* Ginn & Co., 1961, 710 pp. Bureau of Indian Affairs, Institute of American Indian Arts, Santa Fe, New Mexico.

European "discovery" approach. Indians are first mentioned on page 22, "The Indians' high cheekbones, straight black hair, almond-shaped eyes, and beardless faces suggest their relationship to the Asians." Not all Indians have high cheekbones, or almond-shaped eyes, or beardless faces.

"They knew nothing of the white man's idea of private ownership of property. Hunting grounds were claimed in common by the tribe or a group of tribes." The mention of hunting grounds alone implies that this is the only type of property the Indian knew. Many tribes had other properties in common, and some had property by family or clan.

Indians are described as "savage," on page 28 and other parts of the book. Discussing Coronado, page 30, "But no more wondrous works of man than the pueblos of the fierce Indian tribes met their gaze." To describe the Pueblo tribes as "fierce" is ludicrous. They were the first pacifists. Indians "attack"—never DEFEND, (page 40), according to the author. On page 45, "The Plymouth Colony consisted of only a few thousand people scattered in ten small towns. Half of these were wiped out by the Narraganset Indians in King Philip's terrible war of 1675." History relates the courageous struggle of Philip and his people against the depredations and land grabbing of the English colonists, who also sought to impose their religion and culture upon the Native people. A similar approach is shown on page 85, "Pontiac's raiders strike. Terrible Indian attacks and massacres were common during the Conspiracy of Pontiac. Fear swept the frontier until the powerful Ottawa chief signed a treaty of peace at Oswego, New York, July 25 1766." Peace could have been easily obtained and maintained indefinitely, had justice been done to the American Indians. They resisted being swept from their lands, the most militant of the tribes resisted. Failure made it a "massacre."

On page 153, the troubles with the British are described. "Their agents from Canada were furnishing arms and powder to the Indians and encouraging them to resist the advance of the American settlers.

Indian raids and massacres were frequent on the border." No one had to stir up the Native tribes. The major tribes were forced to fight for their land and lives. The same is said of the Spanish, who "continued to stir up the Creeks and Cherokees against our southern settlements." On page 191, "The only heartening event of the summer had occurred in the Southwest. The Creek Indians in Mississippi Territory had been stirred up by Spanish agents from Florida and by Tecumseh's visit. In 1813 they massacred two hundred and fifty Americans at Fort Mims on the lower Alabama River. In this paragraph, it is admitted that Andrew Jackson "compelled them (the Creeks) to sign the Treaty of Fort Jackson, by which they surrendered two-thirds of their lands in Alabama." There is no mention that Jackson and the U.S. government failed to live up to the terms of the treaty, and that the Creeks were defending their land. Jackson's exploits are further eulogized on page 202, when he "swept across East Florida, capturing the Spanish strongholds . . . Then Jackson returned to Tennessee in May, 1818, leaving Florida a conquered province." This remarkable feat was accomplished by murdering the Indian people in that region; some of whom had given aid and armed support to Jackson in his quarrel with other Indian tribes. President Jackson is considered by the Indian people to have been their worst enemy. It was he who violated a Supreme Court decision in the case of the Cherokee removal. It was he who was the instrument of some of the most dreadful crimes and one of the greatest tragedies of American history, the Trail of Tears. Nothing exemplifies the difference between two cultures, two histories, two peoples, more than the renown given to this President.

The gold rush, page 260, is described without mention of the genocide in California. In a similar defense of the white man, we read on page 344, "In 1874, gold was discovered in the Black Hills of Dakota Territory, a part of the Sioux Indian reservation. The Indians were forced to retire before the rush of speculators, who raised the population of the territory 853 percent in a decade." This was an expropriation of Indian lands, when a reserve had been set aside by treaty.

There is no attempt to explain federal-Indian relationships, nor are the treaty conditions described, and the effects of violations.

*RISE OF THE AMERICAN NATION. By *Todd & Curti*, Harcourt, Brace & World, 1966, 880 pp. Bureau of Indian Affairs Schools. Riverside Indian School, Anadarko, Oklahoma.

European approach. While these authors strive mightily to give historical justice to the Indians, the burden of "warring peoples, and aggressors" is upon the Native American (page 94, in which Indians are shown burning a settler's home). These are not photographs and it would be just as much to the point to have drawings or other types of illustrations showing the settlers, gold miners and soldiers massacring Indian women and children. No treatment of Indian culture and history. No treatment of Indian contributions to the "Rise of the American Nation." Description of current conditions and changing policies towards the Native Americans on Page 435 is inadequate.

*THIS IS OUR LAND. *By Patterson, Patterson, Hunnicutt, Grambs & Smith.* L. W. Singer Co., 1963, 474 pp. Public school text, fifth grade.

Following chapter one, which explains the Pledge to the Flag, chapter two states: "The First Americans Had No Flags." Every tribe had its own flag, which flew above the ceremonial house during a time when tribes had joint events, or on top of the tribal house, at other ceremonial times. The tribal flag belonged to the leader (not "chief"—this is a foreign word and has no meaning in Indian culture). These flags were made of cloth. The American Indian Historical Society has many groups of children who come to see the Museum of Indian Arts. There is, on the main floor, an example of an Indian flag of the Maidu people. No wonder the children are so unbelieving, so unprepared to accept that other peoples had other flags, different banners of patriotic allegiance.

On page 19, it is announced, "Most of the tribes hunted, fished, and grew corn and beans. They spent much of their time fighting other tribes. Usually the tribes were small. Often there were several of them living in the same area. Although their ways of living were very much the same, they did not get along well with each other. There were not many cases where Indian tribes banded together to form a nation." These authors have never heard of the Iroquois confederacy. There were also groups of bands forming a tribe.

Improper generalization and mockery is implicit in this statement on page 23, "Baby Brother didn't mind the tight cap he wore on his head, either. The cap was worn to make his head grow long and thin. This shape of head was considered a mark of beauty by his tribe." No specific tribe is mentioned in this description. It is assumed that all Indians of the Pacific Northwest utilized this form of pressure to shape the head. To children, this kind of statement results in titters. The description on page 24 that Brown Bear's father "could have a feast" to celebrate his child's first tooth is sheer hogwash. This implies that a new tooth would be the occasion for a potlatch.

"From the beginning, the Indians were unfriendly toward the settler." This statement on page 58 is inaccurate. The settlers could not have survived very long without Indian help and friendship. In the same sense, page 62 announces, "During their first years in the New World, the Virginia settlers did not think of much but staying alive. A man does not worry too much about freedom when he is hungry, and Indians are shooting at him." Only later, when the settlers began to encroach upon Indian land, did they defend themselves. An improper assumption is made on page 67, "Fortunately, the Pilgrims found un-used Indian cornfields at Plymouth." In many cases, Indians turned over cornfields to the Pilgrims. In other cases the settlers simply took the cornfields without permission. Pilgrims also TOOK Indian corn-fields for their homesites even though the land had been cleared for corn.

In connection with land ownership, page 90 reveals that the English and the French "found themselves claiming the same land." Were these historians treating fact as history, they would know that the land be-longed to the Natives. Another attempt to cast doubt upon Indian ownership and occupancy of the land is made on page 296, stating that the settlers "wanted land to farm . . . the Indians fought the settlers . . . the settlers, on the other hand, saw the Indians as dangerous savages." If this is considered an OBJECTIVE handling of history, then we had better be prepared to listen to "both sides" so far as the Hitler invasions, the Kaiser's war, the march of invading armies across Asia and Europe, and the depredations wrought by pirates, thieves, and crooks through-out the ages. We can listen, of course, but the justice of the matter must be determined sometime. And the attempts of the settlers to reconcile their wants and needs with the actual fact of Indian ownership of this country cannot be justified before the courts of history.

Explanation of the attack by Andrew Jackson and others upon the Indians of Florida is given on page 300, "Spain was weak and could not keep order among the Indians in Florida. The Creeks, Seminoles, and other tribes often went on the warpath against their American neigh-bors to the north." The Florida tribes were protecting their homes; they were insisting upon their right to give refuge to runaway Black slaves; they were waging a defensive war to get the white marauders out of their land before it was too late and they would LOSE their land. Page 305, "The missions were self-supporting communities. Land was tilled for food. Cattle were raised . . ." Why not add BY INDIANS, who comprised the entire labor force?

Even in estimates of population, this text distorts historic fact. Page 308 gives the total population of California in 1848, as 15,000 people. Following massacre, genocide, whitemen's diseases, and starvation, the Indians of California numbered approximately 18,000, a decrease of more than 150,000 over their original estimated population. With 18,000 Indian population at that time, it would appear that the figure for California's population should have been listed at close to 33,000.

Factual inaccuracy in other areas also exist. As one example, on page 310, pemmican is described as dried buffalo meat. It is actually dried pounded meat mixed with other ingredients, still being made today by many Indian peoples.

Page 365, "The new Americans did not want to be unfair to the Indians. Time and again, land was set aside especially for the Indians. 'This is your land', the Indians were told. 'It will be your land forever.' But 'forever' is a long time. The men who had agreed that certain lands should be Indian territory died. Other men took their places. These men said 'Gold has been found on Indian territory. The Indians do not understand the value of gold, so we will take that territory' . . . But the Indians could not hope to win. There were too many of the new Americans, and their weapons were too powerful." This is a blueprint for tyranny.

There is no treatment of the Indian and federal law, or relationships today between the government and the Indians. There is no understanding developed of Indian cultures, current conditions, social structure, or governing bodies.

*LAND OF THE FREE. A HISTORY OF THE UNITED STATES. By Caughey, Franklin & May. Franklin Publications, 1965, 658 pp. Public school basic textbook, eighth grade.

Page 41: "The Californians . . . Although they had no agriculture, they added the acorn to their diet of fish, game, roots, and seeds." That they did indeed have agriculture is amply proved by many scholars who have documented the evidence.

Page 43: Discussing the Eastern Woodlands area, the authors state: "The key traits were corn-growing, hunting, headgear with standup feathers, bark canoes, much use of wood and bark utensils, houses large enough for more than one family, and stress on war, scalping, and torture." The use of the word "traits" to describe the development of technology, agriculture, and a complex society, is certainly not justified. The ability and resourcefulness of such a people to adapt to the environment, utilizing the available food supply, was something more than a trait. The juxtaposition of corn-growing, and headgear-with-standup-feathers is mockery, and improper.

Page 44: "Whenever a whale washed ashore, these Indians had a feast. They also were skilled enough to paddle out to sea to harpoon whales and tow them ashore." If they were skilled enough to paddle out to sea and harpoon whales, it would seem they could have a feast at any time.

Page 44: In connection with the Northwest Indians, "The more of his goods he destroyed, the more highly his neighbors would think of him." The competitive potlatch has been described as inaccurate elsewhere in this book.

Page 49: "As early as Washington's time, our government set itself up as guardian of Indian rights. As recently as the 1950's, the federal government authorized Indians to sue the United States. If the courts held that a fair price for land had not been paid, the United States must pay the difference plus interest." Incorrect. The attempt of the government to improve the position of the Indians resulted in the loss of their land, the destruction of their culture, and general impoverishment. The federal government must authorize ALL citizens for the right to sue. In connection with the Indians, this legislation was passed by Act of Congress on May 26, 1920. In connection with judgments to Indian tribes for lands taken from them, for inadequate payment for such land, or for any other causes, NO interest has ever been paid; such claims have been rejected. When a judgment is made by the federal courts, the funds are placed in the United States Treasury, to be held FOR the Indians concerned, to be disposed of as the Secretary of the Interior and Congress determine, and during the interim, these funds accrue minimum interest.

Page 54: In connection with the Jamestown colonial settlement, "It also was surrounded by large trees, behind which Indians could lurk." This is certainly an uncalled-for remark. So too could other enemies of the colonists lurk, some of whom were their own countrymen.

Page 131: "The fighting (colonial days) most common was between colonists and Indians. Either side might start the fighting. Sometimes only a few lives were lost. Other actions were on a large scale." It would appear a matter of historic justice to mention the fact that the Indians had a reason for fighting—the defense of their land, against the destruction of their economy.

Page 131: "One of the Dutch governors has to his doubtful credit a war; in which most of the Indians of Long Island and the Lower Hudson Valley were killed." This was Governor Kieft, who, it should have been mentioned, is also credited with having been the first to offer a bounty on Indian scalps.

Page 178: Referring to the struggle of the Indians to defend their lands in the Ohio Valley, the authors describe the infamous Anthony Wayne who was sent by President Washington to subdue the Indian people. The story, as related in this textbook is: "Some of the Indians wandered away to get something to eat. Those who waited were surprised at the vigor of the American attack. Disappointed, too, in their hopes for British support, the Indians soon broke off the fighting and fled." To tell it like it was—Wayne pursued the Indians to the British fort of Maumee, slaughtering them at the gates. The British commander refused to open the gates. Wayne destroyed Indian villages, food supplies, and massacred old men, women and children.

Page 236: Relating the story of Indian removal from the southeast, the authors slant the history in favor of the whites, instead of giving an objective review of the facts as they were. According to this textbook, the National government persuaded the Indians to give up their land, to sign treaties which were "negotiated." The narrative ends with ". . . the majority of the Indians moved had to sacrifice part of their property." They had to sacrifice EVERYTHING. The treaties were forced upon the Native people. The removal was at the point of a gun. The Trail of Tears was one of the blackest days in American history, and so it should have been described by the authors.

Page 444: Ishi, the Yahi Indian who was found by residents near Oroville, California, is described as "the last wild Indian in America." What is meant by "wild Indian?" This is a derogatory term. There were no wild Indians at any time.

There is no description of Indian contributions, except inadvertently, and then in practical mockery by juxtaposition with other description. There is no treatment of the American Indians as they are today, where they live, what they are doing, their tribes and communities, their participation in American life and history. This book is definitely slanted to the white-dominated society, so far as the Indian role in American history is concerned.

†YOUR PEOPLE AND MINE. *By Josephine Mackenzie.* Ginn &
Co., 1960, 320 pp. Bureau of Indian Affairs, Aberdeen Area Indian
Schools.

European "discovery" approach. The first English settlement, Jamestown, was settled so that "no Indians could surprise them." And, "now
they felt safe from the Indians." The Indian use of tobacco is made to
appear as an English discovery.

Improper insulting comparisons are made in such sentences as these,
"Peter sat at the table eating quietly with the other Pilgrims. But not
the Indians! They tore big hunks off the deer and smacked their lips
loudly over each bite," (p 77).

Pages 116-121 deal with the Pueblo Indians, who are made to appear
without culture or economy, living a bare existence. Cotton, used by
the Pueblos and grown by them, appears as a Spanish missionary invention. Teaching the Pueblo Indians how to weave, sew, and perform
other household chores, is described as something new to these well-
developed people. It is stated, "The Pueblo Indians liked the good
Spanish priest . . ." when in fact they revolted against them and drove
them out in the most successful Indian defensive action since the beginning of white contact. Irrigation is described as a Spanish discovery,
when in fact the Pueblo Indians had irrigation long before the priests
built their missions.

"The Spanish found the California Indians very much like the Pueblo
Indians but slower to learn." No mention is made of the fact that the
California Indians almost immediately opposed the Spaniards, and generally had to be forcibly taken to the missions. If this textbook was designed to compare various peoples living in this nation, then it has
failed, for the only learning materials are about the Europeans. The
world, the country, the arts and industries are seen with the eyes of the
whites.

It is as though the Native peoples were merely a part of the general
scenery. No understanding can result from such a book, but an ideology
of white superiority is developed in the white child, and a feeling of
racial loss in the mind of the Indian youth.

*†THIS IS AMERICA'S STORY. *By Wilder, Ludlum & Brown.*
Houghton, Mifflin, 1960, 728 pp. Bureau of Indian Affairs schools.
Fort Totten Indian School. Public School text.

European "discovery" approach. Incorrect data exists concerning Indian population (page 113). In the same paragraph it is stated that while the government extended citizenship to the Indians, it has "also permitted them to keep many of their tribal customs." This overbearingly superior statement is typical of much of its contents concerning the American Indian. One might conjecture, if the United States of America is as free and tolerant a nation as such textbooks boast, then the rights of the Natives to keep their customs ought to be taken for granted as one of their inalienable rights.

Describing the life style of the American Natives, it is stated: "It was a simple life. Some of the eastern Indians lived in villages in long houses made of bark. They had no idea of owning land as we do." The same idea is expressed on page 415: "The Indians looked upon these lands as their own." This is as much as to say that the land did not in fact belong to the Indians, and provides a convenient excuse to commit a monumental land grab.

Page 113: "The men made bows and arrows or crude stone axes, and fished for food, and did the fighting. The women planted corn, prepared food, made utensils and clothing, and fashioned pottery and baskets. Children were taught to obey their parents and to endure pain without flinching." Some tribes had this type of division of labor; others did not. That the education of children, their training and upbringing was limited to obedience and endurance of pain, is false.

Pontiac's heroic war to keep the land of his people is described on page 145, as having been waged because the people were angry, "They considered it their land." The treaties made with this government, laws passed against white encroachment on Indian land, are evidence that the land was theirs and was so recognized. The war against the Indians by settlers who wanted their land is called striking a blow "for freedom of the west," on page 173. But the Indian defense of their land is described as "raids upon helpless frontier communities." On page 301, it is stated that "Wayne's expedition settled the Indian problem in the Northwest for some years to come. The white settlers no longer had to live in fear of deadly attacks by Indians." If the United States was supposed to defend the property and lives of the people, one might ask why was not Indian property and life defended, and certainly it was not.

Page 415: ". . . certain Indian tribes continued to claim large sections of land east of the Mississippi. Sometimes they occupied fertile lands which the white men wished to own." The fact that Indians had adopted western technology in many areas, is not mentioned. The fact that Indians also "desired" these fertile lands, that these lands actually belonged to them, is overlooked. Excuses are made for the federal government in the abrogation of treaties with the Indians, with the statement that: "The government acted in good faith, for at that time no one believed Americans would want to settle on the western plains which made up the Indian territory."

This is the same as compelling a criminal to return stolen goods, and then deciding that the criminal needed it more than the victim.

Descriptions of current conditions are phrased so that one has the right to believe that they came off a government printing press under Bureau of Indian Affairs direction: Everybody is going to school; all the Indians are progressing; skills are being learned. Such a rosy picture is painted that the whole becomes a nest of hornets ready to sting the writer the moment hard facts are presented, as they have been, especially during the past few years.

†THE STORY OF OUR HERITAGE: 1100-1877. *By Winther with Cartwright.* Ginn & Co., 1966, 415 pp. Bureau of Indian Affairs Schools, elementary text, Eagle Butte, South Dakota.

European "discovery" approach. But, "There were people here when Columbus came. The Indians lived in a stone age. These 'natives' of the New World had not learned to use iron in making tools and weapons . . ." (See Criteria for discussion of this terminology). The generalized treatment of material culture takes no recognition of the great differences in Native cultures.

Improper comparison is seen in the above sentence contrasting the making of iron for tools and weapons, with the native material culture, which had its own technology. Excessive generalization is found in this statement: "Indians lived in tribes. Most Indians in America lived in small bands or tribes. One tribe generally had little to do with those nearby." Untrue. Trade over long distances with various tribes is too well known to argue this point. Other specimens of generalization and superficiality so that implications of an inferior people can be drawn are: "The education of Indians who lived in what is now our country consisted chiefly of learning tribal behavior and customs, and how to hunt, fish, and fight . . . sometimes a group of closely related tribes joined together into a confederation. The Iroquois, or Six Nations, in New York State were an example of an Indian confederation."

Education, in fact, consisted in the passing on of the knowledge of botany, conservation, natural sciences, the currents of rivers and oceans, and navigation, and a host of other knowledge useful to the living of a people in that age and environment.

Concerning the Chinese people, apologies are made for the sake of conscience. As to the Negro people, "We must never forget that this slave trade was a very cruel business and raised much human suffering. Imagine the terrible effect it had on the people of Africa!" We have not read one statement in any textbook, in connection with the decimation, depopulation, and cruelties practiced upon the Native American. This is not to say that such statements are required, nor even desirable. "Just tell the truth," should be the principle by which textbooks are written.

The section devoted to the Spanish missionaries in their relations with the Indians ignores such facts as forced labor, or separation of families. Instructions for student learning exercises include these: "Many nations have contributed to our country. Make a list of ten places in the United States with French names. Make another list of the places with Spanish names. After finding these places on a map, write a paragraph explaining why the French and Spanish place names are found most often in certain parts of the United States." (p. 96). The omission of Indian names and historic sites in this country is due to the authors' neglect of the Indian role in our history, which is evident throughout the book. The authors say, on page 241, that white settlers "took land the Indians believed belonged to them." This is to deny the FACT of Indian land occupation, ownership and possession.

*THE LIFE HISTORY OF THE UNITED STATES. *By* *Time, Inc.* 12 vols., 1963. Public Schools Eighth Grade Supplementary Textbooks.

The twelve books which are being used as curriculum-related texts in many school districts all over the nation, have this in common: Their treatment of the American Indian in our history is inadequate, inaccurate, distorted, and misleading. No effort in this evaluation will be made to present an exhaustive criticism of the twelve books. Indications of the inadequacy of the books for schoolroom use is shown in the examples cited herewith.

Book One, The New World. Page 9: "These early Americans left no architectural monuments like the Egyptian pyramids, carved no writings into enduring rock as did the Persians and Babylonians, established no far-flung, powerful governmental institutions as did the Chinese. They did not use the plow and the wheel. They had no written language." Besides being an improper comparison, the statement omits one important fact: these early Americans left descendants. The same sort of comparison is made on page 11, "No such empires ever came into being in the vast, almost empty sweep of territory that was to become the United States and southern Canada. Here in the year 1492 the Indian population numbered no more than a million, compared with perhaps 15 million in Central and South America. The utmost diversity and fragmentation were the hallmarks of the North American tribes. In temperament they ranged from the peaceful Pima of Arizona to the belligerent Iroquois of New York." The population estimate is very low. The determination of personal characteristics, whether "belligerent" or "peaceful" is also improper. It is the same as stating that all Americans are warlike, or all Americans are pacifists. The chapter presents no factual information, confining itself to generalities, committing errors such as the use of the word "chief" (no such title or personage) and the word "noble" (no such title or personage).

Chapter 2, page 16, The Indian is described: "He was cruel, and he dearly loved merciless war." No facts are given to substantiate this characterization, which is insulting. Although the Indians are also depicted from the viewpoints of some European artists and diarists, no accurate picture or description emerges of the Native Americans whether by tribe, area, or as to the nature of any of their cultures. In general, an inaccurate and degrading picture is painted of the Indian as warlusting, savage, with indecently-painted bodies. The conclusion left to the young reader is that these people deserved to be replaced by a more "civilized" group, that they stood in the way of progress.

Book Two, The Making of a Nation, page 57, deals with the participation of some of the Indians on the side of the British during the Revolutionary War, comparing the Indians to wild beasts, but does not do a similar service for others in the war. Page 62 describes the Indians as "undependable allies at best," who "massacred" many of the inhabitants. On page 109, the Congress of the Confederation is credited with the great achievement of forming the Northwest Ordinance, which, according to this book, was extraordinarily progressive, but actually was the first legal step to divide up and conquer Indian lands.

Book 3. The Growing Years. Page 14 makes a national hero of Mad Anthony Wayne, who cleared the land of Indians and was responsible for the Fallen Timbers massacre of Indian men, women and children, burning more than 5,000 acres of Indian land. Gleefully, the author cries, "Wayne decisively trounced the Indians, and, for the moment, effectively pacified the frontier." Description is given of the Louisiana and Florida regions before American acquisition by trickery, as a "wild land of riffraff, fugitives from justice, runaway slaves, half-breeds and marauding Indians, whose forays over into Georgia made life hideous," (page 62). These areas were refuges for runaway slaves, who were indeed fugitives from southern justice. The words "half-breeds" used in this mocking way, is derogatory to a people. It is always a strange ploy in the more modern textbooks which make heroes of those who protected the Black people seeking liberty—when these runaway slaves are protected by whites. But when they are protected by Indians then they are "fugitives." The chapter, page 90, is headed "Bold, flamboyant savages of the Western plains." Page 105 relates the exploits of Andrew Jackson, who massacred women and children at Horseshoe Bend, later claiming the slaughter was an "accident." Here he is the darling hero of the frontier, the foe of the Creeks; who were defenders of their land.

Book 4. The Sweep Westward. Relating the story of the gold rush, the author fails to mention the Indians who were massacred, the genocide practiced, and the lands criminally stolen.

Book 6. The Union Restored. On page 10 there is mention of the Negroes who served with the northern forces during the Civil War. There is no mention of those who served with the southern forces, or the Indians who served on both sides, according to their allegiance and interests. On page 145, there is mention of a treaty made by the United States with the Plains Indians, but no explanation that this treaty was distinguished for having been almost immediately broken by this country. The defeat of Custer is termed a "massacre." In the painting reproduced on page 147, the causes for the attack on Custer by the Sioux and Cheyenne are given as resulting "from the refusal of the Indians led by Sitting Bull to remain on their reservations." This is inaccurate and a distortion of history. Struggle ensued as a result of years of hunger and starvation, crooked Indian agents, stealing of their supplies and stores of food, and broken promises and treaties. Their patience finally exhausted, the Indians made a stand against their enemy, whom they defeated in the famous battle of the Little Big Horn.

Book 7. The Age of Steel and Steam. On page 17, reference is made to the General Allotment Act (Dawes Act) which is described as a new Indian policy which "tried to end widespread abuse of Indian land-holdings." It was in fact, an insidious method to deprive the Indians of even more of their reservation land, which succeeded in wresting millions of acres from the tribes. Page 52, by omission, fails to mention the fact that the "hopeful" gold miners who came to territories "bearing the names of Idaho, Wyoming, and Montana," entered lands set aside as reservations for the Indian people—leading to retaliation by the Indians, Page 53, the massacre of 200 Sioux women and children at Wounded Knee is termed a "battle," while the defeat of Custer at the Little Big Horn, in another section of the book, is described as a "massacre."

Finally, there is no mention whatever of the situation of the American Indian today, where the people are, what their conditions are, how they live, their education and culture.

A final evaluation of these twelve books: the books are definitely slanted to the white-dominated society; the Indian appears as a savage, brutish creature and the implication is that the taking of his lands was justified. There is no attempt whatever to present the Native American as an integral part of the history of this nation.

*†EXPLORING THE NEW WORLD (Revised Edition). *By Hamer, Follett, Ahlschwede, & Gross.* Follet Publishing Co., 1965, 496 pp. Bureau of Indian Affairs Schools, Tesuque Day School, New Mexico. Public schools text.

European "discovery" approach. Page 32, "As Columbus and his men began to explore the island, strange people peered at them from behind bushes. They had reddish skin and wore necklaces." The connotation here is that Mr. Columbus found an inferior people who were like brute beasts. On Page 43, "More colonists came over from Spain with more animals and supplies. Unfriendly Indians were killed or driven away." This callous description, without explanation, places the Natives in a subhuman category.

On Page 184, the development of George Washington as a leader is discussed. "He became acquainted with the people of the frontier and the kind of life they lived. He met trappers, fur traders, and pioneers . . ." No mention is made of Washington's contact with the Native peoples, in whom he was intensely interested, whose languages he studied, whose ways he examined carefully, and from whom he learned so much.

The history of Chicago is chronologically listed, but the role of the Indians in the development of this area is ignored. The development of the State of Oklahoma received even more improper treatment. "This land was called Indian Territory. Our government had set it aside as a home for Indians. Most of these Indians had been driven out of other parts of the United States . . . white settlers soon came to the borders of this Indian Territory. They found that some of the land was not being used by the Indians. They urged Congress to let them settle on these unused lands. Finally, our government bought some of this land from the Indians. The government then fixed April 22, 1898, as the day when white men would be allowed to enter the region. What an exciting day that was!" This is a falsification of history. The Indian tribes were forcibly removed to Oklahoma Territory. Treaties and agreements were made guaranteeing them the land forever. They had built businesses, publishing houses, schools, towns, governments. The Oklahoma land grab was one of the most despicable events in American history. To treat it as though the land was taken "because the Indians did not use it" is a historical lie, made with deliberation and prejudice.

Page 337 describes the missions in California. It is not stated that the mission system was a feudal system of peonage and indentured labor. Writing about the gold rush, there is no mention of the Native peoples who were dispossessed. Attitudes toward the Indians, considering them as necessary evils which sooner or later must be "dealt with," persist to this day, as reflected in this statement on Page 342, "In the west, Indians were always a danger. Every worker kept his rifle handy. He was ready at a moment's notice to drop his shovel and pick up his gun whenever the Indians attacked." That the Indians were compelled to protect their land and homes, is hidden from the student; in this way history is falsified in favor of the Europeans.

The acquisition of Texas, Page 294, is handled thus: "Mexico was glad to see Americans settle in Texas because only a few Indians and priests lived there." To belittle the number of Indians who had already settled that part of the country, appears to have been necessary, in order to account for the wholesale taking of their land.

*†AMERICA'S FRONTIER: A HISTORY OF OUR COUNTRY. *By Clark, Compton & Wilson.* Lyons & Carnahan, 1965, 515 pp., Bureau of Indian Affairs Cherokee Indian Schools. Public schools basic text.

Indians are treated as an encumbrance to the nation's progress. Just as clearing the woods was essential to the building of homes, so were the Indians "cleared" to make way for the march of civilization. While a short chapter is devoted (chapter 21) to The First Americans, the analysis of historic, economic and political development, follows the line of white supremacy. "Our nation began as a tiny settlement on our eastern coast and spread across a vast continent. Before the American pioneers and settlers had crossed the continent they had learned many lessons in living in the land. They had to learn how to clear away the woods, to build houses, to plow the land, and to fight off the Indians," (preface, page v).

A conclusion which follows by virtue of the text is that "white settlers," (to which reference is made again and again), were responsible for the discovery, development, and "civilization" of the country, as though the land was useless until the "white settlers" came. A patriot is a person who loves his country. One of the best ways to be a patriot is to know about our own American pioneers and heroes. They were the ones who discovered, settled, and built our country." (p. 1).

Fatuous and unnecessary innuendoes exist in the book, guaranteed to develop reactions of white supremacy through descriptions of Indian habits which were presumably unacceptable to the antiseptic purity of the superior whites. Dealing with French travels "The first Indians that the explorers met were friendly. One Indian took hot fish in his fingers, blew on it, and then put it in Marquette's mouth. We hope the Indian was thoughtful enough to wash his hands, but we are afraid he did not" (p. 43). Not mentioned, of course, is that Marquette and his group were found by the Indians half-starved, weary, lost, and had to be fed like babies.

The fact that in their "patriotic" march to the West, the white settlers relentlessly stole Indian lands and pushed the Natives from one forlorn and barren spot to another, forcing them to fight for their very lives, is treated as "necessary," and the defensive struggles of the Indians are described as bloodthirsty wars of aggressors. The Battle of Horseshoe Bend, in which the Creeks were fighting for their homes and lives is so described. And, "The Sioux . . . were fierce warriors who were always raiding and scalping other Indians of the plains," (p. 223). This is inaccurate, and an insulting characterization. There is no mention whatever of the Trail of Tears, and other forced removals. "The traders on the Santa Fe trail were in great danger from Indian attacks. Many white people began to cross the plains. The Indians knew that their hunting lands would be ruined. The Indians would starve if they could not hunt. We can hardly blame them for hating the covered wagon caravans," (p. 245). This type of "tsk-tsk" treatment is bound to develop a strain of inhumanity in a child. In the same breath the text speaks of a "thoroughfare for freedom" in connection with the Oregon Trail, in which destruction of Indian life and property was the dominant theme.

Kit Carson is eulogized as a great "Indian fighter"—a hero. He "fought against many of the western tribes. He defeated some of the fierce Blackfoot Indians," (p. 251). So too is Andrew Jackson held up as an example of patriotism, heroism, courage—a model for children to follow.

The gold rush is dealt with as an adventurous and progressive development, which brought wealth and the good life for America.

*YOUR COUNTRY AND MINE. By *Brown, Tiegs & Adams.* Ginn & Co., 488 pp. Public schools text.

European approach. Just as almost all other books do, this text makes much of the fact that Indian land and furs were "bought" with an exchange of beads, trinkets, and knives. On page 72, for example, it is stated, "These ships carried cargoes of small gifts, or trinkets, to offer the Indians—pieces of bright cloth, gay blankets, shining knives, and glittering glass beads. Indians took these trinkets in exchange for their rich furs."

Most white people smile in superiority when given such information. It serves to reinforce their belief that they are smarter than the "poor Indian," who is assumed to have been stupid and naive. There is no understanding developed of the difference in cultures, economic values, and social systems existing among the Native peoples. A knowledge of political economy in itself would preclude such ignorance. The fact is that two economic systems were in confrontation: the one, a system of commodity exchange for money; the other, a system of direct exchange of goods. Land was not "sold" among Indian people. What was "given" or "sold" in terms of western economy, was the right to *use* land and the tribes understood that they could at any time have the land returned, is accordance with their social values.

These "beads and trinkets" were in fact a representation of exchange value among the Indian people.

The treatment of the Lewis and Clark Expedition represents the continuing effort of a white-dominated society to prove how clever, how educated they were. On page 72, it is stated that the explorers "hunted out the valleys, streams, and mountain passes." No mention is made of the fact that they were led by Indians who helped them find their way in the new land and often rescued them from certain death in these "explorations."

Concerning the Catholic missions, (page 99), "These twenty-one missions were established to teach the Indians about the Christian religion and to help them to learn Spanish ways of living." The missions were outposts of the Spanish empire. Life in the missions was one of feudal indenture. The Spanish soldiery was one arm of Spanish conquest. The missions were the other.

Discussing the gold rush, the authors mention not one word of the results of this massive land steal: Indians were evicted and dispossessed from their land, which opened up one of the most complex and continuing processes of litigation the country has ever seen.

On page 164, "Food from the soil and sea . . . the colonists planted their first crops of vegetables and corn . . ." Not stated is the fact that they got the corn and other "vegetables," from the Native Peoples.

An error is made on Page 175, "One morning in 1607, as some of Powhatan's subjects were fishing . . . " The tribes had no "subjects"; their leaders were in a position of authority by virtue of approval of the people.

How Pocahontas, "The Indian Princess" saved the life of John Smith is described on page 176. For these many years, the role of both Pocahontas and Squanto have been interpreted according to the white man's sympathies. It is a fact that both these Indian people were not heroes to their race; they were informers upon their own people, helped the invaders in their efforts to grab lands. On page 252, the Sequoia National Forest is mentioned with great pride, but not the man whose name was taken, nor the uses of this great natural resource by the Native peoples. Who discovered Alaska, on page 319, is dealt with in the usual way—some Russian "found" it. Ignored are the Eskimos, Aleuts and Indians who discovered that land, learned how to live in it, and settled it. According to these authors, before white "discovery" there were "only a few Eskimos and Indians who lived there at the time." What is a "few"? The land was populated and settled, and for that type of terrain, there were many Native peoples living well in the land.

The peninsula of Florida on page 63 is described as a place where "robbers and bandits found shelter in Florida, and warring Indians also hid there." Florida was the home of Native people, who in later years "hid there" to escape genocide on the part of the whites.

†° EXPLORING AMERICAN HISTORY. *By Schwartz & O'Connor.* Globe, 1963, 473 pp. Bureau of Indian Affairs Schools. Anadarko Area Indian School, Oklahoma. Public school text.

European "discovery" approach. Page 8, "Columbus found . . . the people of these lands were poor." The word "poor" denotes an inadequate life style, while the Native peoples had plenty to eat, an economy which suited their environment, and a life style which provided their needs.

The relationship between New England colonists and the Native owners of the land is misconstrued, page 49, "The Indians in New England began to fear the march of the newcomers. Indian attacks against white settlements took place more often. The most serious Indian attack took place in 1675. It was known as King Philip's war . . ." The "attacks" were defensive measures of the Native peoples to protect their land and their lives. An insulting comparison is found on page 82, "The settlers on the frontier could never feel safe. There were dangers from wild animals and Indians." This statement expresses the approach and the attitude of the writers. The whole book suffers from this supremacist ideology. "Indians and animals" places the people of the land in the same position as predators who had to be cleaned out. Missing is the reality of Indian life and occupancy of the country.

The fact that the federal government considered the Indian tribes as *Nations* is ignored. No treaties with the tribes are mentioned, nor is this aspect of American life dealt with at all, an aspect which is with us today as well as being a part of our history.

The gold rush is treated as a massive adventure. No mention of the Indian situation.

The march of Europeans westward is dealt with as though the Indians were impediments. The Plains Indians, according to these authors "lived chiefly on buffalo meat," (p. 227). While the buffalo was certainly a basic part of the diet, it was used for clothing, houses, and a host of other necessities of life. Certainly it was not the only food source. The implication is that the life of the native plainsmen was of the most primitive order. Indeed, it was highly complex. Food was derived both from hunting, fishing, and natural vegetation. Trade with other tribes was common, so that the Plainsmen had access to other products, which they did not have in their own environment. Here again, "The Indians fought the newcomers desperately. They attacked (!) settlements and lonely ranch houses. They tortured and killed women and children, burned their homes and stole their cattle. The settlers fought as cruelly as the Indians. Indians were often killed without mercy." This period of American history is handled as though both the settlers and the Indians had rights to the land. Nowhere is there mention that the Native people were fighting desperately to defend their homes and their property.

Falsification exists as well as half-truths: Page 227 states, "As the Indian tribes surrendered they were forced into lands set aside for them

by the government. These were known as reservations. The government gave them food and schooling. Attempts were made to teach
the Indians to farm, but they were not very successful. Even today, the
proper treatment of our Indians is a problem."

To correct the record: The reservations were the most barren lands in
the nation. They were unfit for farming. The schools promised in the
treaties did not materialize, or if they did, they were perhaps the most
abysmal failures known to man. What is the "proper" treatment of
"our" Indians? Why "our" Indians? Are the Native peoples some kind
of natural resource like a mountain or a stream, instead of being human
beings whose land was stolen? Indians learned to farm and raise cattle
so quickly in many areas that they became strong competitors to the
Europeans. It should be explained that the treaties promised land,
then took away the land; then more treaties were made, and more land
taken until finally the Native people were living in the most abject
poverty, their culture destroyed, their property taken by force, with
promises of tools of agriculture; even these promises were broken.

Falsification of history occurs again on page 232: "The last of the Indian territory opened to settlers was the Oklahoma Territory. In 1889,
the government threw open this territory for settlement. Since this
was the last large area that had not been settled, thousands of people
took part in the rush to get land." It is not explained that the Oklahoma Territory was already settled—by the Native peoples who had
been forcibly transported there with promises they would not be
disturbed "as long as the grass shall grow." To make the above statement is the same as implying that the Indians did not settle the land,
and therefore progress, was effected through the whites who *did* settle
the land . A knowledge of Oklahoma's early history would have shown
these authors the extent of sophisticated, successful settlement that had
indeed taken place in the Oklahoma territory, by the Indian Tribes.

There is no treatment of the most serious question confronting this
nation: How to remedy the centuries of wrong done the Native people.
Where are they now? What is their situation today?

*FIVE CENTURIES IN AMERICA. (ABC History Series) *By Drum-
mond, Fraser, & Alweis.* American Book Company, 1966, 657 pp.
Eighth grade public schools text.

European approach. Chapter 2 describes "The America Europeans
Found." Conjectures as to origins of the Native people is by way of the

usual Bering Sea route. "Probably they came in search of game." Perhaps this is so, but "probably" they came in search of a new land, is an equally valid conjecture. Page 52, Spanish rule is described as welcome to the Indians. "The Indians learned many things from their Spanish conquerors," (p. 52). Nothing is said about what happened to the Indians, how they were treated and what happened to them in the feudal camps of the missionaries, or how they struggled against the missions.

A derogatory description of Indian participation in the La Salle expedition is given on page 56: "With twenty-nine Frenchmen, eighteen Indian braves, and a few squaws, La Salle set out in December, 1681." There is considerable eulogy of Andrew Jackson, and misinformation about the state of Indian affairs, on page 274, and this paragraph deserves to be printed in its entirety for its undisguised racism:

"In common with most Americans who had lived on the frontier, Jackson distrusted the Indians. He had fought in many Indian wars. He had seen the results of Indian attacks on white settlements—the mutilated bodies of women and children, the charred ruins of pioneer cabins. Jackson believed that the Indians deserved little sympathy and that serious quarrels could not be avoided as long as Indians and white men lived close to one another."

While this, in essence, is presumed to reflect Jackson's attitude to the American Indians, it serves to make judgment as to the role of the Indian in the life of the country at that time. In relating subsequent events, the text says, "A few tribes resisted and had to be moved by force." The implication is that this action was necessary, and indeed it was not. The removal of the Indians from their Southeast homes was in violation of the Supreme Court decision rendered by Chief Justice John Marshall; it was in violation of treaties, and it was in violation of human and tribal rights.

On page 311, the Treaty of Guadalupe Hidalgo is described, which ended the war with Mexico and made it possible for the United States to acquire Texas, California, Arizona and New Mexico. This treaty had some important conditions in connection with the American Indians in those territories, which are not mentioned in the text. The Indians were to be protected in their rights, and were to be accepted as citizens of the United States if they so desired.

There is no mention of the Indian during the gold rush. On page 442, the march of the settlers to take the west is discussed. The only mention of the Indian case is the assertion that their "hunting grounds" were being taken from them, and "they had to change their way of life." Relating the struggle of the Natives to hold the reservation lands in the west against white encroachment, it is said "Often Army troops showed as much cruelty as the Indians themselves." The difference between the two warring peoples, which is not explained in the textbook, is that the Indians were defending their land, and the Army taking it.

Treatment of the Indian of today is extremely general, sophomoric, and adds nothing to a student's understanding.

*THE ADVENTURE OF AMERICA. By *Fraser and Yeager.* American Book Co., 1966, 404 pp., Public schools text, fifth and eighth grades.

"Europeans discover America," is the subject of Unit One. On page 55, clues to the First Americans are given as "remains of their camping places," describing the American Indians as primitive peoples. The implication is that there are no more Indians living, and this receives support from a failure to deal with the Indians of today.

Page 57: "How did these early people manage to live? Some of them took shelter in caves. To get food, they fished, hunted and gathered wild plants. They made simple clothing from animal skins. In time, they learned to make crude hatchets, hammers, and spears out of stone or bones." Such a statement ignores the economy, technology, and variety of the Indian people.

Page 59: "The eastern woodland Indians worked out religious ceremonies, such as chants and dances, that they hoped would please these spirits in nature. These Indians' religious teachings also helped them to behave as good persons and to help their tribe." This is certainly no description of an extremely complex culture. It is inaccurate.

Page 265: "Also, there was trouble with the Florida Indians, who raided nearby settlements in Georgia. A United States Army officer, Andrew Jackson, followed some of the Indians back to Florida and punished them for their raids. This caused serious arguments between the United States and Spain." Reasons for the Florida Indians' struggle are not given. Their defensive war to hold their land is overlooked. The statement is slanted to the white American. Reasons given for conflict between Spain and America are inaccurate. This was a struggle for land and power between two foreign governments.

Treatment of the Indians at the Spanish missions is inaccurate. The Indians during the gold rush are ignored. A more comprehensive evaluation of this book ought to be made, as a matter of fact, and it is hoped that some scholars will do this. The book is so vastly generalized, so shallow, and contains so many inaccuracies, that little or no learning can result from use of it by the students.

*†THE STORY OF OUR HERITAGE. *By Winther & Cartwright.* Ginn & Co., 1962, 798 pp. Bureau of Indian Affairs schools. Aberdeen Indian School. Public Schools text.

This text shows ignorance of Indian history and cultures. There is no evidence of having consulted any source materials or authentic data. The book, unfit for student use, is bound to do serious harm to the student.

Page 16: "The prairies and the Great Plains which lay west of the forest remained unsettled for three hundred and fifty years after Columbus's discovery. This wide open country belonged to the millions of buffalo which grazed on the grasses . . . Beyond the Great Plains, far to the west, were mountains and valleys covered with forests and inhabited by an abundance and great variety of wild life."

That the land was inhabited by and belonged to PEOPLE, the American Indians, and had been theirs for more than 20,000 years, is not considered. Ignorance of Indian cultures is shown on page 18: "One tribe usually had little to do with other tribes except that a tribe sometimes warred with those nearby." This is inaccurate. Ample data exists to prove that there was extensive trading, wars were not more than skirmishes limited in extent and slight in occurrence before white contact. "The education of the Indians consisted chiefly of learning tribal behavior and customs, and how to hunt and fight." This inaccuracy exists in almost all the textbooks. There was no tribe whose technology was limited to hunting and fighting. On page 19: "Unfortunately this is a sad story, for the ways of the white men were far different from those of the red men." This passage places the conflict between Indians and whites on the sole basis of "ways," or traits, and is misleading. The Indians were eager to learn from the Europeans, to trade for goods, just as the whites were eager to learn from and trade with the Natives. Conflict was based on Indian ownership and occupation of land wanted by the Europeans, usually acquired by force or fraud from the Indians.

Chapter 2, pages 32–51: There is some description of Spanish cruelty and some mention of the use of slavery. However, this chapter does not deal with the encomienda system, except in the vaguest way, and makes no mention of slavery carried on in the Catholic missions. While there is some description of "mistreatment" of the Indians, there is nothing said of their mass slaughter by the Conquistadores. On page 48, it is stated: "On the other hand, there is also much to praise about Spain's accomplishments in the New World ... in spite of their faults, the rulers of Spain made many contributions to the development of agriculture, industry, and mining in the New World ... the mines and shops of the Spanish colonies produced great quantities of precious metals, jewelry, and leather goods ...." Not stated is that such articles were produced by the Indian people.

Page 153 states: "Whenever there was danger of Indian attacks, one neighbor passed the news along to another, and settlers joined together for their common defense." It is implied that the Indians, rather than the whites, initiated force and violence. There is frequent mention of damage suffered by whites, but little or no mention of loss of life and property of the Natives. Page 195: "Even though Clark failed to capture all of the Ohio Valley, or Northwest territory, his courageous exploits put an end to deadly Indian raids on American settlers in that region." The same ideology is expressed in this: "The land north of the Ohio, like that south of the River, was Indian country. When the white settlers moved in they cut down the forests, they killed off the game, they took land the Indians believed belonged to them." No recognition is given of the Indian attempts to protect against trespassers. The use of the word "believed" is an ancient device to cast doubt upon Indian possession of the land. This type of language sanctions the stealing of Indian lands, and is an inaccurate statement of native land use.

The false impression is given in the textbook that the Native peoples moved to reservations voluntarily: "The settlers began moving across and into the Great Plains. To avoid trouble, agreements were signed with the Indians limiting them to certain areas, or reservations."

There is no mention of the Indian plight during the gold rush. There is no mention of Indian removal during the Jackson administration, nor is there any treatment of Federal-Indian relationships.

*†HISTORY OF YOUNG AMERICA. By *Cordier & Robert*. Rand McNally, 1954, 278 pp. Shawnee Indian School, Oklahoma Public School text.

This text supports the illusion of white society that a vast wasteland existed in this country prior to white contact. The text begins the history of America with the Europeans. It is a fact, however, that a complex civilization existed here, based on an intensive utilization of the products of nature; and based on the transformation of such products into articles of immediate use as well as for trade intertribally.

"American history is the story of how people came to the Americas, how their ways of living changed, and how they changed the lands in which they lived," (p. 3). "In America, before Columbus came, there were only Indians," (p. 4).

Learning instructions planned for student utilization in this text include: "Make a time chart. Plan to start with Columbus. The history of the Americas really begins with his voyage in 1492," (p. 38).

The same learning instructions treat of Indian life as though the Natives are an extinct form of life, and actually encourages the young student in the obnoxious act of pot-hunting.

The taking of Indian land is authorized as a necessary step in civilization and progress: "In the pages that follow, you will read often about someone taking possession of land for his country. Such lands were newly discovered. Usually they had few people, and most of the land was unused. . . . When an explorer found such a land, he might claim it, or take possession of it for his own country. This meant that the explorer's country would rule the land," (p. 15).

Misinformation and incorrect data exist in this text concerning the nature of Indian life. "The Indians had no roads—only trails along which they traveled on foot. Indians seldom traveled to the lands or villages of another tribe," (p. 30). Here is shown a lack of knowledge about the considerable trade between tribes over great distances, the unique roadways upon which today the great freeways have been built. The descriptions are inaccurate. Improper comparison is also expressed in the first sentence.

Considerable information exists as to what the first European settlers brought, but no mention is made as to what they took from Indian life.

When Indian accomplishments are mentioned, an utterly improper editorial amazement is expressed, "It is hard to believe that the work (of building stone buildings of adobe) was done by Indians who had never seen a stone building. The Missionaries must have been very good teachers," (p. 180). No mention is made of the great stone apartment houses built by the Pueblos before white contact, and certainly before the Spaniards came.

Falsification of history abounds in this book, in an effort to make events more palatable. Thus the merciless and bloody conquest of the Southwest by Coronado is explained "All the Indians (of Acoma Pueblo) went to live with friends in the other pueblos and left their homes for the Spaniards," (p. 35). An outrageous example is given which condones Spanish inhumanity, when this historic obscenity is described, "Even when DeSoto's men took all the food the Indians had, there was barely enough (for DeSoto's men)," (p. 30).

The condoning of slavery and the slave system is only one of the evil features of this text. "The Spaniards and Portuguese soon found that they could not get enough Indians for plantation workers. They then brought Negroes from Africa to work on the plantations, because these people had lived even closer to the equator and were used to the tropical sun," (p. 41). The Indians are described as lazy, shiftless creatures, "At first the plantation owners thought they could get the Indians to work, but the Indians of the Islands and the lowlands along the coast were not used to hard, steady work," (p. 41). This is outright slander.

Finally, in an effort to be good guys so that everyone would be happy, the authors state "The Indians were right. The pioneers were right too," (p. 112).

Misinformation and inaccuracy exist about the California Indians, and improper comparisons are made between this most highly populated part of the land, and the southwestern tribes: "The Indians of California were much less civilized than the Pueblo Indians of New Mexico and Arizona. They did not even farm. They were skillful basketweavers, but baskets were about the only well-made articles they had," (p. 179). Such ignorance of authenticated data, proving a highly complex life, is unpardonable in scholars.

One could detail errors of information, ignorance of scientific data, and rank racial prejudice in nearly every part of this book. Such a text leaves the young student unprepared for the truths of history and builds up the ideology of a superior race. Utilized in an Indian school, as this book has been and still is, it can only serve to intensify the bitterness and dislike for the white society and society at large—a society which unashamedly falsifies the history of a whole people.

*†LIVING IN AMERICA TODAY AND YESTERDAY. *By Cutright, Clark & Newell.* Macmillan, 1958, 278 pp. Third grade. Public Schools text. Bureau of Indian Affairs, Phoenix area Indian Schools.

This bland, middle-class book is written about bland, middle-class people. While information is contained about the Indian people, particularly in the Southwest, even the Native Americans appear as bland, middle-class people.

The approach is from the white man's point of view and the middle-class white man's way of life. On page 2, explaining what a pioneer is and what an Indian is, the middle-class mother says: "A pioneer is a person who goes first or leads the way. Sometimes they had to fight Indians." The third grade student, who in this case is an Indian child, learns from this book that the so-called pioneers were the first to build homes in America.

Page 110, "Old Timer" explains that, "A reservation is a place where Indians live. When white men first came to this country, only Indians lived here. The whites and the Indians often claimed the same land. They had bad fights. At last the Indians agreed to live on certain parts of the land. These Indian lands are called reservations. Each Indian tribe has a reservation." That Indians were forcibly driven to reservations, is probably too strong a dose for the children, in the eyes of these authors. Life is falsified and diluted, and the young student unprepared to meet the facts of living. Moreover, he learns nothing of his basic history—which is not all bland, nor all middle-class. Errors are made. Not all Indian tribes have reservations, for example.

The middle-class white children, "learning" about Indians from a trading post owner, are told (page 159), "In those days the Navajos did not farm and raise sheep as they do now. They and some other tribes traveled from place to place. They were wild and liked to fight." The culture and lifeways of a Native people are falsified. To describe the Navajos as "wild" is an insult. To state that they "traveled from place to place" is to class them with a society much more ancient than that which was found upon white contact. The people traveled from one part of their own land to another. When the white "pioneers" pushed them from one area to another, conflict developed.

In the same way, the text continues on page 200, "often there was bad feeling between the Indians and the pioneers. The Indians sometimes burned the new communities and killed the white people. Or they came at night and took their horses." No mention whatever of what the white "pioneers" took from the Indians! "Some brave pioneers began to go to the plains to make new homes. They went in covered wagons . . . some of the Plains Indians did not want the pioneers to make farms in their hunting grounds. So there was often trouble between the pioneers and the Indians." This is a nice, stupid and stupefying way to describe a defensive war that took place between Indian and settler, when the Natives were defending their land. However, the pioneers were "brave"; it is not stated what the Indians were.

No sweat, no tears, no sorrow, no problems in this book. Life is covered over as with a misty curtain. Life, for these Indian third graders who must study about themselves from this book, is also entirely unreal. They know better. But the falsification of their life as told in this text, cannot help but leave them confused and torn between what they know and what they are told by teachers who use this book.

*WESTWARD THE NATION IN SONG, DANCE, AND STORY. *By Minugh and Cory.* Franklin Publications, 1965, 256 pp. Fifth and Eighth grade basic history text.

The sixth of the seven chapters in this textbook is devoted to the Alaskan "frontier." While some of the songs of the Natives have been somewhat phonied up, some treatment of the American Native folkways is given.

So far as the rest of the textbook is concerned, it is filled with glorification of the pioneers, the adventuring gold miners, and the settlers whose land-grabbing activities are handled with love and tender kindness and a sense of folk history which has made legend of their exploits. This is not to say that the settlers were entirely at fault in their immoral activities when they usurped Indian land. A study of this Nation's history shows that the federal government encouraged it, and when not encouraging it gave way to the pressure of the land-hungry Europeans— despite the fact that such land had been set aside for Indians "forever."

Outright prejudice is shown in many parts of this book. On page 7, "The people who went first had to follow wild animal paths and Indian trails." (It should have been put in this way, "If not for the Indian trails, the people could not have found their way.") Then, "Those who were not killed by Indians, by wild animals, by bad weather or by accidents along the wilderness trails, came back from the valleys of the Ohio with stories. . . ." This is an assault upon the Indians, who are described as murderers, and ignores the fact of Indian defensive activities along the borders. It is slanderous.

About Daniel Boone, page 8, "Folktales about this frontier hunter and Indian fighter . . ." The story is told of how Boone hunted animals with fire torches. It is interesting to note that in many other books which describe this method as used by the Indian people, they are described as cruel and heartless. If Boone does it, fine. If the Indians do it, horrors! Some of the songs printed in this book are derogatory to the Indian people, treating them as though they were predatory animals. Page 15 offers a chorus, "Daniel Boone on Pinnacle Rock, He killed Injuns with his old flintlock."

Credit is not given to Indian discoveries, lifeways, foods, and other major contributions. Page 37, "Maple syrup, maple sugar and honey were the common sweetenings for the Kentucky pioneer." These were Indian foods which the colonists learned about from the Natives. The smoking of meat is described on page 51, but not the fact that the Indians invented this process. Corn production and harvesting, as well as the harvest festival, are described on page 53, but not the fact that the Indians developed corn and that the corn festival idea was copied from the Indians, the settlers making it into a fun-party. Poetry is offered which treats of the Native as though he were extinct, such extinction being necessary to progress. Page 65, "Where Indian fires once raised their smoke/ The Chimneys of a farm house stand/ And cocks crow barnyard challenges/ To dawns that once saw savage land."

The small-town itinerant tradesman is eulogized as a fearless pioneer, who "seemed unconcerned about unfriendly Indians and wild animals." The juxtaposition of Indians and wild animals seems to be a favorite gambit in books such as these. The itinerant trader knew he had nothing to fear from the Indians, because he was not taking their land—he was TRADING. On page 95, transportation by water is briefly described. The incorrect information is that all water travel and transportation were alike. The two "legends" given in this section are supposedly Indian, but there is no mention as to which tribe had these legends. The same ideology is shown on page 108, in which Indians are "feared" just as animals were. "The boat was the pioneers' only defense against Indian attacks or river pirates." And, "People were usually happy as they drifted along because they were headed for a new home. They often sang, especially when they didn't have to worry about Indians."

Part of the book is in story-form. Thus, on page 141, a story is told about a supposed Indian attack. The lady of the house hears a noise. She thinks, "Indians Or just some harmless animals new to the dogs? It was Indians, as they discovered when a war-painted Commanche climbed the wall and started to jump over. Mrs. Wilson shot her rifle—and missed! What the rifle failed to accomplish, a Negro accomplished with an axe. As fast as an Indian showed above the wall, he was driven back with the axe. This was too much for the Indians. They ran away, contenting themselves with stealing the horses." This is such sheer poppycock that it does not bear refutation.

Kit Carson, in this as well as in other books given to children as food for their mental and spiritual lives, is an incongruous combination of "friend" to the Indian, who knew and was known by them, was liked and trusted by them, and at the same time knew how to kill Indians!

On page 158, he is eulogized in this manner, "He knew how to watch
for an Indian ambush and the place of attack . . . He knew how to keep
his scalp . . . Kit knew how to make friends with Indians. Kit learned
the Indian language. The Indians trusted him. They respected him.
Kit Carson said, "Let us be brothers, and to understand one another.
Let us dwell peacefully in this great and wonderful country . . . America." But, it was Kit Carson who herded the Navajos into captivity, who
fought the Native peoples whenever their interests conflicted with the
whites, even though justice was with the Indian. It is an incredible insult to the logic of the young student, to think he would believe such
trash, or that the Indian student would believe that his ancestors were
foolish enough to "trust" such a man.

When the gold rush is described (page 210) the gold miner is eulogized and his feats glorified in song and dance. Considering that this
was a period of utter shame for America, it would be the better part of
decency to just forget the whole thing, and look elsewhere for folksy
tales about man's bravery and persistence in the sight of extreme difficulty. Still further glorification of the pioneers as courageous people
who conquered the Indians and the wilderness is found on page 225,
"People were hospitable and neighborly on the sod-house frontier. As
the settlers battled against Indians, heat, drought, insects, wind, torna-
does and loneliness, they were drawn together." Does it never occur to
these writers, or to historians, propagandists, politicians and settlers
of other frontiers (perhaps Viet Nam?) that great possibilities existed
of making friends with the Native people, developing mutual confidence, through strict adherence to treaties, respect for Indian land
possession, respect for Indian lifeways?

*TRAILS TO FREEDOM IN AMERICAN HISTORY. *By Coons &
Prater.* Ginn & Co., 1965, 463 pp. Public school text, 5th grade.

This textbook is unique, because at last an author is admitting that
the Indians were "The First Settlers" of this continent. Considerable
space is devoted to the Indian in many phases of the nation's life.
Space is also given to the Indian peoples of South and Central America.

It is quite remarkable, therefore, to find the same ideological inconsistencies and historic errors that exist in other textbooks. The Indians
are always "attacking" white settlers. When a battle is fought, it is the
Indians who "massacre" the whites.

On page 145, the colonization of Virginia is described. But "The

Indians massacred many colonists . . . the settlements spread along the rivers, forcing the Indians to move a little further away." When the Revolutionary War is described, the authors state "there were many Indian raids in the Ohio Valley. Bands of Indians hung around settlements. It was said that a woman could not safely go a hundred yards to milk a cow or a man to water his horse. Many cabins were burned and the families were massacred," (p. 252).

Describing Indian cultures, the authors explain that when the Southwest Indians became farmers, they had more "time to do other things. They began to show an interest in religious ceremonies, in the government of their tribes, and in art." It is a tautology that mankind had religion even before he had the digging stick which preceded the hoe. The Southwest Indians were strongly organized in their own governmental forms as part of the tribe's governing body. The arts of the Indian people, and particularly those of the southwest, are known throughout the world, having begun at such an early age in man's history that exact dating is difficult.

Another falsification of Indian history is found on page 25: "The Iroquois were brave warriors or fighters. They liked to fight and spent much of their time on the warpath." At what stage of history are the Iroquois being described? The Iroquois liked their sports and games, their homes and families, their land and their way of life before white contact.

Dealing with the Native knowledge of their own history, the authors question their oral history. On page 32, they say "The newcomers supposed that the Indians had always lived here. If the explorers asked the Indians about their history, the Indians could not tell them the true story. Their people had been here so long that the story of their coming had been forgotten. They had no written language, so whatever they knew of their past was told in the form of myths or legends. These did not give an accurate story." These so-called Indian "myths or legends" have been more accurate than the misinterpretations of some historians. Their history was woven into every custom, religious observance, and oral transference of the story of their beginning, from generation to generation.

The gold rush is dealt with in the usual fairytale textbook manner. No mention is made of the Indian lands being taken, their food stores demolished, their homes destroyed. The gold miners are described as hardy, adventurous, sacrificing pioneers. The section on the Spanish occupation deals not at all with Spanish treatment of the Indians as feudal slaves.

*†LIVING IN OUR AMERICA. *By Quillen & Krug.* Scott, Foresman, 1961, 704 pp. Bureau of Indian Affairs schools, Juneau Indian School, Alaska. Public School text.

European "discovery" approach. Indian history is not an integral part of the history of America in this text.

"Although the settlers did not know how big a land this was, they saw unused land everywhere," (p. 25). This indicates a lack of knowledge of the different types of land use in varying economic systems. The land was extensively (as opposed to intensively) utilized by the Native people. "Clark's victory over the Indians made life safer in the Ohio country." In the same way, an assassin's victory over his victim might make life safer for the assassin.

Concerning the missions, "Missionaries who knew the language of the Indians came and preached, and Indians came and listened. Many Indians stayed to work on the mission farms and the farms of the Spaniards." This is a distortion of the truth. Many Indians were kidnapped and forced to work in the missions, where they constituted the labor force. Those who escaped and went home were pursued and forcibly brought back.

"The Union Pacific track gangs had to fight hostile Plains Indians and bear the scorching heat of summer . . ." This statement on page 404 fails to mention the fact that the railroad was given the right to take Indian land, and remove them from their homes, despite federal government promises they would remain in their land forever.

A comparison is made between Spanish colonization and that of New England on page 627. The Spaniards "had one purpose in mind—to convert the Indians to Christianity . . . one result of this was that whole communities of Indians became Christians. In our thirteen colonies the Indians were pushed off their land by the whites. In our part of North America . . . the whites had little luck in getting the Indians to work." First, the Spaniards used the Indians as slave labor. Second, it was certainly not possible to get "the Indians to work" in enforced servitude, as the colonists desired. This is not a stigma against the Indians, who were considered to be lazy and shiftless, but rather a credit to their free spirit, which resisted slavery or forced labor. In New England, the colonists did not need Indian labor, and so the method was to "push them off" the land. On the other hand, the Spaniards simply took away the Indian land by force (not Christian conversion).

There is no description of Federal-Indian relations, no consideration of the position of the Indian politically, or in the social system. There is no treatment of the Indian of today.

*COLONIAL AMERICA. *By Fisher and Fowler.* The Fideler Company, 1966, 126 pp. Public Schools text.

These authors have managed to write a book about colonial America, part of a series titled "Story of America," which is entirely free of any information about the Native Americans.

The one mention of Indian influence or relationship with colonial America, is in the caption of a picture showing an early colonial hut, described as being "much like Indian lodges." Considerable discussion arose over this book when it was first presented for adoption in some school districts. The publishers then made some revisions, removing the offensive photographs of Negro Americans who were cast in the role of lackeys. But no revision has been made as to the American Indian. If done, the whole book would have to be torn apart. Other criticisms included the point that this book contains no information of a factual nature. It is sheer propaganda. The photographs display well-to-do middle class people;—altogether a book so unreal that it could justifiably be rejected for many reasons.

*†THE AMERICAN CONTINENTS: GEOGRAPHY FOR TO-DAY'S WORLD. *By Barrows, Parker & Sorensen.* Silver, Burdett, 1959, 364 pp. Bureau of Indian Affairs. Wahpeton Indian School, North Dakota. Public Schools text.

European approach throughout. Ignored completely is the Native existence as a people, their discoveries of plants, uses of foods and knowledge of agriculture; and the Native technology in use of the land.

For example, on page 51, the farmers (European) cultivate "corn in southern Maine . . . Potatoes are another famous crop in a small part of Maine near the border of Canada . . . The markets of the United States get other products from New England farmers. There are blueberries, cranberries, and many vegetables, including carrots, tomatoes, celery, green beans, onions, cabbage and lettuce." Not mentioned, is that this modern farmer got his potato, tomato, beans, celery, and many other products of the soil from the American Indian. While this section deals with New England, the same failure to inform is found in all sections.

On page 167, the use and misuse of the buffalo is treated as though the European "explorers" were the first to reach the western plains. Indian uses of the buffalo are treated as if this was not a technological development, but rather a primitive society's accidental use of an important source of food and other needs. Nowhere is the Indian given credit for inventiveness, discovery of life resources, nor for teaching the white farmers the uses of such resources. An error is committed on page 168: "As the buffaloes were killed off, the Indian tribes of the plains lost their chief means of living. They became dependent on the white people and were settled in areas, called reservations, set apart for them."

Not explained is the fact that the Indian accommodated himself very early to new methods of farming, the use of equipment, the techniques of western civilization. They were placed on reservations because the white people wanted their land. They were assigned land which in most cases was unfit for cultivation; and consequently were dependent upon the government for the simplest needs of life. Despite this condition, many tribes which were removed to reservations managed to make a success of their new land, (Choctaw, Delawares, Cherokees, Chickasaws). Only when the white man again wanted the Indian land, was it taken from them once more, their industries disrupted and their governments dissolved.

Page 183, "Today, men have turned water from streams into irrigation ditches . . ." The Indians utilized irrigation and dug deep wells even in the desert. Settling the west is considered, as though the Natives did not exist there before the whites came. The Catholic missions are described without a single word as to the Indians who were there and formed the labor force. The gold rush is treated without a single reference to the American Indian.

To ignore these events, and to pretend that they did not exist is to falsify history.

†YOUR WORLD AND MINE. *By Grace S. Dawson, Tiegs & Adams.* Ginn & Co., revised edition, 1960. Bureau of Indian Affairs, Standing Rock Community School, Fort Yates, North Dakota.

Relates history of the "ancient world" (European, Asiatic) as beginning of American life, but no mention of ancient world in America, nor of America's original inhabitants. "America was founded and built by people from other lands," it is stated in the prologue; this is the theme of the entire book.

†HISTORY OF A FREE PEOPLE. *By Bragdon & McCutchen.* Macmillan Co., 1967, 834 pp. Bureau of Indian Affairs schools. White Shield School, Roseglen, North Dakota.

More sympathetic treatment of Indians in American history, and their deprivation of land and rights under European settlement than in some other books. Great generalization exists here too, however, and this danger cannot be overemphasized. For example, the decimation of the buffalo is blamed in the most general terms for the defeat of the Indian tribes, and because of their dependence upon the buffalo, it is claimed, the Indians could not exist once they were exterminated. The examples of the Cherokees, Choctaws, Chickasaws and many other tribes who did not hunt buffalo, but built villages, constructed governments, had widespread education, published newspapers and books, is not mentioned. Their loss of land, and their deprivations under white domination are not explained. No information as to Indians of today.

*ONE NATION INDIVISIBLE. *By Heller & Potter.* Charles E. Merrill Books, Inc., 1966, 690 pp. Eighth grade history basic text, public schools.

European "discovery" approach. References to Indians fragmented throughout the text, most of which are such as this, "Indians also proved to be troublesome," (p. 24). Some recognition is given to Indian aid of colonists such as that in Maryland, where the Native people turned over rich crops ready for harvesting to the settlers. Very sketchy and most inadequate treatment of modern Indian affairs.

*WE THE PEOPLE. *By Richards & Isely.* Benefic Press, 1964, 428 pp. Public schools text for 7, 8, 9 grades.

Generalizations abound in this book, not only so far as Indian history is concerned, but in most areas of instruction as well. European culture approach. According to this textbook, the American Indian does not

exist in our society, and did not exist in our history. There is no influence shown upon American democratic thought, nor on American society as a whole, by the Natives. There is no treatment of the American
Indian today. As a result of these important omissions, the book is a
failure.

*WESTWARD THE NATION. *By Shaftel, Johnson, Reeve, Reeve,
  & Taylor.* Franklin, 1965, 265 pp. Fifth grade public school text.

European approach. Indians are mentioned only as "attackers," "hostiles," and impediments to the progress of the pioneers in their westward march. Background is provided in two lines, in which the Indian
is considered in the same sense as animals: "Pioneering white men found
the Indian and game trails and followed them west." According to this
textbook, nothing happens in the Gold Rush except what concerns the
miners, pioneers, and settlers. "Nothing stopped them," this book de-
claims, "not sickness, death, wild animals, or savage animals," (p. 121).

*THE STORY OF OUR COUNTRY. *By Clarence L. Ver Steeg.*
  Harper & Row, 1965, 416 pp. Public Schools Basic text 5th grade.

European approach. Errors in data and improper comparisons exist.
The contributions of the American Indian are not mentioned. The
American Indian today is not treated. Information is generalized.

*†UNITED STATES HISTORY. *By Gavin & Hamm.* D. C. Heath,
  1960, 880 pp. Bureau of Indian Affairs Indian School, Cheyenne-
  Eagle Butte School, South Dakota.

European approach. Incorrect data concerning Northwest territory
and the Indians, (page 179). Removal of the Southeast tribes—the treatment is fair to the American Indian, (page 265). Considerable generalization throughout as to the Native peoples. Indian situation on the
Great Plains—the treatment is fair. No treatment of the American Indian today.

*†THE GROWTH OF AMERICA. *By Liebman and Young.* Prentice-
  Hall, 1959, 468 pp. Bureau of Indian Affairs, Phoenix, Arizona.

The approach is European. Contributions of Indians to American life and to the world, generally not treated, except the admission that the Iroquois contributed to the founding of the nation through the philosophy of their confederacy, (page 49). Fair treatment, page 189, concerning Tecumseh and Indian war. Slanted to the settlers, on page 205. No treatment of the Indian today.

*THE AMERICAN STORY. *By Gavin & Hamm*. D. C. Heath, 1959, 744 pp., Public Schools, elementary basic text.

This book, with a different title, is essentially the same as THE GROWTH OF AMERICA. It has approximately 300 more pages, and is obviously meant for a different type of reader. The colonial section is expanded. A section titled "The Challenge of the Sixties" has been added. Some of the material favorable to the Indian has been deleted. There is great generalization as to the role of the Indian. The approach is European. There is no treatment of the Native American in the world of today.

†YOUR COUNTRY'S STORY. *By Margaret G. Mackey, with Tiegs & Adams*. Ginn & Co., 1961. 558 pp. Bureau of Indian Affairs Schools.

European approach. Generalizations exist about Indians. Slanted to the settlers at the expense of Indian rights. No treatment of Indians in modern America. No mention of contributions of Indians. Justification for taking Indian land "because the settlers needed it." No treatment of the culture, history and lifeways of the Native Americans.

†STORY OF THE AMERICAN NATION. *By Casner, Gabriel, Biller & Hartley*. Harcourt, Brace & World, 1964, 786 pp. Bureau of Indian Affairs Schools.

European approach. Attempts to be "fair" to Indians in several sections of this textbook soon gives way to slanting the history in favor of settlers, who "had to" have Indian land. No treatment of Indian culture, history. Little treatment of contributions. No treatment of the American Indian today. Generalizations about the Native Americans. Struggle of the Plains Indians made to appear merely as a fight to keep their "hunting grounds," instead of the basic reason—which was to keep possession of their own lands.

*OUR UNITED STATES IN A WORLD OF NEIGHBORS. *By Carls, Sorenson, & Haworth.* Holt, Rinehart & Winston, 1964, 472 pp. Public school text, eighth grade geography.

Distortions of fact, omissions which deprive the student of information, and misconceptions, abound in this textbook.

Page 47: "When white men reached the Shenandoah Valley, they found rich land to farm. They also found a well-worn Indian trail that led north and south along the valley floor. It was an Indian warpath." This brings up images of warriors skulking stealthily in the woods, waiting to pounce on the brave settlers and pioneers. Actually, they were trails used to get to hunting grounds, to fishing areas, food gathering places, and for travel to trade with other tribes.

The journeys of Lewis and Clark are explained in detail, but without including the help of the Shoshone woman Sacajawea. On page 58, there is a generalized description of Indian character, as being habitual thieves. "Indian braves were taught that stealing was a thrilling game. Best of all was to sneak something big and noticeable, like a cooking pot, a gun, or a horse. The Indians played this game among themselves all the time." This is a degrading description of the Native people. On the other hand, if indeed they stole cooking pots and other articles, it was a small thing compared to the theft of their land, foods, homes and property, by the settlers. Such thefts are not described in this book.

A ludicrous example of an effort to degrade the Indian way of life, an effort which backfires upon the authors, is found on page 163, in which white bread is extolled as being more culturally civilized than brown "coarse" bread. "Even today," say these experts, "people in some countries eat bread that is no better than the coarse ancient bread . ." This coarse, ancient bread is today highly prized by most people, and is known to be more healthful than the white packaged bread of our "civilized" times.

On page 263 it is stated: "The white men were far ahead of the American Indians, for the Indian still lived in the Stone Age." Certainly western civilization had developed a higher stage of technology, and this was recognized by the Natives, but the implication is that the Indians had no technology, no civilization, no religions. The "stone age" description is derogatory. Indian culture, history, economy, and relationship with the federal government, and his situation today, are not treated.

†IN THESE UNITED STATES. *By Preston & Tottle.* D. C. Heath Co., 1965, 490 pp. Bureau of Indian Affairs School, Busby, Montana.

United States History begins with the immigrants from Europe, according to this textbook. America was in the throes of the "stone age" before European immigration, according to information on page 47. Information concerning the contributions Europeans made, but no reference to Indian contributions. All the misconceptions found in other books, are here. Considerable generalizations concerning Indian history and lifeways exist.

†A HIGH SCHOOL HISTORY OF MODERN AMERICA. *By Shafer, Augspurger, McLemore & Finkelstein.* Laidlaw Bros., 1967. 729 pp. Bureau of Indian Affairs School, Chemawa, Oregon.

European approach. References to Indian part in American history spliced in occasionally, as "Indians were attacking the frontier," (p. 123). "Old Hickory had been an Indian fighter as a young man. He understood the desire of white settlers to take Indian land," (p. 197). Indian resistance to white encroachment in one part of the textbook, (p. 338). There is no description of Indian life. Statements on page 21 are entirely incorrect concerning technology, arts and state of Native cultures. There is no treatment of Indians today, but the "Bureau of Indian Affairs is helping to educate the Indians, relocation finds them jobs," etc. Filled with unsupported generalizations, and inaccuracies.

*THE UNITED STATES OF AMERICA: A HISTORY FOR YOUNG CITIZENS. *By Brown, Helgeson & Lobdell, Jr.,* Silver Burdett Co., 1964, 615 pp. Public schools, eighth grade basic textbook.

European approach. Generalizations concerning Indian culture and lifeways. Indians always attack, are never attacked. Pontiac "starts a bloody war," on page 195, makes him responsible, but not the colonists who took the land of his people. On page 139, we learn that the "Indian allies of King George III were busy with torch and tomahawk through-

out the war." In this description, it is stated that the British paid the
Indians to fight on their side. There is no authentication for this story.
They had cause enough to protect their lands. In the Northwest territory, "parties of raiding Indians were a constant menace to settlers,"
(p. 222). On page 238, the removal of the eastern Indians from their
properties is justified because " . . . the government did pay the Indians
for their land." Treatment of the American Indian today slender and
inadequate.

*†OUR UNITED STATES. *By Eibling, King & Harlow.* Laidlaw
   Bros., 1965, 672 pp. Bureau of Indian Affairs schools; Juneau, Alaska.
   Phoenix Indian school, Arizona. Public school text.

Published in two editions, one for high school, and this one for elementary school use, OUR UNITED STATES reveals the same inaccurate data, the same misconceptions and distortions of fact in both editions. The approach is European; life in these United States begins
with the colonies of New England, according to this book.

On page 136, the story of Daniel Boone is told, in which he, together
with five other families, attempted to settle the land now known as
Kentucky. This area is described merely as "Indian hunting grounds."
The implication is that the Indian people did not possess the land. This
is untrue, and when the Indians attacked Boone's party and attempted
to remove this threat to their liberties, they had historic justice on their
side. Inaccuracy and omission is found on page 137, in which Henderson's fraudulent purchase of land in Kentucky is described. The facts
of this "purchase" are not given, even though history is filled with evidence that Henderson's purchase was a fraud.

The Ordinance of 1787 is described as a "great law," which permitted
settlers to move to the Ohio valley. In this way, the states of Ohio, In-
diana, Illinois, Michigan, Wisconsin and part of Minnesota were
founded. But the authors do not state the truth: that these states were
founded from the lands of the Indian, which were taken from them
with the approval of the United States government in spite of treaties,
promises, the rights of possession and ancient occupancy.

Throughout the book, settlers and pioneers are treated in great detail.
No mention is made of their encroachment upon Indian lands. The
only description of the Indian in these monumental land-steals is that
the settlers had to protect themselves "against hostile Indians."

A section on page 433 deals with the American Indians today, in eight lines.

Andrew Jackson receives historical justification for his treatment of Indians in the removal from their lands in the Southeast. So also is the movement of settlers to Indian lands justified, "because," as the authors state, "they needed it."

AMERICAN HISTORY & GEOGRAPHY

SUMMARY OF EVALUATIONS

Summarizing the evaluations of these forty-two representative textbooks on the subject of American History and Geography, the following determinations can be made:

1: All but four of the books approach the beginnings of American history as European. The four which do not, give the Indians no credit for being explorers and settlers in their own right.

2: None of the textbooks give the Indian credit for discovering the American continents.

3: All of the books contain inaccuracies to a greater or lesser extent.

4: The culture and lifeways of the Indian are not described at all in most of the textbooks. In the others, the Indians are degraded.

5: None of the textbooks describe the culture of the American Indian as a developmental process.

6: The contributions of the Indian are listed in only two of these forty-two books, and then only in a cursory manner, without describing the impact of Indian contributions on national and world economy.

7: None of the books describe the special position of the Indian in history.

8: The religions, philosophies, and contributions to thought of the Native are not described in any of these textbooks.

9: The American Indian today is described in 30 of these books, but in such a generalized, over-simplified manner that no understanding can result. In all these books, there are errors concerning the position of the Indian today.

V

State and Regional History

CRITERIA

1: The general Criteria apply in this area, as they do in the area of American history and government.
2: Errors of omission are particularly unacceptable in a state or regional history. The American Indian should be treated as part of the history of the state or region.
3: Accurate data should be provided as to the tribes, areas of possession, conflicts of the past.
4: Degrading descriptions are not permissible, especially in such terminology as "savages, primitives, hostiles, aimless, wandering."
5: The story of the American Indian today, his situation, locations, and presence in urban areas should be dealt with. His organized groups should be described, his leaders mentioned, and wherever reservations exist, they should be described accurately.
6: The contributions of the Indian to the state or region should be dealt with specifically. The names and stories of outstanding Indian leaders should be part of the pride of the state.
7: Crimes of the white people should not be glossed over or omitted, such as those occurring during the gold rush. They should be described objectively, and the historic reasons for the situation given.

*ARIZONA FOR BOYS AND GIRLS. *By Dorothy F. Robinson.* Connolly Publications, 1959, 176 pp. Bureau of Indian Affairs schools, Phoenix Indian School, Arizona.

What begins as a promising book about a state which has a larger Indian population than any other in the nation, turns out to be one with the usual cliches about "good" and "bad" Indians, which fails to even mention some of the most important events in Indian history (for example, the Navajo Long March), and gives no clear picture of federal-Indian relations.

This usually occurs when a writer is deeply concerned about being "fair" to the original owners of the land and fair to those who took it from them. It just does not work out. If the American nation and the American people are all that great in the way that most textbooks ballyhoo them to be, then surely they can take some historic responsibility.

Indeed this book does deal with some of the various tribes that still live in this state. And certainly Arizona is proud of the Indian people, by and large. But this pride is not without some selfishness, for the Indian tribes with their picturesque ceremonies and their wonderful people are a tourist attraction second to none except New Mexico in the entire country. Not stated is the fact that Arizona was the last state to permit Indian citizenship, which was granted by congressional action in 1924, but not accepted by that state until 1948.

The literary form utilized in this book is facetious, overbearingly patronizing, and in ever so subtle a way instills feelings of superiority in the student who is not Indian. Generally, the students to whom this book is directed are not Indian. The description of the Indians in that region as being "poor" when found by the Spaniards, is not culturally accurate. What is it to be poor? We understand that this means a lack of food, clothing, and homes. The People lived their lives without want, and when food was scarce the country was wide open to them to obtain what they needed. What is meant by this description, probably, is not that the Indians were poor, particularly, but that they were not rich. There were no elements of the desire for acquisition of property, or the hoarding of "things," among the Native peoples, and perhaps this is reprehensible in the context of the white civilization.

Having begun with such good intentions to deal with the Native peoples of the state, the author soon lapses into the usual errors made in textbooks. The Navajos were fighting, and the government had to come in and make them be "good." The Apache people receive exceedingly unfair treatment. They too, had to be forced to be "good."

What is not understood by the author, and what comes through to the young student as a powerful misconception, is that the Apache people were waging war upon invaders. It is incorrect to categorize the Apaches as "nomads" who roamed anywhere they wished. They moved across a great territory, it is true, but the boundaries of their lands were well defined. Both the Navajos and the Apaches receive unfair treatment because of their militant struggle against the European invasion. Particularly reprehensible are the statements on page 73, in which most (if not all) Apaches are judged to be "bad." Cochise is the only exception, but the "bad" generalization is the final result of this author's analysis of a whole tribe of people who were most courageous and militant.

The Hopi fare no better than the Navajo and Apache in this book. Page 84 states that they worshipped "many gods," but does not explain anything more about their religious beliefs and their inherent philosophy. The ritual observances are described; but without explanations, they appear merely "strange."

An unusual concept of Indian land ownership has been developed by this author. The Spaniards (page 99) simply "took" the land from the Indians. The Mexicans retained the land "taken" by the Spaniards. But America BOUGHT the state of Arizona from the Spanish, and this, apparently, makes the whole deal quite proper and legal. The immorality and illegality of taking land, holding it by force, compelling the signing of treaties (as was done in the case of the Navajo) by those who did not have the right to sign treaties, and then penning the people up in "reservations" which could not support them, should be clear to any intelligent person.

In the final chapter (page 153) the author states that "Arizona is rich because of the culture of the people who have lived here. Indians and Mexicans have given much color and fun to our way of living." Is that all they have given? A statement such as this leaves the student (particularly if he is Indian) with a feeling of uneasiness. The question must rise in his mind as to just what the whites want in this day, that they haven't already got out of us?

COLORADO, THE LAND AND THE PEOPLE. By Kenehan. Edited by Mary S. Kaiser. Prepared for the Denver Public Schools Department of General Curriculum Services for the Colorado State Department of Education 1959, 195 pp.

Research for the book, as acknowledged in the foreword, was done by members of the "People of Denver Committee." Fifty-nine individuals were interviewed or furnished materials for the book. Not one was a recognizable authority on Indian history and culture.

Judging from the contents of this state history, the vast body of literature about the American Indian has had no share in preparing for the book. Had the author and committee done so, they might have avoided some of the more obvious errors of fact that have been made.

The Native people before white control, are treated in the same context as prehistoric life, whether animal, vegetable or chemical. They were just there; their lives have some "strange" interest for today; but there is no association between them and the history of the state. The contributions of the Europeans and Orientals who came as immigrants to this land are carefully listed. There is little mention of the contributions made by the American Indians to the history of the State, the economy of the nation, the culture of all America, or the color and Native heritage which this country derives from the original inhabitants of the land.

The story of the Indian is dealt with in a chapter titled "THE STRUGGLE TO POSSESS THE LAND. For many years Colorado was occupied by tribes of Indians who often fought with each other for control of the land. This story is concerned with other people who also desired the land and with the short, bitter conflict they waged to secure it." This presumes that everybody was in conflict over land ownership and is obviously an effort to account for the wholesale theft of Indian land. There is inaccuracy in this statement: ". . . the Kiowa seemed to appear from nowhere . . . No one knows positively when the Ute came. They were here when the other tribes appeared, and their legends state that they had always been here. . . . In reality, they probably moved down from the North where their kinsmen, the Shoshone, lived more than a century before the other tribes arrived; perhaps they had onced lived in Asia and crossed the Bering Strait to Alaska. They were sometimes hunters of buffalo on the plains, but they returned to the mountains after the hunt or after a raid upon the Plains People," (p. 13).

The periods of time, or eras of culture history are so confused here that the story makes no sense. The usual phraseology "Nobody knows where they came from," is utilized to lend an aura of accident to their occupation of the land. The Ute were part of the Shoshone family, one of the great tribal groups that moved into North America from the south. According to most sources, they have been here approximately 20,000 years. It is to be wondered at, that considering this broad spectrum of human history, there are writers who still are conjecturing "where did they come from? how long have they been here?" Such questions can have only approximate answers. And twenty thousand years is a whole lot of years to trace a man's ancestry. The reader can be assured that this is probably one of the oldest groups of inhabitants of the same area on the face of the earth. Of more significance, is that this history of Colorado makes only token effort to inform the readers where the people are NOW in the state. Reservations exist. Indian communities exist. The national headquarters of some distinguished Native organizations are in that state. There is a great deal of Native American activity going on and has been for many years. Some of our most distinguished Indian leaders live there.

Discussing the Plains Indians, whose land was taken, and who were consequently forced upon the land of the Utes with resultant intertribal conflict, it is stated on page 13, "These Indians ranked among the richest, since wealth at that period (1775) was estimated in food, not in money or property." In fact, the so-called wealth of the Indians at that period of their history was counted in HORSES, not food. Traditionally, the Indian people would not have considered food as wealth. Too, the tradition of hospitality would preclude the determination of food as wealth.

"At first, the Indians ate the horses which they called 'mystery dogs'; later they trained them for riding," (p. 14). The horse was utilized immediately for transportation and hunting. The implication here also, is one of distaste and ridicule. They probably ate the animals, too. What's wrong with horsemeat?

Descriptions of the Sun Dance, page 15, are incorrect. The purpose of the Sun Dance, briefly, was to secure material benefits or regeneration of life, the making or renewing of common interests. It cemented the union of the tribe, the loyalty of its members, the patriotism each felt in their country and to their people. On page 16, it is announced that "Children led a carefree life with little discipline." Children did not require discipline. They were brought up to behave themselves, to respect their elders and their tribes, and to guard its history. The second chapter on page 16 opens with these words, "A new interest (concerning the Santa Fe railroad). At first they accompanied the trains; when this proved too tame, they attacked the trains." Such statements have no place in a book designed for use in the classroom. The Indian people attacked the trains when they learned that their lands were the price to be paid for ease of transportation for the whites, not to engage in "a new interest" game.

The mining booms, with silver and gold as the magnet, are handled, with the miners emerging as intrepid adventurers and pioneers who "opened the west." The story of Otto Mears, who made a "prospector's treaty" with the Utes, in which they gave him a huge parcel of land, and a right of way for which he paid them $2 each, is handled in such a way that the Indians are made to say, (by Mr. Mears himself) that the $2 in cash was worth much more to them than millions of dollars "in promises." Mears was tried on charges of attempting to bribe the Indians to sign a "Treaty of Punishment" in connection with the killing of a white man. He was "exonerated" by Secretary of the Interior Kirkwood, and became one of the State's very wealthy men.

The American Indian today is handled in the very "precious" story of one Indian, Bird Neckles, who made good by going into the United States Army, became part and parcel of American white-dominated life, and is set up as an example of an Indian on relocation who became one of the country's good boys. It is filled with platitudes, and does not reflect Indian life.

The American Indian today is handled very briefly, stating that their population in Denver is growing, that they made "contributions" to the general society, and that their conditions are improving as a result of the work of the Bureau of Indian Affairs. Any Indian resident of the state where Indians are living, would know that such generalizations are inaccurate. Besides containing errors, misconceptions, and misinterpretations of Indian history, the book is poorly organized, obviously written for the purpose of glorifying the early miners and settlers.

An interesting and very important footnote to this evaluation, is a consideration of a new book which arrived too late for formal evaluation in this Study. The title is "Human Relations in Colorado, a Historical Record." It was prepared by James A. Atkins, through the Colorado Department of Education, and was published in 1968. This book gives adequate reasons for the efforts of the Indian people to defend their land. Its tone is sympathetic. It strives mightily to give historic justice to the Native, and describes the tribes by name, at the time when contact first occurred between white and Indian. But here too, even in the work of a more enlightened group of people, the Native emerges as something less than a civilized man; his societies and tribes are degraded; his failure to be LIKE THE WHITE SOCIETY becomes an insidious criticism against him. This occurs because there is no basic treatment of the Indians' cultures, their way of life, their concept of land ownership, and their history AS TRIBES, and as peoples. It is stated, on page 41, that the Indians had no central government. Surely this cannot be given as a reason for over-running Indian land! The Utes

are described as "virile nomads" on page 42. The "settlers were relieved
of the gnawing fear of Indian attacks," on page 47. This is a shallow,
generalized, unscholarly treatment of the Native American in Colorado.

*EMPIRE BUILDERS OF GEORGIA. *By Suddeth, Osterhout &*
Hutcheson. Steck-Vaughn Co., 1966, 419 pp. Georgia State textbook.

The center of reference in this book, as to the history of Georgia, is
established in two phrases in two separate sections of the textbook. Page
28 relates that the authors think of the Indians as the First Americans,
instructing the students to "learn something of his contributions (the
Indian's) to the exploration and settlement of this country by Europeans." The second phrase is found on page 368, in which the student
is informed that it is possible to "trace Georgia's history from the opening of the Indian country to settlers, through the years when back-
country farmers grew patches of grain . . ."

Thus, the heritage of the American Indian in the state of Georgia is
reduced to that period in history which was opened by the Europeans,
and his native heritage as a distinctive culture in his own right, is reduced to his usefulness to those who made out of this unique Indian
land a battlefield in which the struggle for power was waged.

There is no information concerning Indian cultures prior to European colonization. There is adequate information revealing the contributions of the Indian people to the white men who took their lands. An
indication of lack of knowledge as to the cultures of the native peoples
of this region is noted in the descriptions of Indian leaders as "emperors," "princesses," or "kings." There were no such titles and no such
political entities among the people of those tribes which possessed
Georgia prior to European contact. There was no monarchy in existence, nor was there a class of nobility.

We learn a good deal about Indian involvement with the Europeans
who came: first the Spanish, then the French, and English; and last the
Americans during the period of Reconstruction. Even today, Georgia
is for Georgians. The pledge of allegiance is to the Georgia flag. The
history is told in the light of Georgia's interests and rights.

The highly benevolent tone of this book is extremely tiresome. Certainly there is understanding of the awful tragedy of Indian removal.
As the authors say, on page 155, "Records of conflicts indicate that important lessons in human behavior are still to be learned." Indeed, this
is a safe injunction to the young student. The Indians are gone. The
country is safe for the whites, who have the Indians' rich lands, their

rich resources, and have destroyed their progressive and complex civilization. These Georgians of today know their history. Just the same, they cannot help but make some feeble attempts to justify their criminal actions of yesterday, and this is done on page 108, for example, when it is explained that Georgia "could claim ownership" to the lands, but "yet the Indians were in actual possession." It was, therefore, necessary to move the Indians out, as expressed in these words, on page 146, "There came to be a feeling that they must be removed entirely from Georgia soil." Thus is justification for one of the cruelest incidents in man's history, when a progressive and civilized people were forcibly removed west of the Mississippi for no other reason than that their lands were wanted by the whites. Andrew Jackson emerges as a man who brought peace to Georgia, one who did his duty in clearing the Indians out of their own land. The broken treaties and broken promises of the United States are painted over in this statement, that the government "gave the Indians the idea (!) they would hold their land permanently." That this was not a mere idea, but a firm and legal commitment bound by treaty and agreement, is not revealed.

There is no phraseology derogatory to the American Indian in this book. But the concepts propounded, the philosophy and ideology of self-important, patronizing dominance of whites, are such as to defeat the process of learning the history of this state. There is a lack of scholarly treatment about the First Americans. Certainly the authors have produced a book that smoothly is "fair" to everyone, including the Negroes who have now come forward in such numbers. A strange commentary upon this most current phase of Georgia's history—that of the civil rights movement which forced the state to desegregate the schools and allow the Black millions to vote—is that it is described, but not one Negro face is seen in the many illustrations. There is also not one Indian who has been given a place of distinction in any part of the book, and it is to be noted that Georgia's "Hall of Fame" is lily-white. Not even Tomochichi is to be seen there, and it was he who made it possible for the first permanent colony to be established when he signed a treaty with his friend, James Oglethorpe, England's first Georgia Indian agent and the Crown's first Territorial Governor in that area.

*KENTUCKY HERITAGE. By *Wilkie & Moseley*. Steck-Vaughn Co., 1966, 344 pp. Public Schools state text.

Unit One of this state textbook contains a preface that says: "We shall begin with the land and the Indians, for in the beginning the land was theirs." The first chapter describes the geography, topography, and natural regions of the State. We find such an opening particularly appealing, since it sets the stage for a regional history with consideration of the environment itself.

With chapter 2, however, an inaccurate statement is made on page 17, that "When the first white men came to the land that is now Kentucky, no Indians lived there." While the authors admit that Indian tribes were there, the fact that no "homes" existed becomes evidence that the Indian tribes did not own the land now known as Kentucky. Here a knowledge of native land use would have been valuable. Indian villages and home sites were certainly not the only evidences of native occupation and possession. Furthermore, there were many spaces in this region, as well as in all other parts of the country, which were jointly used by native tribes. In the case of Kentucky, evidence points to the fact that the area was the joint property of neighboring tribes.

The authors are inaccurate as well, when they explain that when the white men began to encroach upon Indian hunting lands in Kentucky, the natives defended it with their lives, "but still they did not choose to live in the 'Dark and Bloody Ground.' " The facts are these: When Dragging Canoe, the Cherokee leader, resisted the sale of the land in Kentucky to the Transylvania Company, he pointed in the direction of "Kaintuckee" and warned, "You will find its settlement dark and bloody." Many tribes used this area for hunting, and for the available salt licks, which were common property. Although the analogy is of a different time and social order, it might be asked whether the United States may be said to "own" certain lands set aside for parks, dams, public domain. Or, whether their ownership of such "unused" sites might be cause for the taking of such land by a foreign power.

Page 18: Inaccurate information is given concerning the Indians' beliefs and knowledge of the state. The authors say the Indians did not know "who lived there." Indian people of various tribes either lived there or hunted there. In any case, it was Indian land, and those tribes utilizing it for joint hunting purposes knew quite well the story of those who had gone before. There is sheer speculation on page 22, concerning the origins of Kentucky Indians, and beliefs.

Page 25: The authors say the Cherokees sold their land to Richard Henderson and the Transylvania Company in 1774. This is untrue. Henderson's title to the Kentucky land was not approved. The Cherokees, under the Articles of Agreement made in 1730 with England, had no right to sell or cede any land to anyone except the Crown. Certain Cherokees attempted to do so, and were opposed by Dragging Canoe, who refused to sell the land, which was under joint usage by the Choctaw, Creek, Cherokee, Illinois, Kickapoo, Shawnee, Mobilians, Osage, and Quapaw.

Page 34: It is stated that in a party at the salt licks in the state, were "several squaws and an old Dutch woman." This is derogatory. Why not a Dutch wench, or a Dutch squaw, or some similar term of endearment.

Page 45: An incident is described, which in its proper connotation might have developed some understanding of Indian values, but in the context given, develops only misconception and distortion: It is said, that in 1771, the Daniel Boone family traveled through Kentucky, with a rich supply of furs. Near Cumberland Gap, "a band of Cherokees surprised them and robbed them of everything." It is a fact, that the taking of pelts on Indian land without permission was against the law. The whites were warned time and again to stay out of this Indian-owned land. But the "brave" Mr. Boone was a law unto himself, and defied Indian law. This was not robbery.

Page 48: A nostalgic note is struck, filled with sentimental yearning, but it leaves the dispossessed Indian cold, when it is stated that the Boones were turning their faces "westward toward free land and wide spaces." This so-called free land was not free at all. It belonged to the Native people.

Page 87: The destruction of Indian towns north of the Ohio by a body of Kentucky troops in 1782 is treated like a heroic action, "Whole (Indian) villages were leveled as a lesson to their owners to leave Kentucky undisturbed." The Kentucky Long Knives, the authors proudly state, made sure the land was safe from Indian invasion. This use of the English language to distort the true meaning of land ownership and defense of the land by the Natives, is the usual case when whites are determined to justify their crimes.

Page 94: The hardy Kentucky pioneers are lauded for their industry, when it is described that food was grown in their garden patches, with "beans, potatoes, pumpkins and corn planted." No indication is given that these were Indian foods, the contribution of the natives to the people of Kentucky and the world.

Page 123: Attempts of the tribes to regain their lands are handled in such a way as to term their efforts "harassment." The Indians were hostile, the authors say, burning and pillaging cabins, as well as passengers on flatboats coming down the river. In any objective history, these attacks would be correctly described as a guerrilla war to recapture their land.

Page 128: The exploits of General Wayne are described as heroic actions, particularly in his massacre of Indian people at Fallen Timbers in northwestern Ohio. The authors applaud, "Kentuckians were free from Indian attack on the north forever."

*THE KANSAS STORY. *By Isely & Richards.* Harlow Publishing Corp. Oklahoma City, Okla. 1961, 436 pp. State history text.

Indian oral history is degraded in a statement on page one, that since the natives did not have a written language, therefore they lived in a "prehistoric period, and the stories they tell are called legends or traditions." On page 31 we are told that "neither the men nor the women worked as hard as the people do today." Therefore, "the Indians had a great deal of time for parties and games." Descriptions such as these—which are inaccurate as to Indian life—are found throughout the section dealing with Indians of the Kansas region. The names of the tribes are given, their locations are also given in general terms, but there is no other knowledge imparted of their culture and history. In this book too, we find such terms as "wandering" applied to such peoples as the Comanches. There is much speculation as to what the ancient Indians believed or thought, but little knowledge occurs. There is no description of the Indians of today. The handling of the native in this book makes them appear as extinct as the dodo bird.

†THE MISSISSIPPI STORY. *By Richard McLemore and Nannie McLemore.* Laidlaw, 1964, 416 pp. Bureau of Indian Affairs Choctaw Central School, Mississippi.

The theme of "trouble with the Indians" is again repeated. The Native people of Mississippi were a cause of "many difficulties" for the French. The British too had "difficulties." Logic should dictate that foreigners will always have difficulties when attempting to invade another country. It should have been no surprise that the Indian people resisted encroachment.

Having violated every promise made to the Indians, the settlers established a fort. In Mississippi lived some of the most militant and most progressive tribes in the country. It is no wonder that patience wore thin, and on August 30, 1813, the Creeks rushed the white man's fort and destroyed its inmates. According to the authors, page 97, "many of the people, including Major Beasley, were drunk." Notice should be taken that the whites were drunk, not the Indians. Valuable lands belonging to the Creek Nation were finally wrested from them through the successful efforts of Andrew Jackson, who led an army into Creek country in 1814.

This history of the State of Mississippi bends the history on behalf of the European settlers. As a result, according to this textbook, most of the Indian land was finally annexed to the United States government, because "The lands were valuable and would attract immigrants." The Choctaw, who were inveigled into fighting on the side of Andrew Jackson, aiding him to defeat the Creeks, were later repaid for their services by being removed to Oklahoma territory.

The rest of the book completely ignores the Indian people. The original natives still live in that state, some having refused to leave, hiding in remote areas for generations; and many drifted back home from their places of exile thousands of miles away.

†MISSISSIPPI YESTERDAY AND TODAY. *By John K. Betters-worth.* Steck-Vaughn Co., 1964, 420 pp. Bureau of Indian Affairs. Choctaw Indian School text.

This textbook contains inaccurate information, distortions of fact, and many misconceptions. The population estimate is inaccurate. Page 21, the numbers of Natchez are placed at 3,500. In 1682 the French estimated these people at 6,000 at least. The Choctaws are numbered at "somewhere between 5,000 and 10,000." Hodge places the population at 20,000. The Chickasaws are placed at 2,000, but Hodge says the minimum was 2,000 and the numbers more likely were 6,000.

The Chickasaws are described as having a "warlike nature." True,— following white contact. A description is given of the Natchez which is a gross insult: "The Natchez Indians helped to give rise in France to the 'noble savage' idea, which was popular with many Europeans at the time of their settlement of the New World. . . . In the end the French found the Natchez to be more savage than noble, at least when dealing with Frenchmen!" Again, "The daily life of the Natchez Indian was leisurely, except when the tribe was on the warpath . . ." They would have starved in that country if they were "leisurely." They are further described as being "utterly lazy." The culture and society of this tribe is distorted, "Natchez society was anything but simple and democratic." Considering the state of affairs in Europe at this time, it would appear that the Native society was indeed democratic at least in comparison.

Page 34 states, "With the coming of the white man to the Mississippi area, the days of the Indians were numbered. They could not delay for long the advance of white men determined to put their lands to new uses." In fact, the Choctaws and Chickasaws had adopted modern technology, customs and manners, and had prospered before being forcibly removed to Oklahoma. The Natchez were completely annihilated by the French.

A particularly inhuman statement is made on page 34, "Though most of the Mississippi Indians are now gone, literature has dealt more kindly with them than history has . . . Today, Mississippi's Indian heritage is almost forgotten. Very little is known about the Indians who once hunted and roamed the fields and forests through which our highways stretch today . . ."

Falsifications of history take place throughout the entire textbook. On page 67, it is stated that "In South Mississippi a Mingo by the name of Red Shoes allied his tribe with the English. Although the hostile chieftain was finally killed, his tribesmen harrassed the French for many years." Not stated is the fact that this leader was Shulush Homa, whose wife had been seduced by the French (Angie Debo, *"Rise and Fall of the Choctaw Republic"*).

History is distorted in this description of the Choctaw removal, page 126: "On October 18, 1820, Andrew Jackson and Thomas Hinds, representing the United States, and the Choctaw chiefs Pushmataha and Mushalatubbee, concluded the treaty of Doak's Stand. In this treaty the Choctaws gave up their tribal lands in Central Mississippi and the lower Delta area. The Choctaws were given other homes west of the Mississippi in Indian Territory." The truth: This treaty was not ratified. The land to which the Choctaws were removed was already occupied by white settlers. The treaty is noted for the fact that the Choctaws requested the United States agent to destroy all liquor near Choctaw settlements. A subsequent treaty was negotiated in Washington, D.C., in 1825. The Choctaw delegation consisted of Mushalatubbee, Apukshunnubbee, Pushmataha, McCurtain, Folsom, and Pitchlynn.

The degrading statements made in this book about the Native tribes, the misinterpretation of their history, the unabashed "white supremacist" approach throughout, is enough to condemn the book as a text. More likely to produce learning and authentic information would be an accurate and substantiated, authenticated history of the native people who once lived and possessed the State of Mississippi. Until that is done, at least Angie Debo's *Rise and Fall of the Choctaw Republic* should replace this book.

*MISSOURI, MIDLAND STATE. By *Collins & Snider*. Ramfre Press, 1967, 442 pp. Senior high school and Junior College State history.

Unlike most other books of this type, "Missouri, Midland States," opens with some information about the earliest inhabitants. Chronologically accurate though this may be, the statement on page 7 is insulting, "The Osages were described by some travelers as being filthy. They were said to be greasy and disgusting objects with dirty buffalo robes thrown over their shoulders. The women, if possible, were more filthy and disgusting than the men. The Indians never cleaned their food before cooking and eating it. Wild game would often be cooked and eaten with the blood and dirt of the hunt still upon it." These are outright insults.

The early "explorers" were bent upon proving the Natives to be savage, unclean, and in short nothing but brute animals—the better to lay claim to a land they could use to advantage. Another falsification is committed with the statement on page 40, "The Spanish deserve a great deal of credit for their treatment of the Indian during the colonial period. They were usually considerate and kind and treated the Indians with politeness." It is a fact that the Spaniards bilked the Indians every chance they got.

Visitors who came through Missouri during early expeditions, in fact, described such tribes as the Osage, as tall, handsome, well-mannered people, who taught the visitors how to make hominy. When first contacted by the whites, these people had advanced far enough in agriculture so that they had four kinds of corn and four kinds of pumpkins among other products. These people traveled far for trading purposes.

The Indians generally are described as aggressors: savage and hostile to the whites. But the characteristic of the "settlers" who attacked Indian villages and made war upon tribes for purposes of taking their land, is considered adventurous, brave, examples of a true pioneer spirit. A sampling of this ideology is given on page 90, "It took strong-hearted men to carry on this commerce with the Southwest. The great wagon trains were constantly beset by danger. Warlike Indians roamed the prairies keeping constant lookout for possible attack upon unsuspecting travelers. The wagon train had to be continually on the alert to protect lives and cargoes from these marauders." At some point in history, there must come a time when the words "attack" and "defend" are explained to the student with a degree of objectivity. Page 187, the Pony Express route "was infested with hostile Indians and bandits . . ."

The devious description method is utilized when, on page 271, it is stated, "The Americans did not settle on villages as did the French, but moved out into the villages and 'squatted' on public lands." In other words, these Americans took Indian land, built homes and fences, and regularly interfered with Indian economy. It is, however, admitted that the Indians of this area had "well developed native Indian cultures" which were overrun and supplanted by the early Spanish from the South and Southwest, the French from Canada and the Great Lakes region, and the English from the East."

†OKLAHOMA OUR HOME. *By Daisy L. Moore*. Harr Wagner, 1955, 390 pp. Bureau of Indian Affairs. Chilocco Indian School, Oklahoma.

A European approach is shown in this book. The book is quite obviously written for the white-dominated population, white-dominated schools, and Indian schools dominated by white supremacist ideology.

The history of Oklahoma begins with Coronado, in the Foreword. This will be a surprise to many Indian children, whose great-grandparents were born in that state, and who know that Indians of certain tribes had possession of that area long before Coronado; Indians of other tribes had joint use of the area for hunting purposes; and many Indian tribes used the region for thousands of years before Coronado was born.

An excuse is found for military surveillance of Indian land and tribes. On page 76, because "of such warfare among the Indians, the United States government established military forts in Oklahoma. This was done to try to preserve peace among the Indians and make Oklahoma a better place to live." No mention is made of the government's policy of giving land to one tribe, then giving the same land to another tribe—thus provoking conflict between the tribes.

The passage of the bill which provided for the opening of unassigned lands in Oklahoma for white settlement, is hailed on page 161. This was accomplished through trickery, in which a rider was attached to a current Indian Appropriation Bill, on March 2, 1889. There is no mention of the renowned Indian leaders who built Oklahoma. There is no mention of the great progress made by the Tribes before the opening of the unassigned lands, or of the contributions in literature, art, industry made by Indians of Oklahoma. There is no notice taken of the current situation of the Indian people of the State of Oklahoma.

*†OKLAHOMA, THE STORY OF A STATE. By *Edward Everett Dale.* Harper & Row, 1963, 448 pp. Concho Demonstration School, Oklahoma. Junior High School.

A good deal of information about the Indian tribes of America, and particularly many who were forcibly transported to Oklahoma in the early 1800's, is made available by the author.

This author has a mistaken conception, however, in connection with the early occupation of the territory now called Oklahoma. He states that there were very few Indians in the area. The fact is that certain tribes utilized the land as hunting sites, and certainly this is as much to be considered "ownership" as the huge King ranch and other ranches with vast holdings, which was at one time Indian country in Texas. Objection is also taken to the designation of certain Plains tribes as "fierce and warlike. They painted their faces, dressed in buckskin leggings and moccasins, lived in round tents called tepees, and depended upon the flesh of the buffalo as food," (p. 21). This statement is derogatory, and does not reflect a basic knowledge of the Indian Plainsmen who embarked on a defensive war against the invading whites at an early stage of the contact, until vanquished by superior arms.

Page 24: "At last the Five Civilized Tribes agreed to give up their old government and to divide their lands so that every Indian might have his rightful share." This was done by deceit, as historic evidence shows, and is in contradition with the rest of this text, which explains more fully what happened. Objection is also taken to the observation on page 26, ". . . the study of Oklahoma history begins with the coming of the first European people into the Mississippi Valley . . ." As already noted, these lands were the property of a number of tribes, and the history of the state, therefore, should begin with them.

The author describes the white travelers, including the traders, in this way, "Early traders were, in a sense, quite as much pathfinders as were the official explorers. It is true that they kept no record of their travels and made no reports as to what they found, but they did learn a great deal about the streams, mountains, and trails of Oklahoma, consequently, they were able to give valuable information to the explorers sent out by the government," (p. 88). It is peculiar that no writer of the white race, to our knowledge, has designated the American Indian as a "pathfinder." When pressed, it is stated that they kept no records, consequently cannot be considered in that class. How then, does this author justify considering the traders as pathfinders, and fail to describe the Native Americans in that light. Incorrect data is given on page 95, in noting the Indian population.

Misconception as to the culture of the Natives at the time of white contact must arise as a result of the author's description of them, for on page 95, he says, "At the time that the first Europeans came to America, the Indians were living in what is called the Stone Age of civilization." To grant the author a full degree of excuse for this error, it is quite possible that he is unfamiliar with more current nomenclature. The stone age in man's development designates an entirely different type of culture, technology, and social organization. Primitive man had different cultures, different values, a different technology. Far better is the designation "Pre-literate." However, we cannot remain charitable when on page 96, the author says, "Like most primitive people, they believed in dreams and omens, and in charms to ward off sickness or death. They told stories to explain the origin of things they did not understand—thunder, lightning, rain, hail and snow, or the rising and setting sun and the changing moon." Many other peoples advanced to a considerable stage in their development, believed in dreams, omens, and attempted to explain the origin of things in the natural life about them. It happens even today, in more sophisticated religions.

The section titled "The Pattern of Society" gives considerable value to the work of Indian artists, writers, and poets. It is too bad that some of the prominent and distinguished personalities of Oklahoma who are Indian are left out of this listing, such as the Tallchiefs, superb ballerinas; and Louis Ballard, distinguished musician and composer.

†OUR FLORIDA. *By a committee of Teachers of the Public Schools, Dade County, Florida.* Steck-Vaughn Co., 1962. Four soft cover books approximately 60-70 pages each, elementary grades. Bureau of Indian Affairs schools, Miccosukee Agency, Florida.

Book 2 deals with the Seminole Indians of Florida. It contains descriptions of Seminole dress, houses, the hairdoes of the women and the work of the men. Information is of an extremely general nature. There is no discussion of the culture, history, or current situation. Seminole lifeways are indicated in so general a manner that on the one hand the children in the public schools will learn very little; and on the other hand the children in the Indian schools will be bored, for it tells them very little if anything about their own people. Many changes have taken place in Seminole life within the last ten years. It is not reflected in the book. The text is generally very unsatisfactory. Book 3 deals with the early Indian tribes. Treatment of their culture is more informative than that given the Seminole, and despite some errors and inaccuracies, the three pages of general description should produce a desire for further study, and that is the best that can be said of this book.

EXPLORING MINNESOTA. By Harold T. Hagg. Follett Publishing Co., 1958, 160 pp. Public schools of Minnesota.

This textbook is described by the publishers as a "new Unified Social Studies" book. On page 6, is given the ideology which guides the author in developing the study of the state: "Our state was the home of the Indians long ago. They hunted in the forests and fished in the lakes. Then white men explored Minnesota and discovered its wealth and beauty." This is to set the Native Minnesotan on a plane of simple natural resources. Untrue. The Indian had long ago explored this region, and they were well aware of its wealth and beauty, or they would not have fought so strongly to retain possession of it.

Improper comparison between modern and ancient Indian life is made and inaccuracy is found, on pages 30 and 31, when it is explained that the Indians were "nearly starved" in the winter, and that because of the hardships of Indian life, "many Indians died young." There is no substantiation of the picture drawn here, of an impoverished, meager existence, in which the people were starving. Improper comparison exists when the author states that the Indians "did not use other resources in the way we do now." The Indian way of life is further described as to compare unfavorably with American modern civilization, in that they made houses of bark and skins "instead of lumber, nails, brick and concrete, as we do now." Clothing, says this author, "was made of hides and furs, not of cloth." The implication is that Indian life was so crude, and their products so "primitive," that it is a blessing we now have those beautiful things like lumber and cloth. Not stated is the fact that the early white comers imitated Indian ways, utilized Indian manners of dress, including hides and furs from which they learned to make moccasins and jackets; and even imitated materials used in the house building customs of the Natives. The author, in comparing the world of more than a hundred years later, with that of the Natives, whose economy was highly complex in their stage of society, has sought to diminish the Indian, and to show the students how great the country is now as compared to the Indian days; how rich and wonderful and smart we are today.

The Indian is blamed for the destruction of their own lives, because with the acquisition of the horse, they were able to make an industry of buffalo hunting, (page 33). It is not recognized, in this book, that the Indian way of life was destroyed because his land was taken away, his game destroyed by the whites, and his forests stolen to make part of white-owned property, by fraud and thievery, so that his economy was shattered. The religions of the Indian people are oversimplified to such a degree that no understanding results. Which tribes he is talking about, in describing the various forms of worship, is not revealed by the author. What the explorers did (Americans) to find routes of travel, climate, soil, and plants, is explained, on page 41. But it is not explained that these things were learned from the Indians.

On page 7, it is stated that the "real settlers" of Minnesota were: ". . . pioneer loggers, farmers, businessmen, and other workers." If this author refuses to consider the Indians as the first Native settlers, what, we wonder, does he consider them to be? How Minnesota became a territory is also in the category of history falsified by generalization and omission. Page 57 explains that for many years Minnesota "was Indian land, not open to white settlers." But, in 1837, the Indians "sold" the lands to the United States Government, which made possible the settlement of the territory. Untrue. Indians were compelled to sign a treaty which gave almost the entire state of Minnesota (then occupied and owned by Indian tribes) over to the government. On page 122, we learn about the Europeans who made the state rich and great. There is no mention of the American Indians, who still live there. Only in a photograph showing a Chippewa girl harvesting wild rice, is the Indian treated as part of the population of the state.

THE TEXAS STORY, By Ralph W. Steen. Steck-Vaugn Co., 1960, 470 pp. Public schools state textbook.

This book has a European approach. The history of the Indian in the state is fragmented and spliced in as incidental to the story of the European-oriented history of the state.

On page 1, with bravado and superiority, the authors state, that "Texas history, as the term is generally used, means the history of Europeans and their descendants in Texas." It is made clear, in the words that follow, that the textbook does not deny the existence of Indian tribes who lived in that region for thousands of years, before the Europeans came. The book, say the authors, "simply recognizes" that in that state today, only a few towns, several counties and a river or two have Indian names, and that is all the evidence remaining, of the original people of the state. "The customs and traditions of the tribes have long since been forgotten," it is stated. Furthermore, they say, with utmost gravity and smugness, "There is little in the civilization of modern Texas that can be attributed to the Indians."

Phraseology which condemns the Indians as aggressors and interlopers during visits of Spanish voyagers (rather than the facts being in the opposite direction) are expressed in such statements as this: "All of the vessels were wrecked or lost along the Texas coast, and most of the men fell victim to disease and to the Indians." The same first chapter relates the voyages of early Spaniards, who were directed to fabulous cities by the Indians. Mockery is expressed in these "tales," and anger because the Spaniards did not find gold, but there is no expression of the possibility that to the Indians these were indeed cities of fabulous wealth; that wealth, in the eyes of the Natives, was not the glittering gold sought by the early Spaniards, but something else entirely.

White supremacist racism is expressed throughout the book, in such words, on page 31: ". . . the Indians of East Texas were at least semi-civilized and were quiet indeed in comparison with their wild brothers of the plains." On page 56, and the succeeding pages, the story of Spanish attempts to establish missions is related. These were largely unsuccessful, due in part to the refusal of the tribes to give up their lands, and due also because of the history of mistreatment to which the Indians were subjected in the missions. The failure of the missions is treated as though the Indians were stupid, lazy, uncivilized, brutal, and incurably "savage." The Native people are treated as "nuisances," not in the more charitable generalized sense, but in descriptions giving chapter and verse of racism. The Karankawas are described as "blood-thirsty;" all of the tribes are said to have been imbued with one desire— the stealing of horses. Without the slightest feeling of historic injustice, the authors describe the relationship of Texas' early white settlement in connection with the Cherokee people, in such a way that it becomes quite clever to have cheated them of their land. By implication as well as by explicit description, it is related that the Cherokees were promised title to their land, but that for years this was not done, and the promise remained unfulfilled, in spite of the fact that both the whites and the Cherokees signed a treaty on the basis of guaranteeing them title to the land, in 1836. The Texas Colt, a newly developed gun, is described as a great technical accomplishment, because it "proved to be remarkably well adapted to fighting Indians on the plains," (p. 154). When the whites of Texas "founded two reservations" by "donating" land for the purpose, in 1852, they are described as failures, largely because the Indians "were not interested in agriculture." The author is talking about some of the most advanced tribes in the nation!

The wholesale destruction of the buffalo, when on the one hand white profiteers found a ready market for buffalo hides which could be made into expensive leather; and when buffalo bones became profitable as agricultural fertilizer, is treated as a fine positive result. The loss of the buffalo made it "impossible for the Indian to roam the plains at will and easier, therefore, to keep him on the reservation," (p. 299).

These are a few examples of racism, prejudice, supremacist ideology, expressed in the most unabashed way, by the author. Two small reservations still exist in the state of Texas. Without a doubt, the Indian is still part of the Texas population, but nothing is said of his conditions, or his situation in the world of today. The general reaction of the reader must be: "Thank God, Texas in all her glory and great genius, was able to get rid of the Indian problem by getting rid of the Indian." To say that the data utilized is inaccurate, would be impossible. No data are utilized. There is nothing but bold, brazen generalization—twisted and broken without factual reinforcement, spitting prejudice at every turn and with every word as to the first Americans of this land.

That such a textbook should have been accepted by the Texas educators; that it should be permitted to remain without litigation as libellous, and an example of the vilest type of racism, is to be wondered at.

† OUR PACIFIC NORTHWEST: YESTERDAY AND TODAY. *By Babcock & Babcock.* McGraw-Hill, 1963, 444 pp. Bureau of Indian Affairs schools. Public school text.

This textbook is used in the states of Idaho, Washington, and Oregon. According to these authors, the history of the area begins with Marco Polo in 1271, and continues with the travels of Europeans seeking the Northwest Passage. After "establishing" that the Europeans discovered the Pacific Northwest, the book deals (almost as an afterthought) with the original inhabitants, on page 66.

The treatment of the original inhabitants is extremely simplistic, the principal interest of the authors being to determine the general physical characteristics of the Natives. This description is generalized and does not show the variety of peoples who settled that area. Over-generalization appears on page 67, when the Indians of these three areas are divided into two main groups: the inland group, and the coastal group. While some general conclusions may be drawn from such a division, as to the material culture of the Native people, such conclusions are not valid as to their culture, religions and traditions. Hostility between the tribes is described as part of their culture. There is no indication of the time in history when this is presumed to have occurred — whether before white contact, or following contact with the Europeans.

An aura of stupidity is lent to the people of the coastal region, on page 68, when it is stated that Indians took large quantities of salmon from the streams, and "What they could not eat fresh, they smoked or dried for winter use." The implication is that they ate until they could eat no more, and THEN STORED the food for future use. In fact, their principal concern was to lay aside food for the winter. On the same page, it is stated that acorns were one of two staple foods. Describing this food, it is said that it was "cooked into a tasteless but nourishing food." Acorn is one of the most desired foods of the Indian people, even today. Many Native people will go miles to a festival or a ceremonial event, because they know their hosts will have acorn gruel, bread, or soup. One might ask: tasteless to whom?

On page 123, there is a description of the Indians' reactions to the white man's "possessions — his firearms, mirrors, burning glasses . . . " This interest is described in such a way as to diminish the intelligence of the Native people: "They wanted to learn more about it so that they, too might possess the secret of the white man's magic." This is untrue. They knew that they were confronted with new technology, and that life must change for them. The Natives, whenever they made a treaty with the United States government, insisted first of all on education. Does this represent the "primitive" reaction of a "primitive" people, who believed the whites had some sort of "magic?" On page 142 the authors explain the Indians' reactions to religious practices and draw improper conclusions from their recital of prayers or singing of hymns: "The Indians probably thought that by following the white man's instructions, they would learn the secret of the white man's powers." This, again, is to diminish and degrade the intelligence of the Native people, who were well accustomed to prayers, sings and chants in their own religions.

On page 78, there is a description of the rearing of children, including the practice of flattening the head, which some tribes did. The authors say: "The children of the inland tribes did not receive as much care and attention as those of the coastal tribes." In the first instance, some tribes did practice the head-flattening technique in child rearing. However, it is made to appear that all tribes did, and this generalization is improper. In the second instance, how did these writers determine that the children of the inland area did not receive the same care and attention as those of the coast? This is such a specious, palpably ignorant statement that it is an insult against the Native people.

These descriptions are false: "The purpose of owning slaves was not for their economic value but for their prestige value. Ownership of slaves was a sign of success in war or of sufficient wealth to purchase them. In some cases, slaves were sacrificed to demonstrate that a chief was so wealthy that he could afford to destroy his valuable possessions . . . Generally slaves were not badly treated. True, they did the hardest work and ate what was left after the family had dined. However, they lived with the family and they were not beaten or starved." There is ample evidence that the slaves had an entirely different social position than slavery implies in the sense of western civilization. That any were killed for purposes of prestige is a falsification.

The potlatch is described on page 83. This ceremony is explained as it has been falsified and distorted for many years. The Indian war of self-defense in the Northwest is treated as a "massacre" if they won, and as a victory if the whites won, (p. 196). The story about the Indian named Lawyer is false. He was not a chief. True, he was named chief by the state's governor. But he was never recognized by his people. In this book, Lawyer is treated as a hero, defending Governor Stevens and informing him of a Cayuse plot to rebel. Lawyer has been memorialized in a monument on the campus of Whitman college, and this is the white man's way to repay a traitor to his people. Textbooks are presumed to tell the truth. If there is question, or conflicting opinion and evidence, it ought to relate both sides of the story. The famous speech of Chief Looking Glass before the great Indian Council on June 8, 1885, should have been published, in which he exposed Lawyer as a traitor. This was no internal quarrel. It was a deliberate attempt on the part of the state government to foist a Trojan horse in the midst of the tribes. The treaty signed by Lawyer was denounced by the Native people, who refused to approve it.

There is no mention in this book as to where the Pacific Northwest Indians are today; how they live and what they are doing to improve their lives. Nor is there mention of the continuing treachery of the state and federal government, as witness the ligitation over fishing rights in the state of Washington. A serious criticism of this book, in all aspects, is that it generalizes about Indian culture, customs and conditions. One never knows what tribe the authors are writing about.

* DISCOVERING NEW MEXICO.   *By Crosno & Masters.*
The Steck Co., 1950, 354 pp. Public schools text.

Published nearly twenty years ago, this book is still being circulated by the Steck-Vaughn Company. It has been used for a long time, and for that length of time the young people of New Mexico had an opportunity to digest its propaganda. Written in narrative style, the book is so bad a piece of English that it should have been condemned on that basis alone. So far as the history of the state is concerned, the approach is strongly from the point of view of the white man. From the "outside looking in" the whites examine the Indian history of this most Indian-populated state. This is the only textbook examined in the entire study of TEXTBOOKS AND THE AMERICAN INDIAN which may not actually still be in use. It has been chosen as an example of the sort of trash that has been fed to our young people these many years. The Pueblo revolts are treated like savage "massacres" by the Indians. At best, this textbook is a tourists' guide to the state and the Indian people of the area.

* THE STORY OF CALIFORNIA. *By David Lavender.* American Heritage Publishing Company, 1970, 352 pp. Public schools, 4th grade.

Highly generalized information about the American Indian is contained in this book. The pictures of the Native people, with very few exceptions, show them to be uncouth, brutish beings. Improper comparisons are made, probably with the idea of involving the imagination of the young students, so that he might "relate" to Indian lifeways. On page 46, for example, "The big problem for Indians everywhere was food. They could not buy what they wanted to eat."
Incorrect information is presented in the statement that the Yuma and Mohave Indians were "the only Indians who raised crops in California," (p. 52). Discussing the Yurok Indians of northeast Cali-

fornia, the statement is made that they built "strong houses" out of trees that had fallen down. The implication is that these people had no way of felling trees. They had highly developed skills in bringing down even the big redwoods.

On page 124, we learn: "In many ways the Indians who lived in the missions had much to be thankful for. They did not need to spend long hours hunting or finding acorns. The cooks at the missions prepared meals for everyone. When the food was ready, a bell rang. The Indians gathered at a central place, and the food was passed out to them. They were also given clothing to wear. Before, they had been almost naked." This might have been a place to make a proper comparison. For example, the student might be asked: How would you like to be put in a lineup and have your food passed out to you? Information is given on page 127 about the "Mexicans" who believed the Indians should have some of the mission lands returned to them, and the statement made regarding secularization is this: "The Fathers had been right about one thing. The Indians were not ready to work for themselves. They had not yet learned responsibility. With no one around to give them directions, they did not work at all. They did not plant their fields. They did not watch their animals. They traded their property to Mexicans for foolish things that they soon wasted. After their land was gone, the Indians did not know what to do. They had forgotten how to live in the old ways. They were not ready for new ways. Only a few were able to join the tribes that lived in the hills." Not mentioned is the great Mexican land grab, as great perhaps as the American land grab which took place some years later. Not mentioned either, is the treatment of the Native people following secularization. They were driven out of the missions, left without food, starving and homeless. Most of their people were killed, or died as a result of the white man's diseases. Their homes in the native lands were taken by the Spaniards or the Mexicans. Homeless, landless, driven from place to place, one of the most degrading examples of "civilized" man's treatment of the American Indian occurred in connection with secularization in California.

On page 101, an explanation is given as to why the Yuma Indians killed the soldiers and prevented construction of the mission in their country on the Colorado River. The reason given is that the Spanish settlers came with a thousand animals and these animals ate all the Yuma vegetables they had planted. This was only one of a long series of insults which included the rape of Yuma women. The Spaniards attempted to end the religious observances of the Yuma people, to ignore their most respected traditions and lifeways, and treated them as brutes capable only of experimentation in the teaching of Christian religion.

Life at the mission is described thus: "The Indians liked the food. More and more of them came to live near the missions." The missions grew to be more than churches. They became little towns." This is very precious, to be sure, but far from the truth. In sentences and explanations such as this one, the author is attempting to ride two horses at the same time. On the one hand, he is trying to remain on good terms with the Catholic historians; on the other hand, he is attempting to satisfy the demands for historical justice now being heard from Indian scholars and Native historians. He is not alone in this type of fun and games. The section on the American Indian today is very general. Where the Indian people are, what they are doing is not described.

* CALIFORNIA RANCHO DAYS. *By Helen Bauer.* Doubleday & Co., 1953, revised 1969, 128 pp. Public Schools supplementary text, 4th grade.

"None of the Indians were given money for their work. What would they do with money? Did not the ranchero give them food, clothing, and a place to live?" This is only one of a series of outrageous superior, racist statements made by the writer concerning the Indians of California during the time of the Rancheros, when in fact the Natives worked as serfs on the ranches of those who occupied the Indian lands. There is no mention that the early land grants, both Spanish and Mexican, took Indian land without compensation, or that the Americans, following the end of the war with Mexico, engaged in one of the most massive land steals in history. "The Indians traded otter skins for whatever they could get." This observation on page 23, is demeaning. They traded for what they wanted, and they knew quite well what they wanted. These are examples of some of the errors committed. An opportunity for explaining the transition from feudal labor in the missions to another type of serfdom, itself in turn transitory, is missed here, and the book is a mere glorification of the ranchos.

*CALIFORNIA'S OWN HISTORY. *By John Caughey.* Century Schoolbook Press, 1965, 302 pp. California State adopted textbook.

"People came to California ten or twelve or fifteen thousand years ago." Modern estimates place the figure at closer to 25 thousand years ago, (p. 12). "We do not know just where they entered our state. We know they came on foot and that their coming was part of a very long walk." Modern scientists consider that they came by boat as well. On the same page: "They also enjoyed some things that we would not think of eating. They smacked their lips over fat worms and toasted grasshoppers." This is facetious provincialism. The worms and roasted grasshoppers have been food for many other peoples besides the Indians, for many thousands of years. The connotation is that of a "strange" people, not like other human beings. Page 13, on housing, "That means three or four houses, and one more to bathe in." They had no bath house. A sweat house is probably meant, which was also a ceremonial house.

Innuendo which attaches to a vulgarized people is found here: "Old California was full of fleas—hungry, biting fleas. Everyone says so. If the fleas got too bad, all an Indian had to do was burn down his house and build a new one," (p. 16). It is questionable that an Indian person would burn down a house. Fire was dangerous. About the fleas: "Everyone says so"—but who is everyone? And what period of time is the author writing about?

The section on the cooking of acorns is treated so casually as to deprive the young student of the true meaning of this discovery, which could be compared to the discovery of the use of wheat. It made available a staple food for thousands of years to come. It should not be treated facetiously, (p. 22). On page 25, we learn "The large number of languages gives a good hint that these people did not do much traveling. They did some visiting and trading with their close neighbors." Evidence supports the fact that they did indeed do a great deal of traveling, to places as far away as three or four hundred miles and further.

"In almost every tribe, more fuss was made over a girl when she became a woman," (p. 31). What is "fuss?" On page 86, describing the Yuma "massacre" the author states that the Yumas, "pounced on these few Spaniards and killed almost every one of them. They also burned two mission stations that had been located nearby and killed the four padres." There is evidence both in records and the oral history of the Yuma people that their women were raped by the Spanish. The destruction of the hated Spaniards was the result.

In the chapter dealing with life at the missions, page 92, it is said that "Many more Indians chose to be mission Indians. The smallest of the missions now had several hundred Indians. The largest had as many as two thousand." After several additional paragraphs relating the role of the padres in teaching the Indians, the author remarks: "How the padres did all this teaching is hard to imagine." More strangely still, the statement is made on page 93: "The Indians at the missions ate more regularly than they had when they were wild. The padres took care of them in many ways. The Indians had the feeling of being part of something much bigger than the old Indian village . . On the whole, they must have felt better off than before." All evidence points to the contrary, and it is extremely difficult to account for such statements by this eminent historian. Facts are plain for all who care to examine them that the Indians were forced to come to the missions, were forcibly brought back when they escaped, that mission life caused a sharp decline in the birth rate and a sharp increase in deaths.

Another falsification is contained on page 119, "The vaqueros had to guard against Indians from the mountains and the desert. They were known as the 'horsethief Indians.' They usually ran off the horses rather than cattle, because they liked to eat horses. These Indians were more trouble than the bears and wolves and mountain lions." This is a rank insult against the Native Californians. They used horses for transportation, for hunting, for the same things everyone else used them for.

Inaccuracy exists on page 136: "Sutter brought with him a German, a Belgian, an Irishman, and an Indian boy . . . He also brought eight men and two women from Hawaii." In fact, he brought nine men, as Mr. Henry Azbill knows personally, since he is a direct descendant of one of these men, being half Hawaiian and half Indian—and in full possession of actual facts concerning these people whom Sutter brought. "Sutter had to be careful because of all the wild Indians around him." In fact, he had armed guards more to guard against the Mexicans and Americans than against the Indians, most of whom were friends. The gold rush in California is treated from the white man's point of view. Indians were mere impediments on the rush to the mines. As this author explains on page 168, the miners had a hard time getting to the mines, "Then came a hard climb to the Pit River, past dangerous Indians." This book contains many errors, besides misinterpretations and distortions of Indian life.

*CALIFORNIA AND THE WEST. *John W. Reith, Editor.* Contributors: A. Fish, J. Hart, P. Moss, G. Pearcy, Jr. Reith, A. Rhodes, W. Wake. The Fideler Co., 1969, 400 pp. Public Schools fourth grade text.

General failure to understand Indian culture, history and technology is shown in this textbook. Errors include but are not limited to these: Page 48: "The first Californians came to North America from Asia." Scientists now state that they came from a number of directions and not always on foot. Page 49: "The village leader was called the chief. There was also a group of wise older men, called the council." The word CHIEF is an Anglo creation. There was no such word or type of leadership among the Indian people. Page 49: "Only a few Indians in California were farmers . . . The only California Indians who used any of their land for farming lived along the Colorado River." False. Many Indians farmed, had sophisticated irrigation systems, and had excellent methods for storage of food. Page 49: "Indian women and children gathered berries, nuts, roots and seeds." The division of labor was different than that in other tribal regions. All the family worked at whatever had to be done, whenever it was necessary to do it.

Page 50: "They ground the kernels (of acorn) between two stones . . . usually the meal was soaked in a basket." Untrue. Acorn was ground in stone or wood mortars, depending on the area. The meal was not soaked in a basket. Page 53: Indian houses of the Central California valley "were called wickiups." Untrue, not by California Indians. Page 53: "Indians lived near the redwood forest . . . found fallen trees in the forests, they split the trees into rough planks and used the planks to build their houses." False. They selected good trees in the forest, felling them with stone tools and splitting them with wedges of stone, or other materials. Page 53: "In the dry lands . . they covered this framework (of homes) with palm leaves." False. Only in southern California (Palm Springs and Coachella Valley) and even there this usage was limited. Page 53: "Most tools were very simple." False. The drills, knives, arrowheads, scrapers and so on, were certainly not simple and not simply made, as any informed person knows. Page 71: "The padres soon learned how to talk with the Indians." Slanted implication. The Indians also learned how to talk with the padres. Most Indians learned to speak both English and Spanish, and were thus linguists of their own Indian tongue and the two foreign tongues. Page 72: "Many thousands of Indians came to live at the missions." Untrue. Most of the Indians were forced to come to live at the missions. They represented forced labor.

*CALIFORNIA MISSION DAYS. By *Helen Bauer*. Doubleday & Co., 1951; revised, 1969, 126 pp. Fourth Grade Public Schools, supplementary text.

Written from the point of view of the Spanish missionaries. On page 22, we learn that "In return for gifts, the Indians showed the newcomers where to find water." This insidious insult against the Native people is an indication of the rest of the book. Evidence shows that at this time the Indians were friendly. After they learned of the threat to their freedom and their lands, they turned against the priests. On page 26, relating the story of Mission San Diego, "When the Indians did come, they were warlike . . . About a year later, a hundred Indians were living at the mission. No one thought there was any danger. But one night hundreds of warlike Indians came with clubs and bows and arrows. They came quietly into the church and took the padres' robes. Then they yelled and set fire to the church and all the other buildings. Before many minutes, every building was on fire." The approach in favor of the Spaniards is clearly shown, and the position of the Indians who stood to lose their land and were protecting themselves against forced labor, is not indicated. The language itself is derogatory.

The attitude that the Indian people did not know how to govern themselves without the padres is shown here again and nothing is said about what the priests learned from the Indians, which was considerable. Life at the missions is not described. There is no discussion of the type of labor and the social system in existence at the missions, which might have been of some scholarly value to the students. Treatment of the building of Mission Dolores in San Francisco is inadequate, inaccurate. The Indians disappeared from that area faster than at any other of the 21 missions in the state, or were killed. Word had reached them of the results of missionization, and those who remained went into the hills and combined with other tribes almost immediately.

The Mission Dolores was actually peopled by Indians of other localities and other tribes, from as far away as San Diego. These people were forcibly transported from their homelands and compelled to work at the San Francisco mission. An error exists concerning Mission San Jose. Confusion is shown between this mission, and the pueblo of San Jose. The chapter on Mission San Miguel states, "Governor Pico sent word to the Indians to come back (to the mission) or the land would be sold." Since the Indians knew they would be killed if they attempted to return and claim their land and property, it is no wonder they refused to "come back." (If indeed Governor Pico—one of the most notorious land grabbers in California history—"sent word" to them.)

CALIFORNIA, A HISTORY. By Mabel Young Williams. Harr

Wagner, 1965, 211 pp. Public Schools text.

Inaccuracies as to customs exist. Page 12, "No one could hunt on
land that did not belong to his own tribe." With tribal permission, they
could. Another inaccuracy, page 16, "They left no writings to tell us
how they lived. But they did leave other things, however, that help us
learn about their lives." There are many living Indian descendants of
these people who know how they lived. On page 19, another inaccuracy
refers to a 'long house' used by the California Indians. No Indians of
this region had such a term. "Each sweat house was built partly below
the ground." Not true, this only came later, with the advent of a new
religion and then not all the tribes followed such a construction. "Most
of the houses were covered with mud and weeds." They did not use
mud. They built on a framework of poles, the roof being constructed
of interlaced branches, brush, and other woody materials, then covered
with soil.

"The Mohave and Yuman tribes lived near the Colorado River. They
were the only California Indians who learned to plant seeds. They were
the only California tribes to grow their own food.'" This, on page 22 is
inaccurate. Many tribes planted seeds for tobacco, beans, squash, corn,
cotton, and melons. On the same page, the description for making acorn
is inaccurate. There was no such belief as the word "witch" implies. Belief in spirits did exist. The description of the shaman being "rich" is
inaccurate and betrays an ignorance of both the literature on the subject and the knowledge of the people themselves.

"The first thing most Indian children learned was swimming." Not
true, only among tribes living near water, and many tribes lived away
from water. Some of the sheerest tripe has been written into this book,
as "beliefs" of the Indian people. To note them all would take pages
of explanation. Suffice it to say that a STUDY of the literature alone
would have avoided such blunders as this author has made as to the
history and culture of the Indians who lived in the region we now call
California. Description of the guessing games is inaccurate. The statement that the California Indians did not have numbers (page 45) is incorrect. On page 120 it is stated that the Spaniards taught the Indians
how to grind grain on a metate. This is a Spanish word, and Indians
used the rock pounding and grinding method long before the Spaniards
came.

Information that the Indians lived well in the missions is also incorrect. Facts prove otherwise. "The Indians had better food and clothing than they had ever had. They were more comfortable than they had

ever been." Such propaganda is actually an insult to the intelligence, when there is documented evidence to the contrary. As to the missions, feudal forced labor existed, with all its evils. The statement referring to "wild Indians" on page 126 is gross insult. What is "wild?" A reason for granting lands which belonged to the Indians, to the white settlers, is given on page 169. "The government was giving away large grants of land. There were no white settlements on the valley . . . He (Sutter) might be able to keep the wild Indians away from Spanish settlements." So much of the information given in this book is inaccurate, distorted, and unsubstantiated, that the book may be judged as absolutely unacceptable. Other information, such as is well known among Indian people still living today, is not even mentioned. Such as, for example, that at Sutter's Fort Indians were fed from a trough.

In dealing with the gold rush, beginning with page 213, there is no mention of Indian sufferings, rape and genocide, etc., which also exist in the record as documented evidence. This author writes as though the Indians were dead, for on page 277, it is stated, "Some of these (new) laws would seem very surprising to the Indians and the early Californians."

WE, THE PEOPLE OF CALIFORNIA. By Hegland & Petteys. Franklin Publications, 1965, 172 pp. Eighth grade basic text, California public schools.

European approach, which opens the history of California with Cabrillo. After several visits by Europeans, the authors say, "California lapsed back into sleepiness . . The Indians . . lived as they had always lived, meagerly, off the land, moving short distances with the seasons, each tribe largely isolated from the others, all cut off from the powerful Indian nations to the East across the Sierras," (p. 7). The Indians lived well in an economy suited to their needs. They moved when it was necessary, and traveled great distances for trading purposes. The tribes were well aware of other tribal societies and were not isolated. They were less "isolated" than were whites who came to this country in the sixteenth century and had no methods of transportation.

According to these authors, the Spaniards first developed irrigation ditches. Untrue. The Indians, particularly of Southern California, had developed sophisticated irrigation systems long before. As to trails and paths, on page 9 we are surprised to find that the Spanish missionaries built the paths which "were used by engineers, a century and a half later, to lay out some of our state highways." This will come as a surprise also to the many scientists, anthropologists, and Indians who know otherwise.

Population (page 12) is considered only in the white context, which these authors say was approximately 10,000 "exclusive of Indians." A pass is made for oriental friendship, on page 15, "To our shame, we later enacted laws that no Oriental could own land, but these laws have been repealed." No consideration whatever is expressed for the Native peoples of California whose land was taken. "We, the People of California," obviously means We, the White people of California. The book discusses government, some minimum of attention being given to the so-called minorities. There is no treatment whatever of the growing Indian population, their situation, problems, and where they are today.

*STORIES CALIFORNIA INDIANS TOLD. *By Anne B. Fisher.* Parnassus Press, 1957, 108 pp, adopted for elementary use as curriculum related text, State of California.

Coyote stories are told largely for adult sophisticated entertainment. This is particularly true of California coyote stories. To prove this point, the reader need only glance at the authentic translations of almost all coyote stories, done by linguistics departments of universities. Nevertheless, this author chooses to utilize them for the pleasure of children. This is a common error. While such behavior among the white persons who choose to write about Indians amuses us, we are not amused by this author's dedication. The dedication states "For all boys and girls who like Indians and Animals." To say that this is an insult would be to explain only a minute part of the anger and hurt felt by Indian people reading this insensitive combining of the animal world with the human.

*CALIFORNIA GOLD DAYS. *By Helen Bauer.* Doubleday & Co. Revised 1968. Fourth grade supplementary book for public school use.

The gold miners are glorified beyond all evidence to the contrary as to their character, reasons for coming, and way of life. On page 92, "It was surprising that there was not more trouble. The miners were men of all kinds. All had to work together. A hundred thousand people in the wild, rough life of the gold mines! Whoever they were, every man had an equal chance. All had to play fair and follow the rules. This was a true democracy." If democracy was really represented by the hanging committees, the vigilantes, the kangaroo courts, and the killing of a man without trial, then democracy is not understood by this writer. If justice and democracy mean the attempted genocide and extermination of a whole race of people, because they stood in the way of gold, then this type of democracy is not for human beings. There is not one word of criticism of the gold miners. The Indians are mentioned only inadvertently. There is no explanation of Native conditions, land stealing, their way of life, and their intense suffering under the rule of the Great God Gold. No understanding is possible, as a result of this book, about the condition of the country during the days of the gold rush. The descriptions of how gold is mined, how great and adventurous it is, can only send the young student into a mercenary dream world. The book as a whole is unrealistic, inaccurate, and a Chamber of Commerce tract to glorify the gold miners.

LIFE IN AMERICA: ALASKA. By Stuart R. Tompkins. Fideler, 1966, 127 pp. Public schools fifth grade geography.

Some information, but little or no understanding of the land, the people, their history, or their current situation. This is a geography text, of course, but some background is needed in this field as in others, and it is lacking. Arts of the Native peoples are treated like a mere casual craft. No description is given of the beautiful artistic works of the Natives, not only in carving, but in other artistic fields. This book is a vapid "chamber of commerce" type tract. It does not impart either information nor knowledge.

THE OTHER SAN FRANCISCO. By David F. Selvin. The Seabury Press, 1969, 163 pp. Offered as supplementary text in public schools of the San Francisco Bay Area.

The book is inaccurate in many respects concerning the Indian people of the area. On page 7, it is stated that "Life made no heavy demands on them." The implication is that all the Natives had to do was to stretch out their hands, whereupon food, shelter and clothing would fall into their laps. The contrary is true; they needed and had a complex organized society in which full advantage was taken of the land's natural riches.

"Early visitors" to California are quoted as saying that the Natives were "squalid and listless . . . as primitive and backward as could be found anywhere on the face of the globe." This degrading description is quoted from a writer, whose contacts followed missionization, and it should not be made in a book proposed for school use. The statement that they "relished grasshoppers, insects, snakes," is implicitly derogatory, if given without further explanation. On page 8, generalization about the women of the tribes, who "occasionally threw a wrap of deerskin around their shoulders," is puerile, not descriptive of Native attire.

Page 11. It is stated that "Intermarriage was not only accepted but encouraged." This is inaccurate. Intermarriage was tolerated by the "lower classes, or soldiers," but certainly was frowned upon by the "Gente de Razon." The objectives of the missions, given on page 23, are sheer propaganda. Not even the Spanish overlords believed this. The missions were outposts of Spanish dominion, and Christianization was part of the process to subdue the Natives, to make certain of a stable labor force. On page 24, paragraph 2, the Indian appears as some kind of a fool, because "Little rewards and food were often enough to persuade them to lend a hand in clearing land or erecting the mission buildings." They did this, because they were friendly at first, believing that these people wanted only to LIVE on the land, not to OWN it. The life at the missions is described so that the Natives were mildly punished if they refused to work, and generally they worked well and happily.

The facts about the Mission Dolores in San Francisco are these: Nowhere else in this region, where 21 missions were established, did the Indians die out faster, or disappear more swiftly than they did here at Dolores. Most of the inhabitants of the later Mission Dolores were forcibly transported from other mission areas, and became nothing better than feudal slave laborers. On page 29, it is stated that "soldiers frequently used to round up new recruits" from among the Native peoples. It should have been stated, that this happened ALL the time. A particularly inaccurate statement, and one derogatory to the Indians of the area, is made on pages 29-30, where it is said, concerning secularization and "distribution of the land to the Indians," that "Where distribution was actually made, gambling, thievery, and sheer fraud soon relieved the unsophisticated Indian of his share." This is a half-truth. The Native people were driven from the missions, left without food or shelter. The idea that they themselves resorted to gambling and thereby lost their land, is derogatory. They never were allowed to take their land.

While attempting to display some sympathy for the Native people of this area, the author commits inaccuracies; his data are incorrect; the information is so shallow and overgeneralized that little or no resemblance is found to the truth about the history of the Indian in San Francisco. A particularly crass example of this is the treatment of the Indian in the chapter on the gold rush, starting with page 50. "The Indians," this author states, "lived out their time in California ignorant of gold." That the Indians certainly knew about the gold, is shown in the fact that *Indians* led miners to places where gold was to be found. To the Natives, gold was not a commodity; and it had no place in their economy. Furthermore, there is no description of what the gold rush did to the Indians in dispossessing them from their land, homes and food-gathering, hunting and fishing areas.

*FIVE BOOKS IN GEOGRAPHY. Fideler Co., 1966. Fifth grade public schools texts.

These books are used in public schools as basic texts. Evaluations indicate that they all contain errors, misinterpretations, omissions, and distortions of history.

The five books have no actual information concerning the Native peoples of these geographical regions. The treatment is bland, uninteresting, and ignores most of the facts students need to know in order to learn. The current situation, where treated, is a mere token of explanations that need to be given. Federal-Indian relations are not discussed.

There is an enormous opportunity in the study of geography to contrast the type of geographical divisions existing before white European contact, so far as the Native peoples are concerned. Tribal territories, common grounds for hunting and fishing, lands utilized in some areas for clans and families which were tied together in loose tribal entities— all this is of supreme interest, and will teach the development of mankind to the student so that it becomes a fascinating subject. Political as opposed to geographical boundaries could be treated here. How and why the lands were divided among the tribes, so that all had a share in the bounties of nature and an opportunity to develop an independent economy—these are of great interest, but they have not been treated.

GREAT PLAINS STATES. *By Walter Havighurst.* 1966, 164 pp., Book
4 of the series.

"Because of the great stretches of treeless country and the warlike
Indians who lived there, most of the plains remained unsettled until the
middle of the nineteenth century." Not mentioned is the fact that the
Indians were still fighting for their land. This item on page 41 displays
the same ideological tendency as all other books do—that the warlike
"qualities" of the Indians prevented settlement. More in the vein of
historical truth would be the admission that they were fighting for
their homes and land. Page 128 has this description of the locality of
the Missouri River. "Across the river from Bismarck lies the town of
Mandan. Indians from nearby reservations frequently are seen on its
streets." This is the remark of an idly curious but entirely uninformed
person about Indian life and culture.

THE SOUTH. *By Jerry E. Jennings & Marion H. Smith,* 1965, 276 pp.,
Book 2 of the series.

"Scientists believe that the people we call Indians first came to America from Asia," it is stated on page 54. Other ideas should be mentioned, such as those of some scientists who consider that the first people
came from a number of places. In the section titled "The Revolution
and the New Nation," page 66, the "United States forced many tribes
of Indians to give up their lands. This was because settlers who were
now moving into territory west of the Appalachian Mountains wanted
more land." The book does not mention that the Indians of this area
had adopted the best of European technology, manners, and customs,
and in some cases, even the religion. They were a prosperous, progressive, well-to-do people who were developing a unique type of society,
retaining the best of their own culture. "People and Citizenship," page
78, almost all other peoples resident in the area are mentioned except
the Native Americans. Discussing "social problems" beginning with
page 78, there is no mention of the Indian role in the present society.

THE MIDWEST. *By Walter Havighurst,* 1965, 196 pp. Book 3 of the
series.

"Why is the Mississippi River important?" receives some historical treatment, but there is no description of the extensive and unique original use of this body of water by the Native Americans. The author admits, "As more settlers came, the Indians living here were pushed westward. At the Mississippi River they resisted, and in 1832, the Black Hawk War was fought. After their defeat in this war, the Indians in the Midwest became peaceful, except for a last uprising in Minnesota in 1862." The implication, judging from the complete context of this part of the book, is that the Indians had to be defeated in the interest of progress.

Page 63 discusses the people of the Midwest. "The earliest known inhabitants were the Indians." While it is true that the Indians inhabited the region, it should also be made clear that they were the first settlers here, with an economy and a social structure different from the Europeans. When discussing life in the midwest today, and how it evolved from the past, the author deals with recreation, but fails to mention that many recreational forms were taken from the Natives. According to this book, which barely mentions the Indian people, the Indians had no life or culture. There is no treatment of the current situation of the American Indians. Page 159, "Northeastern Minnesota is still wild land, but it has contributed greatly to the development of America." No mention that the NATIVE PEOPLE of this area contributed to the life of the region, the nation, and the world.

*THE NORTHWEST. By *Walter Havighurst*. 1964, 64 pp. Book 1 of the series

"Much of the land was the home of the Iroquois, a federation of five united tribes," (p. 38). The Indians owned *all* of the land in this region. On page 39, the time-worn legend is stated, "The Dutch bought Manhattan Island, at the mouth of the Hudson, from the Indians." The Indians had no knowledge of such a political-economic system as the sale of land. According to their social system and philosophy, land could not be sold. "Most of the Iroquois Indians took the British side in the war and attacked the frontier areas. . .," (page 44). The reason for this choice should be given: The British treated the Indians better than the colonists. "Scotch-Irish settlers moved into the frontier areas of Pennsylvania, where they cleared the land and fought the Indians." This item, on page 59, fails to mention that these people took Indian-owned land, who were then forced to fight. Discussing the various crops of the Northeast, no mention is made of Indian contributions such as tobacco, corn, arts, inventions.

State and Regional History

SUMMARY OF EVALUATIONS (31 BOOKS EVALUATED)

1: Errors of omission appear in all the textbooks.
2: The American Indian is treated as part of the history of the state in only one textbook, "Oklahoma, The Story of a State," Hale, Harper & Row.
3: Degrading descriptions in one form or another, appear in all the books evaluated.
4: Most of the textbooks contain little if any information about the Indian of the state today.
5: Specific contributions of the Indian are lacking in 25 of the 26 books. The one exception is the book on Oklahoma, above mentioned, which contains a minimum of such information.
6: The story of white encroachment is glossed over, not mentioned at all, or generally excused, in all the textbooks.
7: All 26 textbooks contain inaccuracies, in one degree or another.

VI

Government and Citizenship

CRITERIA

1: The concepts of the general Criteria are applicable.

2: The developmental treatment of government in the United States should include the influence of Native democratic thought and society.

3: The development historically and politically, of Indian-Federal relations should be described, including the federal laws, territorial ordinances, Acts of Congress, and conflict between the cultures.

4: Treaties with the Indian tribes should be treated as part of the history of this nation. Information should be included as to the history of such treaties, and the status of the tribes, which was that of foreign nations.

5: Important Supreme Court decisions, and critical cases in the courts should be part of the information given in the book, so that the student may understand the developmental process of the Indian role in the government of our country. Indication should be provided that such litigation is still continuing. The basis for such litigation should be explained.

6: When the family as a unit of society is discussed, the developmental process of the Indian family, historically, economically, and socially should be treated.

7: Indian reservations, rancherias, and other types of land ownership as they exist now, should be described. The areas, locations, and population of the reservations should be given. The current situation of

the American Indian as related to the United States government
should be described accurately and objectively. The truth should be
told. Such conditions as Bureau of Indian Affairs schools, which are
federally controlled institutions, at variance with democratic educational thought, should be described. At the same time, possibilities
of change ought to be discussed from all points of view, not merely
that of the author. Particular effort should be made to ascertain the
Indians' points of view.

8: Indian participation in government, agencies, contributions to
democratic thought and processes, should be described.

†AMERICAN GOVERNMENT IN TODAY'S WORLD. *By Robert
Rienow*. D. C. Heath & Co., 1962, 752 pp. Bureau of Indian Affairs
Schools. Standing Rock Agency, Fort Yates, North Dakota.

The textbook begins with a description of the United States as a
world power. "By accident of birth we are Americans." This may be
true for Americans of European descent, but it is a specious note with
which to start the *Indian* student upon a study of American government.

As a whole, the book could well be a handbook for lobbyists. Every
aspect of government, political life, political parties, departments and
sub-departments of governmental agencies, committees and sub-com-
mittees is dealt with. Certainly the Indian people need lobbyists, and
might be better off if there were some. But in the teaching of government and its functions—as they existed in early times, as they developed,
and as they are today—this book is a mass of confusion.

Further, it is particularly distinguished for its omissions of important
governmental functions. Particularly as these concern Indian life today, Indian history, and federal-Indian relationships throughout America's history.

There is no mention of treaties, least of all in connection with treaties
made with tribes and groups of tribes. There is no description of the
functions of the Bureau of Indian Affairs, and how the Indian people
are directed through this federal agency. Very little mention is made of
the Native Americans. A very interesting statement is made concerning
"What leadership means. World leadership is a product of power. It
stems from a nation's capacity to produce—from the efficiency of its industry and the richness of its resources. It comes from the people's com-
mercial drive, their ability to trade. It grows out of the initiative and

unity of those people, their dedication to their own political and social system. It is a reflection of their military possibilities, the stick they wield. 'A man without a stick will be bitten even by a sheep' is an old Hindu proverb. World leadership is a compound of strength and prestige." To the Indian student who shares the philosophy and peace-loving nature of his people, and as well to any student who believes in spiritual and humane values, this is an extraordinary statement of a brutal nature. It speaks of a society that is selfish, heartless, pragmatic; one which reveres efficiency and power above all else. Perhaps that is really the way America is.

*†GOVERNMENT IN OUR REPUBLIC. *By Brown & Peltier.* Macmillan, 1964, 749 pp., Bureau of Indian Affairs Schools, Sherman Indian Institute, Riverside, California. Public Schools text, senior high school.

These authors find it possible to state, on page 4, that "In one sense, the only Americans are the American Indians. Only the Indians, as the Europeans found them here . . . inhabited the same land and inherited the same customs and traditions over centuries of time," and still fail to include the Indian as an integral part of American history and governmental concern.

On page 5, the stage is set for placing the Indian in a "minority" bag, so that major attention and information is devoted to the immigrants of European background. "A few of us had American Indian ancestors but most of our ancestors came here in just the last few hundred years." And so, when describing these varied persons of different nations who came here, they were made to "find" in this book, only others of different nations. "The Asians who came to the United States across the Pacific settled in greatest numbers on the West Coast. There they found many descendants of Spaniards and Mexicans, as well as adventurous easterners who had traveled across the continent as pioneers," (p. 7). There were thousands of Indians in the West at this time. It would appear reasonable to assume that they "found" *them,* but this is not mentioned. Again, on page 15, to answer the question "What is an American?" the authors mention all nationalities but the Native American. On page 17, it is stated that "in 1790 there were fewer than four million people in America . . ." but it is not explained that the majority of the people at this time were American Indians "not counted." In fact, it could not have been otherwise. And yet, population estimates of the Indians living here, mention only 800,000 Indians. This is an interesting fact in our history, that the Native Americans were at one time the MAJORITY of the population, yet never treated Europeans as "minority groups."

Since the approach is bent in favor of the European-derived population, it is therefore not surprising that the Indian in our governmental agencies and part of our whole political system, is overlooked. Information on this subject is found in casual references relating to citizenship (acquired in 1924), and the functions of the Bureau of Indian Affairs. But this statement, on page 596, best illustrates the approach to the Native people, "The Department of the Interior . . . is responsible for 'conserving' one of the nation's rich human resources—the Indian population." This is so insensitive a statement that it does not deserve even the anger which it evokes for considering a race of human beings as "resources."

Factual error is shown on page 598, in this statement, "The United States undertook, in the treaties and subsequent laws, to protect Indians against their enemies and to respect the borders of their reservations." In fact, the treaties with Indian tribes were largely instruments of a gigantic land grab, in which the Native peoples gave up huge portions of their land, often all of it, in exchange for some acres of rock and gravel upon which nothing would grow. Some conditions of these treaties included the protection of hunting and fishing rights, educational services, health services, and the right to live in peace as nations within the American nation itself. The fact that these treaties were broken, the land taken whenever Europeans wanted it, and that this is still being done, is ignored. This is in effect a falsification of our history, a failure to explain the current problems of government. The role of Congress in the affairs of Indians today is not dealt with.

Description of the role and functions of the Bureau of Indian Affairs must have come from the BIA's propaganda department; it falsifies the actual situation. It is stated on page 600, "The chief function of the Bureau of Indian Affairs is to make itself unnecessary, either by fostering the assimilation of Indians into the population generally, or by helping the tribes to attain self-sufficiency . . . The Bureau also helps Indians to learn the techniques of self-government, and those Indians who leave their reservations are assisted in finding jobs and making adjustments . . . Through the Bureau of Indian Affairs we have gone a long way to clear (our) conscience." This is a misstatement of the role of the BIA and what it actually does. This agency is not diminishing; it is growing. At no time in the history of the nation has the Bureau helped the tribes "to attain self-sufficiency." If this has happened, it has been despite the BIA. It should be stated that through the BIA this nation has managed to continue its failure to solve the Indian situation, rather than to "clear the conscience" of the American people.

It is a strange commentary upon those who write textbooks on government and civics that in most other areas, there is an effort made to state simple facts, to describe actual processes and actions. But when these writers describe the American Indian, only opinion is expressed, propaganda. This writer has never seen a textbook which quotes an Indian authority. They go directly to the Bureau of Indian Affairs for information, and since this governmental agency is in the business of perpetuating its bureaucratic control over Indian affairs, the information is sharply slanted.

Tribal governmental forms, the relationship of Congress to the original Americans, the reservations and how they function, the relationship of Health, Education and Welfare to the Indian tribes and reservations —these are all a part of the process of American government. They should be dealt with, in an objective way, giving the facts instead of propaganda.

*CITIZENSHIP AND GOVERNMENT IN MODERN AMERICA.
By Bard, Moreland, & Cline. Holt, Rinehart & Winston, 1966, 466 pp. Public Schools text, 8th grade.

Background and approach is European. Development of the colonies and their forms of government is dealt with historically, but not indicated is another type of society in existence at the time of white contact. The structure of our government from its beginnings should include the influence of the philosophy of democracy as shown in the Iroquois confederacy, the Confederate Creek, Natchez, and Powhattan nations, and the Pequot-Mohican Confederacy.

An opportunity is missed to explain Indian-Federal relations. Page 50, when Section 8 of Article 1 of the Constitution is discussed, this section should have been more clearly explained. It states, for example, that Congress shall have power "to regulate commerce with foreign nations, and among the several states, and within the Indian tribes." The fact that the tribes were treated as nations at the time of the signing of the Constitution, is a matter of importance in understanding our government, its history, structure and operation.

Another opportunity is missed to develop understanding on page 66

(Congress has wide powers in governing the people). No explanation is made of federal-Indian relationships, the role of the Bureau of Indian Affairs, the contradictions existing between American democracy and the governmental operation in connection with Indian affairs. Page 365, the family is dealt with: "Historians have emphasized the importance of the role played by the family in settling our nation. It served as a cohesive force for settlers, direction and purpose as they worked their way westward." Here the conflict of the two cultures should be explained, their economic systems which were in conflict as well. The Native family was of a different social order than the European; it was not the "primitive" social entity which most textbook writers imply.

Some sympathy is expressed for the Native peoples in a photograph with a caption on page 388: "The true natives of America, the Indians, suffered greatly at the hands of settlers who took and developed their lands." The implication is that the Indian people did not develop their lands, when in truth their roads, care of forests, types of agriculture, irrigation, and uses of waterways, had developed over thousands of years and served the purpose of their economy well. The caption continues: "No longer free to wander, today most Indians live on reservations . . ." The words "free to wander," imply the same type of existence that animals have, and would appear to justify the settlers in taking the land, "in order to develop it."

On page 389, discussing the Bureau of Indian Affairs, "The Indian Bureau which was established, sought to replace mistreatment with education, health programs, and gradual acceptance of the Indian as a full-fledged useful American citizen." The Indian Bureau was first established under the direction of the War Department, the purpose being to keep the Natives under military control, and to ease the settlement of land by "pioneers" who took away their property. The gradual acceptance of the Indian as a "useful citizen" implies he was not useful, when in fact the settlers would have been unable to exist in this land without the help of the American Indian.

The definition of what a minority group is, page 393, is open to dispute: "Members of a minority group usually have one or more of the following characteristics in common (1) language, (2) certain physical characteristics, (3) religious beliefs and practices, (4) distinctive dress and customs . . ." In fact, the most important distinction of a minority group is that they lack one basic item: Power. The textbook definition would incline the student to search out these peculiar minority people to see if they had the same dress, the same language, or the same religious beliefs and practices. The Indians, for example, do not today have dress which is different from any others; most are Christians, and most speak English.

*CIVICS IN ACTION. *By Gross, Devereaux.* Harr Wagner, 1966, 406 pp., Public School Text, 8th Grade, Social Sciences.

The first page of the text gives this book away as a European "discovery" oriented one. "Americans have come from every part of the world . . . Look at their names: Dubois, Swaboda, Chan, Goldstein, Olson, Welch, Diaz—these speak of many lands. People have poured into the United States by the millions." How about Stands-in-Timber, Walkingstick, Blue Cloud, Costakik, Qualla? These are Native names and probably are not as important to authors of a European-oriented text.

"We are still trying to guarantee the political rights of everyone. American Indians, our original inhabitants, were not granted full citizenship rights until 1924." This is a long time to take for citizenship to be "granted" to people who have been the original owners of the country. Why should America have such a hard time guaranteeing rights? This should be explained.

The statement is made on page 144, that "From time to time the federal government has protected states against invasion. In 1817 federal troops protected Georgia from invading Indians." That the state of Georgia was founded on Indian land, under the protection of the federal government, is one fact the authors either did not know, or chose to ignore. The fact that the supreme court of the United States upheld the rights of the Indians—in this case the Cherokees—of Georgia, to full occupancy of their lands, a decision which was flaunted by the president of the United States, Andrew Jackson, and the state of Georgia, certainly bears mention. This is no mere distortion of truth. This is a falsehood.

On page 166, it is stated that the Department of Interior "has charge of our public lands. It supervises Indian affairs . . ." It is the Bureau of Indian Affairs which supervises Indian affairs of reservations and federally-directed schools, under the direction of the Department of the Interior. "The Fourteenth Amendment says all the people (except untaxed Indians) must be counted." This statement on page 186 ought to be explained. The phrase was inserted into the amendment in order to assure that Indians could not vote, nor could they be counted as part of the population.

"The American standard of living is one of the highest in the world. Americans owe this good fortune to several things. One is that we live in a land of rich resources. But the Indians lived here for hundreds of years. The same resources were here then. Yet the Indians never reached a high standard of living. They never developed or put to use the riches of the land. The United States, using the same gifts of nature, has become a wealthy, cultured nation . . ." This is like comparing apples and porcupines. Such improper comparisons violate historical principles, and have no basis in logic. It would appear that such authors as these are willing to stretch logic to the breaking point, in order to make the belief stick that America is the most, the richest, the greatest, the biggest, the best. Nobody loves this country more than the Indian. But the Native also recognizes the rights, accomplishments, and contributions of others. Contributions of the American Indian to culture, economy, philosophy, religion, health, medicine, are not even mentioned.

†UNDERSTANDING OUR GOVERNMENT. *By George G. Bruntz.* Ginn & Co., 1961, 73 pp. Bureau of Indian Affairs Schools.

A high school textbook on government which does not deal with federal-Indian relationships can hardly be recommended for comprehensive study in American government. This book deals with the Indian in two short sections:

In 16 words on page 313, it is explained that the Department of the Interior "has charge of 350,000 Indians still living on reservations." Even the phrase "has charge of" would be a matter of questioning by most modern high school students. They might ask what kind of "charge" is implied? How is it managed, justified, implemented? The population of Indians on reservations is inaccurate. Close to 450,000 still live on reservation land, and the general population is higher. Too, many Indians living near or even far away from their reservations are affected by jurisdiction of the Bureau of Indian Affairs.

The only other section of the book in which the Indian has a part in government is on page 348, which describes the test case of an Indian in New Mexico, who in 1948, sued to challenge a law of that state which did not permit Indians to vote. "He was not permitted to register on the ground that 'Indians not taxed' could not vote." (Article 1, Section 1 (3) of the Constitution.) Miguel Trujillo appealed to a Federal District Court and on August 3, 1948, a decision was given declaring New Mexico's law unconstitutional on the grounds that it violated the Fourteenth and Fifteenth Amendments to the Constitution.

From 1912, when New Mexico entered the Union, until 1948, the State denied Indians the right to vote. Furthermore, when by congressional action in 1924, all Indians were given the vote, New Mexico (and Arizona) denied the Native people that right. In more recent years (1968), Indians of the Navajo reservation were denied the right to vote. When the matter came before the district judge, he ruled against the Indian people who were challenging the right of the county to deprive them of their vote. He stated that "the Indians did not show enough interest" to be allowed to vote.

There are many areas of government which affect the Indian people directly. Explanations should be given concerning the contradiction existing in actual fact, between the avowals of the United States government concerning democracy, and the existence of such restrictive regulations as those in *Title 25—Indians,* which supposedly protect the Indians, but act as a brake upon the independent development of their economy and leadership. There is little information, and no relationship whatever to American government, so far as the Indian is concerned, in this textbok.

*†PROBLEMS FACING AMERICA AND YOU. By *Kidger & Dunwiddie,* Ginn & Co., 1959, 635 pp. Bureau of Indian Affairs Schools. Institute of American Indian Arts, Santa Fe, New Mexico. Public Schools Text.

Indian history is part of America's national beginnings, as well as part of current American history and problems. This is the burden of *Textbooks and The American Indian.* The text under consideration is an example of failure in this regard.

In chapter 1, dealing with democracy, there is no criticism whatever about the failures of democracy so far as the Native Americans are concerned. In chapter 4, dealing with "intercultural understanding," the Indian is completely ignored. Describing the debt owed to other nations and other peoples by America, most nations are mentioned, but not the Native Americans, (p. 100). Chapter 5 deals with the farm situation and the development of farming in the west. There is not mention at all of the way the west "was won", by taking Indian lands. But there is a statement on page 108, that "in the early part of the nineteenth century, military triumphs over the Indians opened the Ohio Valley as well as the lower south to settlement." These triumphs were predatory, and Indian land was taken despite existing treaties.

Chapter 10 (conservation) contains no historical background which gives the Native people credit for inventing a sophisticated irrigation system, and developing conservation methods which today are being considered as more effective than those used heretofore by the whites.

In the chapter on education, (page 351), there is an opportunity to mention Indian education in relation to Dartmouth College, which was founded as the result of Indian people collecting funds for this Institution. There is no mention at all of problems and differences in the education of Indians. In the chapter on taxation, there is no mention made and therefore no understanding can be acquired, of the fact that reservations are not taxed. Individual Indians off-reservation pay income taxes and other taxes just like all other citizens. On page 539, in which treaties and treaty-making powers are discussed, there is no mention of the treaties with the Indian Nations, which have always formed a basic part of our national problem, and our national picture. In the concluding chapters concerning modern problems of the American Nation, there is complete silence as to the problems and the complex situation regarding the Native Americans.

*†MAGRUDER'S AMERICAN GOVERNMENT. *REVISED by Wil-
liam A. McClenaghan.* Allyn & Bacon, 1964, 760 pp, Bureau of Indian Affairs Schools. Albuquerque Indian School, Public Schools Text.

This ancient textbook, first written by Frank Abbott Magruder (1882–1940) has been revised to bring it up to date and probably to make it more palatable to the modern taste. Published first in 1917, it has long served its purpose of whipping up patriotic fervor for the first and second world wars, and ought to be retired.

The approach is European. The language is full of extraneous patriotic phrases such as "hallowed, mighty pillar, lofty, abiding faith." Today, more than ever before, a nation will stand or fall upon its actions, not upon the flamboyant words of propagandists. In its current forty-eighth edition, however, this textbook retains its sole advantage, that of being a mechanical and exhaustive treatment of every aspect of government, its agencies, and its officers, without developing an actual understanding of governmental structure and processes.

True to its propagandistic quality, this book follows the usual line of treatment of the Native peoples, as though they were impediments, as on page 30, "These early pioneers who cleared the wilderness and fought off the Indians had to hack out their own economic future in the new world."

In the chapter dealing with citizenship, the author fails to explain why the Indians were not permitted citizenship until 1924, and also fails to mention that not until 1948 did all states allow the Natives to vote.

Page 243 deals with "the commerce power." In considering the first Article of the Constitution, in which Congress was given the power to regulate trade with Indian tribes, an explanation of this section is given in a footnote in which the tribes are described as being "viewed 'very much' as they did foreign nations . . . they also realized the importance of keeping firearms and firewater from them. Later, when the transcontinental railroads were built, Congress had the power to grant rights of way through Indian lands for railroads." Not mentioned is the fact that the Native peoples had ownership of their lands, and that this was the reason Congress was compelled to treat with them as nations. Not explained is that the white men made "firewater" available to the Indians, in order to corrupt and degrade them. Also not stated is that with the building of the railroads, additional land was taken from the Indians, treaties were violated, and promises broken.

Dealing with the functions of the Department of the Interior, page 359, it is stated, "Nowhere on earth has nature been so generous than in the United States. The early settlers, and the millions who followed them, found a land of almost unbelievable natural wealth. They found an entire continent of vast forests . . beneath the rich soil they found seemingly inexhaustible deposits of coal, iron, oil . . ." Nothing is said of the human race found on TOP of the rich soil—the Native people of the country. Nor that the land was rich and fertile because the Natives cared for it, respected and treasured it. On page 369 this statement is false: "In general, the Indians proved ill-suited to our way of life." This ignores the Native achievements in learning western technology. Their many successes under their own leadership are ignored.

*†OUR CHANGING SOCIAL ORDER. By *Gordon & Rienow.* Heath, 1967, 469 pp. Bureau of Indian Affairs schools. Stewart Indian School, Nevada. Public Schools text.

"The problem of the Indian is less one of social discrimination than of cruel economic mistreatment. Except for a few reservations where oil has been found, the typical Indian reservation consists of undesirable, cut-over or desert land which cannot begin to support the numbers trying to live on it."

This is, of course, a fairly accurate statement, but extremely limited. In the content of this book of 469 pages, it is inaccurate. Historically, mistreatment existed in the social and political sense. It also resulted from the clash of two economic and social systems. Currently, mistreatment is still of a political, economic, and social nature. The Indian people of the State of Washington (as an example) would be surprised to learn that their struggle to retain their fishing rights was entirely economic. Their fight to retain their treaty rights is primarily political, with economic results. The Indian people of such reservations as Pine Ridge, Rosebud, or Fort Hall are discriminated against as part of a social order of racism. The failures of Indian education, the abysmal ignorance existing in the textbooks about the American Indian, is no economic problem. It is of a social and political nature.

In our present society, there is no group, or problem that is so basically interlocked with every question concerning Our Changing Social Order, as that of the American Indian. This part of our society has been overlooked in a book that should have dealt with it exhaustively.

†BUILDING CITIZENSHIP. *By Ray Osgood Hughes, revised by C.H.W. Pullen.* Allyn & Bacon, 1957, 654 pp. Bureau of Indian Affairs Schools.

Just as other books on citizenship which have been examined, this one fails to undertake an explanation of the realities of life. There is a great deal of propaganda and patriotic verbiage. The ideal situation is described, but the exceptions which are rapidly mounting and causing the current state of unrest in our country are not dealt with. The fact that the exceptions far outweigh the rule is not taken into consideration. As an example, the denial of voting privileges to many Indian Americans as well as to many Black people, is not explained. What is needed is a dynamic treatment of citizenship, its changing characteristics, its problems, discussed frankly and without fear, and a discussion of the direction of American democracy from the many points of view which are now emerging in our country. These are general evaluations.

As to the role of the American Indian in our society, the question is dealt with in two sections, on pages 75 and 199. In the first section, there is a bare mention that the Bureau of Indian Affairs operates under the

Department of the Interior. In the same section, racism is treated. There is this admission: "That treatment of the Indians by the whites as they moved west is the worst blot on the story of our expansion across the continent. The usual: "Today, however, the status of the Indian has changed . . . Schools have been established . . a rehabilitation program of nearly 90 millions for the Navajo and Hopi Indians has recently been passed by the House of Representatives . . But there is still much to be done . . " Having made these statements, the author goes on to ignore the Native Americans just the same as usual.

*†CIVICS FOR AMERICANS. *By Clark, Gruenewald, Edmonson & Dondineau.* Macmillan, 1965, 580 pp. Albuquerque Indian Schools. Public School Text, 8th Grade.

In no other area of the learning process is the American Indian so badly neglected and misinterpreted as in the teaching of civics and government. Contrary to the belief of many educators, this is an area in which the status of the Native American needs to be explained.

In the history of this nation's development, the Indian has presented the most complex questions concerning the democratic process. When considering the structure and operation of federal and state governments, the position of the American Indian presents not merely a "problem," but a direct challenge to democratic philosophy and operation.

For instance, in this text, it is explained that one "becomes a citizen" usually "by being born in that country." How, then, can the student be made to understand the reasons for failing to grant the Native Peoples of this country their citizenship until 1924, two states (Arizona and New Mexico) refusing to grant such rights until 1948? And then, only after a court case was decided in favor of their right to vote.

Only one section of the book deals with the American Indian. On page 190, it is stated that, in connection with "the Indian problem . . . none of us can feel proud of the treatment that has been accorded them. Our ancestors took their land from them and drove them from their hunting grounds. Over the years, our government made many agreements and treaties with them, but these were often broken." This casual declaration of responsibility for one of the greatest land steals in all history is inadequate. What is needed is an understanding of the reasons for this phenomenon. Nor is there any attempt to explain the nature of government in this land before the whites came, or what they utilized from Indian democratic philosophy, or the relationships with Indian tribes as reflected in governmental policies and structure. This is a part of America and its government. It deprives the student of an important facet of knowledge if it is ignored.

On page 191, the authors say, "In recent years the government has tried to make up for the past ill treatment. Today most Indians live on reservations, special land set aside for them . . . the Federal Government through its Bureau of Indian Affairs maintains about 200 schools for them. Today Indians are encouraged to leave their reservations and live as other Americans do. When they do, they have some of the same difficulties that other minority groups face." Such an explanation is not learning. In fact, the BIA is the oldest governmental agency and the biggest bureaucracy in the nation. How do the Indians on reservations live, if they do not "live as other Americans do?" This would imply some sort of an existence in limbo; what kind of schools are these Federal schools? In fact they represent a direct antithesis to the democratic process. Why?

When the student reads in the newspapers about such things as "per capita payments to Indians," or litigation in connection with land claims, or the taking of great masses of land in Alaska and elsewhere, how can he understand these things—if the textbooks ignore them?

*CONFLICT, POLITICS, AND FREEDOM. By *Quigley & Longaker.* Ginn & Co., 1969, both student and teachers' editions. Public schools text.

This textbook requires a qualified, open-minded, well prepared teacher. Written according to the inquiry method, it presents broad possibilities for stimulating thought among the students, and for developing more profound understanding about systems of government than has hitherto been the case. It is an excellent basic textbook in the search to solve today's problems in education.

Having said this, the question of the textbooks and the American Indians remains to be discussed. Strangely enough, although this book utilizes new methodology and has every opportunity for a successful program in teaching, it fails completely in dealing with some of the most important questions of our time. Not the least of these questions is that of the American Indian. Completely lacking from this text is any consideration of Indian and federal relationships. There is no utilization of some of the most outstanding decisions in connection with

American democracy and democratic thought, which would have given soundness to the text.

The Supreme Court decisions of Chief Justice Marshall particularly present an opportunity to discuss some of the most important issues facing democracy—both historically and for today. A recent decision of Justice Tobriner, of the California State Supreme Court, concerning the use of peyote in the religious practices of the Navajo people, are only two examples of such materials which the authors have failed to use.

One may ask: Is the error of omission not less a falsification of history, than the commission of inaccuracy itself? The authors have missed a unique opportunity for discussing the most basic concepts of "conflict, politics and freedom" in omitting from this textbook all consideration of the role of the American Indian in this nation's politics, its continuing conflicts, and its yearning for freedom.

*YOUR RIGHTS AND RESPONSIBILITIES AS AN AMERICAN CITIZEN: A CIVICS CASEBOOK. By *Charles N. Quigley.* Ginn & Co., 1967, 130 pp. Public School text.

The methods of open discussion, the questioning of accepted formulae, and exploring the thought-process of the student himself in the study of civics and American democracy is fully utilized in this book. Contrary to most civics textbooks, this one does not spout patriotic platitudes, but strives to relate our laws and the interpretation of our laws, to the problems of our times. So far so good.

Sixty-nine cases at court are examined in the book, so that the students may be able to discuss actual instances of some part of the democratic process. There are many cases dating from the times of the Plymouth Colony. There are historic incidents which are described as background so that the cases at law may be considered in a frame of history and living human beings. American democracy so far as law and thought are concerned, is explored.

Only one thing is missing: the American Indian as part of the fabric of the democratic process. The Indian as a challenge to all our democratic processes and thought—this is omitted. It is no specious consideration that prompts this question. Too, it is not the demand of some complaining minority to be recognized, that prompts this question. This question challenges all of our democratic thought, our democratic processes, when by omission, a whole race of people may be ignored, and the only Native inhabitants of this nation shoved to the backwoods of history, law, and democratic processes. The plea of the Grand Council Fire of American Indians, which has been reprinted as the opening part of this book, is not some sort of a plaintive wail to be "recognized." It is the demand of a vital segment of the American people to put an end to segregation of thought as well as deed, the discrimination against ideas as well as persons. Democracy is rotten to the core in America, if this type of omission is permitted to continue.

THE UNITED STATES CONSTITUTION IN PERSPECTIVE. By Claude L. Heathcock. Allyn & Bacon, 1965, 322 pp. Bureau of Indian Affairs schools, eighth grade civics and social sciences supplementary textbook. Public schools text.

In all the 322 pages of this book, a manual on United States government and our constitution, there is no relation between governmental processes, agencies, and the American Indian. There is no relevance nor association between the Constitution and the special position of the American Indian, nor is there any explanation of federal-Indian relationships, whether historical or current.

The influence of Indian philosophy and democratic thought upon the making of the Constitution is completely ignored. There is no mention of treaties and treaty making with the Indians. Discussing some important decisions of the Supreme Court, there is no mention of the very important Supreme Court decisions concerning the American Indian, some of which have changed the course of this nation's history. The complex relationship of the Indian tribes with the federal government is not discussed at all.

In this supplementary textbook, every section and subsection of the Constitution is discussed. Only one matter is omitted, the meaning and purposes of these two parts of Article 1.

On page 165 it is explained, in connection with the powers of treaty making, which belong to the President of the United States with the advice and consent of the Senate, "The Supreme Court has held that not only does a treaty repeal an existing statute repugnant to it, but a new statute likewise repeals a standing treaty repugnant to it. This means that treaties have the same legal standing as acts of Congress, that Congress may repeal a treaty by passing a law contrary to its provisions, or that an existing law may be repealed by the terms of a new treaty. Thus, when a treaty and an Act of Congress are in conflict, the newer of the two takes precedence." This interesting information might be a good subject for discussion as to whether the principles of democracy and international responsibility can be maintained in a nation which does not honor its treaties. The textbook discusses voting privileges and rights. The Negro received the vote in 1876; women in 1920; the Philippine people in 1917. But it was not until 1924 that the Indian received the vote. The textbook should discuss this.

*†PROBLEMS IN AMERICAN DEMOCRACY. *By Patterson & Little.* Macmillan, 1961, 656 pp. Bureau of Indian Affairs schools. Public school text.

In the introduction, the authors describe the purpose of this high school textbook in these words: "It is a survey of those issues in our contemporary civilization which have been most persistent and a satisfactory solution of which seems essential to the preservation of the democratic way of life."

That this lofty goal is not fulfilled in the book, is shown throughout its pages. According to a statement on page 42, the new government of the United States "placed great power in the hands of the American people, in fact, greater power than had ever been given to any people in the history of mankind." This is inaccurate, for the American Indian, the Native of this land, was refused liberties granted to all others; he was not permitted to vote and was not even counted as part of the population. Slavery, too, was a recognized way of life for the new government.

"Our diverse and increasing population," page 335, describes all the immigrants who came to America, but fails to mention the Native Americans who were here and have been a part of this civilization then and since. There is no treatment of the American Indian and his "social problems." The problems in American democracy, which certainly include as a major part, the "problem" of the American Indian, who has been and is even today denied his full rights as an American citizen, are completely ignored.

†COMMUNITIES AT WORK. *By Preston & Clymer.* D. C. Heath &

Co., 1964, 280 pp. Busby, Montana Indian School, elementary grades

This textbook combines a study of geography, social science and history. The suggestions to the teacher are good. Activities can be planned with consideration for an active learning process. The last part of the book deals with four major types of Indian cultures: Woodlands, Plains, the Southwest, and the Northwest. It is explained that these are only part of the tribal cultures existing side by side with pre-European tribal groups being studied. While the idea is good, the fact that there is no mention or even suggestion that these tribes are still alive and growing today is an omission creating inaccuracy. The tribes themselves are not mentioned in the text—merely their area. It is stated that in the main the Indians of these four areas had a culture very similar. Just the same, the failure to state the name of the tribe being dealt with ignores the basic fact of Indian life—the tribal society, and utterly defeats the purpose of the book.

Certain errors exist which need not have occurred. Among such errors are these: " . . the men wove cloth," (p. 248). Men and women both wove cloth. On the same page, "The women built the pueblo houses." The family built the houses. Page 256: "In Kachina dances, men and older boys played the part of the Kachinas." These were danced by the dance clans, not by ALL men and boys, as the above statement implies.

In the section dealing with information for the teacher, chapter 12, the Pueblo Indian environment is described. Not mentioned, in connection with statements concerning their dry lands, is the fact that these people utilized irrigation. Information for chapter 11 states "The Blackfoot tribe settled down in the area that is now South Dakota. The Blackfoot (or Dakota, as they called themselves), is the tribe presented in this chapter." The name of these people is BLACKFEET; they were called SIHASAPA, not Dakota. On page T-104, trade is discussed, but only in connection with the woodlands Indians. Even though it is stated that "Many Indian tribes made trips to distant villages in order to trade or barter . . " the reference in the section "for discussion" implies that only the woodlands Indians traded, whereas all the tribes traded. For example, the Pueblo Indians traded with Pacific coast tribes of southern California.

VOICES OF CHANGE. *By Sydney M. Larue and William T. Larue.* Century Communications, 1970, 216 pp. Public schools text, grade 4.

This series of books, embodying new ideas in teaching techniques and materials, has an over-abundance of illustrations which is most disturbing, since so much undue emphasis is thus placed upon visual instruction. Fourth grade students can usually read texts at that age, and should be required to. The book examined in the series is "California—Land of the West." With reference to Native peoples, it is stated on page 20: "Nomadic hunting tribes lived on the Great Plains." To make sure that the students understand the word, the definition "Wandering" is given on the same page. The Plains Indians were not nomadic. Relating the modern world to the ancient, it is stated on page 74, "Tall buildings stand where forest creatures once lived . . " This implies there were no people on these sites. Why not say, truthfully, "where the Natives once lived their own lives in their own way." According to this book, the Indians made no contributions to the state or country. There are some few words to indicate the Indians were here, but little more.

SOCIOLOGY. By Paul H. Landis. Ginn & Co., 1964, 531 pp. Phoenix Indian School. High school text.

SOCIAL LIVING. By Paul H. Landis. Ginn & Co., 1963, 451 pp. Chilocco Indian School, Oklahoma; and Anadarko area Indian schools, Oklahoma.

SOCIAL LIVING, revised edition, is the elementary version of SOCIOLOGY. The two books are basically the same so far as approach is concerned. General subject matter is also the same.

The criticisms of these two books are much the same, except that the errors are so much more compounded in the higher level book. According to the author, "Sociology does not answer all man's questions about himself, but it does answer many of them. It deals with man in his relationship to others." If this is the purpose of sociology as a study, then the author has failed to deal with the subject as it relates to the Indian student. Since these two books are used in the Indian schools of Oklahoma, we must judge them on the merits of usefulness to Indian children.

Part One contains the usual generalizations about heredity and environment. On the other hand, objection is hereby taken to the description of "civilized" life, in the examples quoted of certain individuals who, when raised in an animal state, failed to "adjust" to civilized ways of living. Hence a girl found alone in a forest "caught fish and ate them raw. She climbed trees and uttered only wild cries. It was hard for her to adapt herself to civilized life. She was placed in a convent and learned something of French embroidery work and domestic science." We believe this to be an improper example. Most Indians were considered "uncivilized" and are still so considered. We think the comparison might better be made between animal behavior. Whether human behavior is always "civilized" takes us into another field entirely. Objection is also taken to the use of "primitive" when describing pre-literate society. This word denotes a society without technology, without complexities of language, and without organized social structure. Indians have also been termed "primitive."

A gratuitous insult is offered to farm people by an excerpted article on page 51, which describes the problems of people moving from rural areas to urban centers. "They often pay exorbitant amounts for poor quarters . . The situation is only partly explained by low incomes. 'For no more money than they're paying for slum apartments,' a social worker said, 'a lot of these families could move into the suburbs and perhaps buy a house. But they simply won't consider going away from their own people.' " If this is a social worker, she is in the wrong business. Anyone who has lived in the slum of a city, knows that it is a superhuman effort to leave. There is fear of debt, an insecure job, of being rejected, and fear they will not be able to hold up their end economically once the move is made. This description has been made often of Indians who move to urban centers.

In the SOCIAL LIVING book, the Indian is mentioned here and there, in a most general way. There are, however, numerous opportunities to make comparisons with Native Indian life. But many descriptions are given of Egypt, Asia, Africa. More relevant would have been examples from this country, with the Native Peoples of the land and their cultures utilized for comparison. Even when the opportunity is so palpable that to ignore it constitutes an error, there is no mention of Indian life and contributions. For example, on page 59, an excerpt is given from an article titled ONE HUNDRED PER CENT AMERICAN. The writer quite properly explains, in a humorous way, all the things that modern man uses, without thought that its origins are with other peoples, other places, other cultures. And so, his pajamas are mentioned "a garment of the East," his tailored garments . . derive from . . the ancient nomads of the Asiatic steppes . . his china is from China . . his fork is a medieval Italian invention . . his coffee is from Abyssinia . . his orange is from the Mediterranean . . " and so on. All examples are taken from Europe and Asia. The author could have added, with more justification, that a great number of his useful articles were taken from the Indian. For instance: tobacco is from the Indian; his basic and most important food product economically, is corn from the Indian; he enjoys squash, beans, or melons, from the Indian; he takes pleasure in canoeing, from the Indian. His town is named Seattle, an Indian name. He comes home and reclines in a hammock, borrowed from the American Indian. He goes to the movies and eats a bag of peanuts, borrowed from Indians. He gives his children some chewing gum, and fails to recognize that this is a gift of the American Indian. The products, items of enjoyment, articles of necessity, are legion, and all these come from the Native Americans. Why not describe THESE contributions?

An error, unfortunately not uncommon, is made in the text on page 105, of SOCIAL LIVING, "Among the Zuni Indians of our Southwest, to get ahead of the other person of the tribe was very much frowned upon." This is such an oversimplification that it is incorrect. "Among the Kwakiutl tribe of the Pacific Northwest, on the other hand, was found one of the most competitive tribes on the face of the earth. They went to great extremes to outdo a competitor. At the Potlatch feast, men of about equal wealth competed with each other in giving away their wealth and property." This is a popular misconception and is best answered by an authority on the subject, NOT Indian. "The true rivalry potlatch, which has been interpreted by others as being socially disintegrative and even as a manifestation of psychic abnormality, we have shown to be basically a technique for resolving conflicting claims of presumptive heirs. In a broad sense, it was simply a process at civil law. It likewise provided a channel for emotional release by the parties in conflict. To let off steam in controlled surroundings appears to have made possible the preservation of a very important behavioral value standard, one that strongly opposed intragroup physical violence in conflict situations. The rivalry gesture seems to have operated constantly as the same sort of a release mechanism. Our position, therefore, is that these specializations of the potlatch complex were not significant as deviants from the areal norms. One might even interpret them as highly consistent with the fundamental function of the institution, that toward social integration." (Page 133 TO MAKE MY NAME GOOD, Drucker, University of California Press, 1967)

Finally, we must evaualte this book as being irrelevant to Indian life. More than that, it is a middle class approach to the problems of life, and would be almost impossible as a useful tool in solving the problems of everyday life ... for Indians as well as for people of other ethnic backgrounds, (including whites) unless they were of middle class status.

Another error which should be of concern to scholars in determining the usefulness of these two books is that made on page 201 (SOCIAL LIVING) "There was no government, as we think of government, in very early societies. There were no written laws, no courts, and no designated rulers. Custom, religious requirements, taboos, and tradition provided for order in such a group." What does this author consider to be "Very early societies?" Such a generalization leaves conjectures — wide open at both ends. It is up to the reader to tailor this generalization to his own preconceived misconceptions. "Early society" could be Indian Native society. This was certainly not without government. Because government is not in the form of written laws, shall we consider the governed to be any the less governed? On the contrary, unwritten law, in man's history, has had more effective a hold on man's behavior than the currently WRITTEN laws, which are more distinguished by their violation than by their observance. Tribal society was highly complex, and each man, woman, and child knew the limits and depths of his rights and privileges.

In SOCIAL LIVING there is one-third of a page devoted to the American Indian today. The approach is: "Much more needs to be done." In the book by the same author, SOCIOLOGY, a great deal of space is devoted to "other cultures" and other cultural heritages. Asia, Africa, and other FAR OFF countries are compared. But here in our own land, where there is ready-made cultural heritage which has continued its life despite all efforts to destroy it—this heritage is not even discussed. Describing the most important forces in social change, the author, (page 181), lists five items: rapid cultural growth, extensive population movement, urbanization, mechanization and industrialization, and secularization. One important element left out is that of leadership — man's hand in guiding his own destiny, and the leadership of a group, of an individual, of a cultural and ethnic entity. Without this, change cannot be for the better, and can only drag mankind backward step by step. For the Indian, leadership is here — modern, knowledgeable and indisputable, even in the process of evaluating books on sociology, which seek to teach our sons and daughters how to live, and teach them only middle-class generalities.

There are some strange contradictions in thought and ideas which upon analysis seem semantically so unsound that perhaps a good course for teaching students who complete the reading of SOCIOLOGY, would be that of logic. For example, page 251 has this statement opening Unit Six: "Government is the ultimate authority. It can demand loyalty until death. It is the final appeal in disputes. And in democratic social orders it is the servant of the people in achieving their need for protection, for progress, and for material well-being." Somewhere, we have lost this author, because these ideas just don't hang together. For example, if Government is the ultimate authority, how can it also be the servant of the people. Without further explanation, this idea is mere verbosity.

†PRIMARY GRADE BOOKS *used in Bureau of Indian Affairs schools. Six books evaluated.*

†BILLY'S FRIENDS, *McIntire and Hill,* Follett, 1964, 159 pp.

†BILLY'S NEIGHBORS, *McIntire and Hill,* Follett, 1964, 160 pp.

†AT HOME. IN THE NEIGHBORHOOD. AT SCHOOL. Respectively 72, 191 and 96 pp. *All by Hanna and Hoyt.* All by Scott, Foresman Co., 1964 and 1965.

†TOM AND SUSAN, A SOCIAL DEVELOPMENT PRIMER. *By Hanna and Hoyt.* Scott, Foresman Co., 1951, 93 pp.

These readers have the same general characteristics, therefore the editors have chosen to evaluate them together as examples of books used in these grades by Indian children in federally-directed schools. No doubt the same books are used in the public schools. But the concern in the case of these six primary grade books is what happens to an Indian child who is subjected to this type of teaching.

The six books show no relationship to the normal everyday life of the average child. They show no relevancy to the life of an Indian child who has been sent to a federal school, most generally from a reservation. The illustrations without exception depict a middle class child, in a middle class family, living a nice middle class life, complete with automobile of the latest vintage, with refrigerators, supermarkets, and fenced houses with lawns freshly barbered. Several of these books display the faces of some kind of a human being having Caucasian features, tinted a sort of brown. It is impossible to discuss the use of the English language in the primary readers. This has become some sort of black magic, understood only by the "specialist." Since one fears to argue with such specialists, attention is given to the "understand-ings" as listed in one of these books. Here we learn that "children can contribute to the work involved in keeping the yard attractive." One wonders what kind of a "yard" the children of the Eagle Butte, South Dakota, Indian School have. "Children can contribute to the work of keeping the family car clean . . . The community provides parks of different kinds for recreation, children can be of help in the communi-ty by picking everything up after a picnic . . . children can contribute to the work which having a fireplace in the home necessitates." This sort of thing occurs in the primary grade book TOM AND SUSAN, who talk like no other children ever have talked in all the world. Pic-nics, fireplaces, cars, yards, parks—all these are practically non-existent in reservation country. There is nothing in this book that can be util-ized in the learning process of an Indian child. What results is a baffled, mystified, hurt child who feels he has been unable to understand what he thinks is probably a terribly simple thing.

The book titled AT SCHOOL is another idiotic piece of pap. On pages 36 and 37 is pictured an ideal classroom complete with beauti-ful blackboard, modern chairs, children with plenty of room, watering flowers, and writing at modern desks. Naturally all of them are white. Naturally, all of them are very well dressed. And naturally, the Indian child will find no relevance in this picture of middle class life, to his own life. One certainly does not expect to see dirty clothing as an illustration, a dirty and ill-cared-for classroom — but something closer to life would be in better taste, even if good photographs must be used. Certainly a closer identification of the child with his environment should be illustrated. This book, the authors state, contains 188 different words. Of these, 76 were used in a preceding book. Now this is Book One reading level, and the words which have been introduced are "He, she, me, hello, good, room" and others, usually of a one-syllable type. These are little children, granted, but in many countries such little children can read by the time they are ready for Book Two "level." There appears to be a lack of understanding or confidence in the learning abilities of children, in all these six books.

We are wondering what has happened to the upsurge in educational innovation and anticipated upgrading of curriculum and instructional materials which had its beginning ten years ago with the Space ex-ploration. These books certainly do not show the improvements ex-pected. It was thought, at that time, that children might even begin to study simple mathematics in the primary grades! But here we are feeding them pablum.

IN THE NEIGHBORHOOD, is another book of the same character as those discussed above. The child is shown "David Hall's Neighborhood," a pretty little town with plenty of space, a barn painted red, and six cows quietly grazing. There are fenced, and mathematically well laid out lawns and gardens. Young Master Cruz's neighborhood is the Albuquerque, New Mexico, Indian school. He has probably never seen such an atmosphere. He wonders how and what he can learn from all this. A little girl comes running grasping a white doll. A white father works in a well-kept cornfield, where each stalk of corn is so utterly perfect and unnatural as to be a joke if the child happens to know farming. Doubtless it is even middle-class corn! A brand new, shiny car waits outside the cornfield to bring the father home, or to bring the children to the father. The father paints the outside of the house with a brand new, modern spray machine, wearing a business suit and hat. No doubt this is to advertise the spray machine, but it certainly does nothing to teach anything to the child. The father, Mr. Hall, is a farmer — a farmer who works in the fields with the most up-to-date equipment.

Even the cows in this book could win beauty contests. No cows ever looked like that. Another neighborhood described as an example, is that in a town where the houses are closer together, but still as unreal as a coyote in a dog kennel. Still another neighborhood is one in a big city, an urban area. Here we have a library, one that actually bestows such gifts as dolls upon the children. There are television sets, boys on bicycles, and Caucasian faces, some of which are stained muddy brown.

Contrast these books with those used in France, Germany, Russia, Mexico, and other lands. We here in America are so far behind in this field that we are back in the dark ages. Little children are learning algebra, writing, and reading well-sustained sentences with meaning. Here, if these books are examples, the people speak in jerks, each word an exclamation mark.

We are concerned with the general learning process of *all* children in connection with this situation. But particularly we are concerned with what is happening to the Indian child, who has some contradictions to resolve anyhow, between his culture and that of the white society, between his language and that of the dominant race, between what he considers valuable and what the western world considers valuable. Contrary to the beliefs of many educators, the Indian child needs a challenge, even competition, to bring out the best in him. Of course, it would be wrong to generalize. There are exceptions. But learning is a challenge, and no amount of regurgitation by someone else will teach any child what it is to learn.

Torn between two worlds, the Indian youngster cannot help but grow up in a sort of limbo, another "problem child" to do research on, perform psychological tests with, turn into a guinea pig so that the white-dominated society may find out "what is wrong" with him, when all the time there is something very wrong with an educational system responsible for this kind of intellectual indigestion.

*†TODAY'S PROBLEMS. *By Ray Osgood Hughes, Revised by Pullen & Reed,* Allyn & Bacon, 1965, 634 pp. Bureau of Indian Affairs, Muskogee Indian School, Oklahoma. Public schools text.

This is a mediocre, conventional textbook dealing with the surfaces of today's problems rather than with the causes or even with the problems themselves. The section on the Indian problem is superficially sympathetic but takes an obviously superior and "things are not so bad," attitude.

Page 22, "Our population has never been evenly distributed over the country, and the westward movement of the people into unoccupied territory has been one of the tremendous influences upon our history." The term "unoccupied territory" to describe Indian land ownership is incorrect and misleading.

Pages 31-34, "Our country's national origins," which discusses the immigration of people from various foreign countries, completely ignores the existence and occupation of a large population of Native Americans. The pronouns "we" and "our" used throughout, obviously refer to the white population to whom the book is addressed, and for whom it is written.

Page 37, "The new school shown here was built under a government program to provide more adequate educational facilities on our Indian reservations. These Navajo children are enjoying the school playground." This conveys the impression that all is well in the Native American schools. No mention is made of the large teacher-student ratio and other inadequacies.

Page 38, "Happily, the situation has improved since then." Although the preceding paragraph enumerates injustices done to the Indians historically, the paragraph with this opening sentence and those following try to mitigate the injustices and hardships which the Indians still face today.

"Many of the Indians live on reservations set apart for their exclusive use." This implies that the Indians do not own their own reservation land but have been granted it as a privilege. In actuality, the reservations represent a pitifully small fragment of the Indian-owned lands which they were able to save by treaty negotiation from white usurpation. A fatuous, simpering type of patronizing verbiage exists on Page 39, "Just what is best for them we are not always sure." Why not let them decide for themselves, might be a good idea. The same attitude is expressed on the same page "A few Indians of that tribe have found themselves in the situation of having more money than they could spend wisely." No doubt many whites also have money which they do not spend wisely. Why should any man or any governmental agency have the power to tell another man how to spend his money? This passage is typical of the approach in the text.

There is no basic explanation of the historic relations between the federal government and the Indians, and why this situation is diametrically opposed to democratic practice and philosophy. These must be dealt with, and the student must be trusted to understand and be allowed to learn from these conditions in our country today.

†COMPARATIVE POLITICAL SYSTEMS: AN INQUIRY APPROACH. *By Minella Schultz.* Holt, Rinehart & Winston, 1967, 306 pp. Bureau of Indian Affairs Navajo Schools.

The approach exemplified in this new political science textbook is interesting and appealing to the teacher seeking more dynamic instructional methodology. The first unit undertakes to compare two political systems: one is a temporary and spontaneous system set up at a German prison camp. The other considers the political system of a Cheyenne society in the mid-1800's. The rest of the book deals with comparisons in various aspects of national life between the United States and the Soviet Union. A final unit is given on rights and liberties in a democracy.

In all four political systems such questions are discussed as leadership and institutions, decision making, the ideology and role of the citizen, and in the case of the two major countries, the comparative process of attaining leadership. More complex questions are raised, naturally, when considering the United States and the Soviet Union.

There is no extensive bibliography. In connection with the unit of study under discussion in this evaluation, only one source is given

—that of Llewellyn and Hoebel, THE CHEYENNE WAY. As suggested readings, the author offers FOUR WAYS OF BEING HUMAN, by Gene Lisitzky. The object of this learning method is to induce the student to question himself, the instructor, his fellow students, and the source materials suggested. Raising such questions as his intellectual background, social affiliations, and natural talents permit, the student is encouraged to work out for himself the answers to queries such as would develop a better understanding of his subject. A description of this method is probably redundant to the readers of this evaluation. However, there are so many "new" types of instructional methodology now being experimented with, and so many have elements of worth as well as elements of uselessness, that it is felt some brief description is needed. The inquiry method certainly has advantages in the hands of an excellent teacher, well grounded in the particular subject being taught.

In the case of the comparative study of the Cheyenne people, it falls far short of the desired results. Some of the reasons are, in our opinion: Without sufficient background in the culture and history of the Cheyenne (or any Indian tribe) there is no point of reference upon which to build an understanding of the current status, upon which is based the comparative study. Five stories are given, all of them concerning the way of the Cheyenne at a time when they had removed or been removed from their original culture for nearly 200 years. The culture and traditions described in these five stories retain some of the old and some of the relatively new. Here is a society in transition, confronted on the one side by different cultures within their own original orbit—that of various Indian cultures—and by a European culture with which they are attempting to cope. How do you evaluate a society in such transition, changing so rapidly that changes may be anticipated practically overnight? How can you make a comparison of this society's political system, when that system is in a state of change? We believe that the treatment as shown in the stories about the Cheyenne, is static. It lacks depth. It shows a failure to understand the whole picture. Few comparisons can be made under such circumstances. To attempt such comparisons, the student should undergo a serious study not only of the Cheyenne, but of the Sioux with whom they made an alliance; with the Crow and other tribes, with whom they fought. Why they fought, and the lessons to be drawn from the conflict of the western civilization which caused them to fight—the cause being the helter-skelter removals of tribes to lands already occupied by other tribes, as one example.

We think this methodology certainly has merit. But we must evaluate the book now being discussed as inadequate and inaccurate. It does not develop any understanding of the Cheyenne, of their culture, their form of government, their basic values, and their situation even at the moment in the mid-1800's which is that moment in time that these people are being compared. The whole point is: do we LEARN anything. Do any understandings develop? Or, are we studying comparative political systems as abstractions, as intellectual exercises? The purpose of education is to learn, to acquire knowledge, to understand, and to develop a hunger for understanding through knowledge and experience.

Page 17 states, "By 1830, the Cheyenne had enough horses to adandon their villages for the more profitable life of the hunter." They left their villages in the region of Minnesota, only to build other villages on the Plains. The implication is that the Cheyenne became a nomadic people with the coming of the horse. They intensified their hunting activities, true. They found themselves in possession of a huge source of food and raw materials, with the intensification of bison hunting that came with the horse. But they remained permanent settlers upon their own land, whose boundaries were claimed by them. If they claimed land which they had no right to, there was war. If other tribes claimed their land, there was war. If other tribes trespassed upon their land, there was war. The whole matter revolved around whose land this was. And the reason this was so, was due to the fact of property upheaval which came with the Europeans, who scrambled tribal land possession to the detriment and ultimate chaos of the Native peoples.

The one example given, of misinformation concerning the Cheyenne settlers, only shows what kind of trap the inquiry method can be, without a great deal of preparatory work as to the culture and history of the people being studied. For, we are well aware of facts, information, history, and the current situation when we discuss a group of modern men caught in a prison camp; or countries like the United States and the Soviet Union. These peoples and these nations are in our immediate consciousness. But Indian history and culture is still deeply unknown, and misunderstood by most Americans.

The fact is, the author did not know enough about the Cheyenne to put the inquiry method to use on behalf of the learning process in their context. And this is true of any method or system of study. Actual "hard" knowledge must be at least 100 times the measure of the pinpoint of learning explored.

†LIVING IN THE SOCIAL WORLD. *By Quinn & Repki.* J. B. Lippincott, 1956, 536 pp. Bureau of Indian Affairs schools.

A look at the authors' evaluation of marriage and love will disclose how outdated this book is. On page 294, the student is told, with remarkable seriousness: "Evidences of widespread and increasing interest in matrimony may be found in the marriage records of the nation . . . romantic love, which sets the traditional pattern for choosing mates in the United States, frequently leads young men and women to conclude that their own personal mating experiences are different. . . This unguided course of selecting a mate through 'blind love' seems foolish." The book, like others in the study of sociology, skirts around the most important and practical questions of modern life.

In connection with marriage, the young Indian student wants to hear about such matters as inter-racial marriages, intertribal marriages (the Navajo people have until modern times frowned upon marriages outside of the Diné and even outside of clan restrictions). Instead he is fed the usual pap about "biological restrictions, cultural restrictions, basic common interests, freedom of the individual, and tolerance of one towards the other mate."

In discussing the various forms of economy, page 324, the authors state, "Some groups of men live directly upon the bounty of nature. They merely collect from nature those supplies which she furnishes ready to be used immediately. They save nothing for the future. Their work consists of picking berries, digging roots from the ground, killing game, or catching fish." The inference is obviously to the Native American culture, even though the authors do not state which culture they are referring to. This is the usual description of Native life in America before European contact, given by those who don't know much about it. The fact is, that human beings who know enough to "pick berries, kill game," and so forth, will have a technology all their own, well suited to their way of life. The idea that technology does not exist in such forms of economy as make use of natural products, is a fallacy.

On page 405, another fallacious statement occurs, "In order for democracy to prove successful, the minority must accept the rules passed by the majority, otherwise everyone might follow his own desires, thus making sovereign control through law impossible." This is so simplistic that it is false. It may be so in formal law, but it does not work in a situation of social change, in which minorities do NOT have the support of a majority of the voting population, but in which they are striving mightily to make needed social changes—such changes not always being the result of simple modifications of laws. The impact of action is too well known for students to be kidded into believing that there is no way other than to "wait" for change. Life, as it has been in practice these last ten years, has proven different.

In connection with cultural heritage, and transference of cultures from generation to generation, the information is extremely general, and the one great example (with its own unique problems and lessons) of the American Indian is not dealt with at all. One might ask the authors: Which culture are you talking about?

This textbook has very little of use to offer the young Indian student. It has very little of practical value to offer the nonIndian student in the public schools. Its generalizations are long since recognized for what they are worth—not much.

AMERICAN PROBLEMS TODAY. By Robert Rienow. Heath & Co., 1965, 726 pp.

GOALS OF DEMOCRACY. By McCutchen, Fersh, Clark. Macmillan Co., 1962, 664 pp.

THE CITIZEN AND HIS GOVERNMENT. By Robert Rienow. Houghton Mifflin, 1963, 344 pp.

CITIZENSHIP & GOVERNMENT IN MODERN AMERICA. By Bard, Moreland & Cline. Holt, Rinehart, and Winston, 1966, 466 pp.

PROBLEMS OF DEMOCRACY. By Edna Bohlman and Herbert Bohlman. Holt, Rinehart and Winston, 1964, 438 pp.

PROBLEMS OF DEMOCRACY: POLITICAL, SOCIAL, ECONOMIC. By William E. Dunwiddie, Ginn & Co., 1967, 705 pp.

These six books have been chosen for combined evaluation because they show the same tendencies and failures. All are high school texts in social sciences. All are currently being used in Bureau of Indian Affairs-directed schools: the White Shield School in North Dakota, the Institute of American Indian Arts in Santa Fe, New Mexico; in the schools of Phoenix, Arizona; Standing Rock, North Dakota Indian Agency; and other schools attended by Indian children. The books are also utilized in many public schools all over the country.

The most important failure of these books is that they are completely irrelevant to Indian history, and the current Indian situation. For, when the young Native American looks around him from the vantage point of his Indian school, he will see federally-dominated lands, federally-dominated school administrators, federally-evaluated and adopted text-books, and federally-dominated ideology in "thinking about" his relationships with the outside world. He is the child of an Indian reservation, where life has no resemblance to what he is reading in these books. Questions propounded for his mental exercise in solving social "problems" are not his problems. At this point in time, and in this particular school, he has little reason to care about these problems. Perhaps there is some small element of information that comes across, as to how to complete an income tax return. But nobody tells him that usually his people do not have income to make out tax returns about, and that if his father is working on tribal property, his income tax return is an entirely different matter.

He will learn, after he leaves school, that his parents may have part ownership in a judgment fund, awarded to them as the result of litigation in the courts whereby his tribe may have been paid for lands taken from them. He will also soon know that the amount generally paid for his land is so little per person that it isn't worth talking about. He will learn that this fund which has been granted to him and to his people as the result of a lawsuit, will often not be paid to his family or to an individual, because the decision of Congress has been to leave the money on deposit in the U.S. Treasury, to be paid out "for education, health, and sanitation." This is all very laudable, but the results of bureaucratic control over education, health and sanitation can be described as failures.

The young Indian student will be taught that all are entitled to freedom of choice in all aspects of their lives. But he will know that there is no choice about going to this particular school.

Two of the six books contain a mere minimum of information about the American Indians. These are *Problems of Democracy* by Bohlman, and *Problems of Democracy* by Dunwiddie. Both books have a highly generalized section on this subject, not more than a page. There is no doubt but that the information has come from the Bureau of Indian Affairs, because EVERYTHING is being done to change the Indian "problem" from a bad problem to a good problem! The other four books contain only the word "Indian" in two or three places, as part of a listing of the Department of the Interior responsibilities.

What of the nonIndian student in the public schools, who reads such books? They will have absolutely no understanding of the role of the Indian in present society, nor of their role in the near and distant past.

Errors of omission or commission are also made in all six books. In *Citizenship and Government,* there is proud verbiage about all the dams being constructed by the federal government. Nothing is said about the fact that most of these dams have been and still are being placed on Indian lands, thus depriving the people of more property. In the same book, page 389, it is stated, that indeed the Indians have suffered much, but "The Indian Bureau . . . sought to replace mistreatment with education, health programs, and gradual acceptance of the Indian as a full-fledged, useful American citizen." The purpose of the organization of the Indian Bureau was to maintain police control over the Native Americans. Only quite recently has the BIA applied itself to improve conditions, education, and opportunity. These efforts have resulted largely in the development of a huge bureaucracy, at great administrative cost, and not much more.

The book titled *Goals of Democracy* gives the Indian one word on page 148: "Collective naturalization by treaty made citizens of inhabitants of the Louisiana Territory and Alaska. Congressional action gave citizenship in 1917 to Puerto Ricans, and in 1924 (tardily) to American Indians." The Indian child will ask "Why tardily?" The public school child will merely wonder. The book titled *American Problems* plays it safe and does not mention the Indian at all. Notice is taken of the Illinois Manufacturers' Association, International Woodworkers of America, Jewish Family Service, League of Women Voters, Dag Hammarskjold, National Automobile Dealers Association, Catholic Welfare Conference, Citizens Commission for the Public Schools, For a Sane Nuclear Policy, Conference of Christians and Jews, Conference of Family Relations, Water Pollution; and so on. There is, however, no mention of the American Indian, his organized groups, his tribal entities which are today engaged in activities giving pleasure and gain to many American citizens; nor of his schools, his family life, his heritage of conservation and love of nature.

According to Professor Dunwiddie (Problems of Democracy) the Allotment Act was a failure, because "the Indians, used to tribal life, did not know how to manage their separate holdings efficiently. No one taught the Indians farming, and the allotments were too small for ranching." Only the last statement is true, for anyone who has ever raised cattle would know that you cannot raise cattle on 160 acres of land. As to the Indian being ignorant of farming, this is untrue. The problem was, then as now: no tools, poor land, no water, no funds for purchasing of seed, fertilizer and other things so essential to farming. That the Indians "did not know how to manage" their affairs, is another falsehood. Burdened by debt, placed on arid land, without tools, seed, or water, or decent housing—how can a man "make it?" Reference, in the same book, on page 192, to the Bureau of Indian Affairs "relocation program," which presumably trains and educates the Native Americans to find a place and an occupation in urban areas . . . this whole program is an enormous farce, a fraud on the people, a failure.

The Bohlman *Problems of Democracy* book, on page 277 states: "NOW, however, real efforts are being made to help the Indians gain economic self-sufficiency and fuller participation in American life." This is untrue. ONLY where the tribes have insisted upon, fought for and gained independence and reliance upon their own leadership have gains been made. These areas are few. For the rest, the story is always the same. Some group of white (and sometimes even Indian, as well as Negro) bureaucrats come in, tell the people what to do and how to do it, usurp their leadership and initiative, then leave to make a five-hundred page report. These are the facts of life, and not one of these six books in the social sciences deals with such facts.

There are three thousand three hundred and forty three pages represented by these books—an easy estimate of one million, six hundred and seventy-one thousand, five hundred words. An enormous number of words and pages of irrelevancy to life as it truly is, for the American Indian.

†BUILDING OUR LIFE TOGETHER. *By Arnold, Banks & Smith.* Row, Peterson, & Co., 1960. Bureau of Indian Affairs School.

First published in 1939, this book has certainly not undergone many changes. It is so out of date, that it would appear the Bureau of Indian Affairs would have retired it long ago. Filled with the usual platitudes about "Citizenship is the practice of good building . . ." There are, according to the proud boast of the publisher, more than 200 illustrations in this book of 384 pages. This, combined with the art work, chapter headings, and other paraphernalia, brings to a bare minimum the amount of information contained in the textbook. In all these illustrations, however, it might be worthy of note that all the faces are white, all the buildings are "great," or lovely little middle-class houses, and all of the nation's problems can be solved by "good citizenship."

It is time that this federal bureau retired such books, so that Indian children need not be subjected to trash disguised as instructional materials.

*THE SOCIAL SCIENCES—CONCEPTS AND VALUES. *Prepared by the staff of the Center for the Study of Instruction, San Francisco.* Harcourt, Brace & World, 1970. Public school grades 1 through 4.

The trend shown in this series of textbooks is interesting and methodologically progressive. Attitudes and approaches in connection with the American Indian as part of classroom study show change for the better. However, incorrect data are still being utilized; improper comparisons are still being made; and inaccurate conclusions are still being drawn, even in the "new approach" books. These books in the social sciences embody the "discovery approach" to instruction.

Any system of study is as good as the information being presented. In the case under consideration the following information is incorrect: Teachers' edition, grade 3, Blackfeet, "Boasting was another form of behavior for the Blackfoot warrior. The warrior was expected to count coup, that is, to brag about how many horses he had captured or how many of the enemy tribe he had touched," (p. 4). This is an incorrect conclusion. Are the Blackfeet being described before white contact, or after? Are they being described during the time when they were being driven from their lands, or when they were living at peace, before the Europeans came? The Blackfeet man took a justifiable pride in accomplishing those things which in the eyes of his people were true accomplishments. No more than this determination ought to be made. In this section, the Blackfeet are described as nomads, without settled homes or lands. These tribes had their clearly designated lands, whose boundaries were known and protected against trespass.

Because their lands were far-flung and encompassed many miles of plains and prairie, does not make them nomads. Another misconception is the attempt to describe the Blackfeet societies as "clubs." It is understandable that some means of "relating" ancient cultures to modern images of such institutions as the special clubs is wanted. But the Blackfeet societies were no more like clubs than are academic senates like sewing circles. It is stated in this textbook, that "Boys and girls joined clubs in the Blackfeet bands. These clubs taught them their roles in the tribes." This is an improper comparison, from which incorrect conclusions have been drawn. The young people learned from their parents, from older people, from leaders of the tribe, and not alone from the Societies. In any case, the Societies were for adults and young persons of special abilities—certainly not for children. An example of a correct treatment of a Society, in the light of what happened to them, is the description on page 215, the Cherokees.

Even though the situation is highly generalized, certain main concepts do come through. Not so in connection with the description of the Nez Percé, who are represented entirely by the speech of Joseph, their leader, stating that he will "fight no more forever." This statement has been challenged as untrue by many Indian historians and leaders. Moreover, it also leads to misconceptions about the Nez Percés, standing by itself as it does in their history as they fought for their land, (p. 214).

A concept which starts out to make sense, but falls on its face in utter disarray in the light of the facts of history, is that treaties and agreements were made "to prevent conflict," (p. 224). How then, do the authors of this book explain away broken treaties, broken promises, as the facts of history show has been the case with Indian treaties and agreements? Explanations of this concept are entirely too general; they do not prepare the student for more accurate information. The authors and publishers need to clean up their data concerning the American Indian, and even in the most progressive instructional materials, given inaccurate data, misconceptions will result, and the learning process be distorted and retarded.

Good supplementary materials, if properly utilized and made available, may be able to compensate for the omissions in this textbook. But no amount of supplementary materials can compensate for the inaccuracies, distortions, and misconceptions which exist.

*WHAT IS MAN? Man in California. *Findings from Research.* Franklin Social Sciences Program. Public schools Grade 4.

This series of books suffers from the same incomplete data, inaccuracies, and improper conclusions that others do. The material is very general concerning Indians, despite the sympathetic approach and the obvious effort to give the Indian a place in modern life. The contributions of the American Indian to American Life are not treated with any degree of importance; they are merely mentioned.

The choices made in describing such contributions are haphazard, and limits the view and concepts of the students. In the same series, (Big Book), with reference to the year 1781 on page 147, "There was no racial discrimination at this time," (in California). There was discrimination and prejudice towards the Indian people in California at this time. There is a section on the American Indians in this book, (page 140). But the information is oversimplified, generalized. The tribes are not mentioned at all, so that their names are not known to the students.

*OUR WORKING WORLD: FAMILIES AT WORK. *By Lawrence Senesh.* Science Research Associates, 1970, Public schools text for grades 1–3.

This, too, is a new series based on new technology and new instructional approaches. It fails. The pictures and cartoons take up nearly the entire book. No doubt this is done in order to compare favorably with the current trend of American youth to "read" the cartoon books rather than writing. In such a book, supplementary materials for teachers must be of the highest quality, and training of teachers must become highly specialized, if this type of book is desirable. The illustrations are for use with recorded lessons. No reading skills are developed as a result of this system. Rather than this, more emphasis should be placed on the development of reading skills, learning skills, to meet the new challenges of modern society. There is a section on the Eskimo, Pueblo, and the Bushmen—all put together as though part of the same "primitive" society. The treatment is inadequate, oversimplified, generalized. Other information, concerning the division of labor, play and recreation, the use of free time, is not incorporated with Indian lifeways. Here good materials are available which could become an integral part of the teaching process. But no indication is given of the possibility of such use. The rest of the books in this series are very inadequate and not useful for the teaching of the American child. All sorts of information is given about the peoples of other lands, but practically none about the Native Americans of this land.

*LEARNING TO LOOK AT OUR WORLD: MANKIND IN TIME AND PLACE. *By Cooper, Sorensen, & Todd.* Silver Burdett Co., 1961, 310 pp. Public schools text.

Part of a series of three books in a social studies cycle, this textbook introduces the pupil in intermediate grades to the world setting in which his "education will take place," according to the authors. Consequently, the earth, living in the United States, and in various other countries, is described.

Missing from the book is any discussion of the Native peoples of the North American continent, where the pupil's education "will take place." Social studies in this book, therefore, is not related either to the problems, the issues, or the background history of the country or the continent. In one chapter, in which Alaska is discussed, there is no clear differentiation made between the Native peoples; Eskimos, Indians or Aleuts. Their cultures and economy are extremely generalized and simplified. Improper and invidious comparison is made between the Native economy and that of modern society, on page 34, "The Indian people along this coast had not learned to grow crops." Statements concerning the Indians and Eskimos of Alaska today are inaccurate, page 38. It is stated here that "The Indian people in the villages no longer carve totem poles." Untrue. They still maintain their arts, including that of totem pole carving.

Describing the capitol of the United States, "Washington and the World" is discussed, but no description is given either of the past or current political or economic relationships between this country and the Indian tribes.

Government and Citizenship

Social Problems

Summary of Evaluation (38 books evaluated)

1: What distinguishes these books on government, citizenship and social problems (social studies, sciences, etc.) is the ordinary, garden variety lack of knowledge. At best, only the surface is scratched relating to Indians in the course of government, as a developmental factor in our country.

2: Inaccuracies exist in all the books.

3: Omissions of important facts of Indian influence upon and participation in government distinguish all of the books.

4: There are many distortions of Indian life, wherever any mention is made of the Native American.

5: The new "methodology" books are responsible for the same errors of fact, inaccuracies, misconceptions, as the others.

6: Federal-Indian relations are not discussed in any of the books. Neither are treaties discussed.

7: The role of the Indian in the government of today, his special place in the litigation, courts, and agencies of the government today, is ignored.

8: The conservative "social studies" books are noteworthy for their complete lack of relevance to life in general, and to the life of the Indian in particular. These books are primary sources of misconception about Indians; in part, they are also most probably the sources of much inner conflict occurring among Indian youth today.

VII

American Indians

CRITERIA

1: Accurate, objective data should replace the usual "dream world" of an author's fancy as to Indian life, culture and history.

2: Degrading descriptions of the American Indian should not be utilized, whether by use of such words as "savage," or by implication and innuendo.

3: The history and lifeways of the Native Americans should be described in a developmental sense, instead of the usual static, generalized manner.

4: Oversimplification and generalizations should be avoided, and the description of the Indian peoples as tribes and entities of considerable variety should be emphasized.

5: Most histories treat the American Indian as though the only relevant matter was his relationship to the whites, and to the European society. Indians within their own society, with consideration for their internal and changing situation, as well as their intertribal relationships, should be accurately and objectively described.

6: The general misconception of most persons today is that the Indian has disappeared. The contrary is true. It is a fact that Indian societies still exist. Treating them as extinct is to put blinders upon current history. Changes have come about, but the Native societies and social mores continue to exist.

7: The Indians of today should be accurately described: where the people are, what reservations and communities they occupy, what their economic situation is, what their educational conditions are, and their political position as well. The relationship of the Indian to the federal government should be treated in a developmental way, his contributions to society and the world at large should be named and described. Such Native contributions should not be limited to those of material culture, but recognition should be given to the philosophy and democratic thought for which the Native American was known before white contact. His religious beliefs, his yearning for knowledge, his human and spiritual traits, should be given consideration.

8: If conjectures are made, such as those considering origins of the Indian people on this continent, then these should be on the plane of objective scholarship, and all sides of the question should be noted. Implications and innuendos of Indian practices and customs should be avoided, and the facts given. Improper, invidious comparisons should be avoided, as to Indian life and modern western life. This is certainly unfair to the Native American, who lived in a society of his own making with his accepted and well developed complex cultures as the standard for his behavior and customs.

9: When European-Indian conflict is described, the causes for such conflict should be given. Indian land ownership should not be treated as though they did not in fact own the land, for historic and current litigation proves the contrary, and may be brought in evidence to make the author of such a statement look like the fool he is, if this is done.

10: Many Indian people have entered the western world, and have made significant contributions. These should be noted and recognized. Many others prefer to cling to the old traditions, and these should be respected.

11: The facts should be told without fear, about the treatment of Indians by Spanish missionaries and gold miners. The feudal slave labor system in the missions should be explained. So too, should the facts of the attempted genocide of Indians during the gold rush be faithfully told, as part of history. No attempts should be made to gloss over such historic facts. Everything has been said already in the textbooks, blaming the Indian for conflict, "massacres," and hostility. That these were brought on by white intrusion, invasion and harassment, is never mentioned. Now let us tell the students the whole truth instead of half of it.

†INDIANS. *By Edwin Tunis.* World Publishing Company, 1959, 157 pp. Bureau of Indian Affairs schools, including Chilocco Indian School and Anadarko Area schools.

On the page facing the title page, a drawing is shown of a Plains Indian village, the caption of which reads: "Lodge of a Plains Indian village. The two boys at the left are training as future horse thieves by stealing meat from a drying rack. Their instructor is their mother's brother. He is beyond the teepee, mounted." Since illustrations are done by the author, this one can certainly be considered as part of the ideology of the book as a whole.

Page 17: "It is thought to be highly unlikely that an idea will be duplicated independently by a people who are cut off from the normal chain of contact. In the light of this, it is believed that our Indians either brought their basic ideas with them, learned ideas from other Indians who had imported them originally, or had contact long after migration with Asia, Polynesia, and possibly with Europe . . ." That similar or even identical ideas have originated and still originate simultaneously in entirely different parts of the world, and by entirely unrelated persons, is so well known a fact that it appears redundant to explain it. Examples of such instances arise continually. Why could it not have occurred by independent invention, as well as by borrowing, or as learned ideas.

Page 20: "It would seem reasonable for the people in any one section of the country to speak a similar language, but that would be too easy; the Indians mixed things up." This derogatory and uncalled for comment belittles the Indian people. One might ask, how does it happen that Italians and Greeks who live side by side in the same apartment house in a big city, TODAY, do not learn one another's language.

Page 21: The translation of the Dakota name is given as "cutthroats," although other sources give it as "adder, or enemy."

Page 21: The text is laced with facetious remarks, probably meant to be smart or funny, all of them in very poor taste. An example: "The Indians of the western Plains developed a formal gesture language by which tribes of differing speech could communicate. Though it wasn't known far outside that area, probably any Indian could have understood it pretty well, since much of it was pantomime and any Indian was a good actor." The Indian sign language is a universally recognized, practical means of communication the world over. To handle it so cavalierly is insulting.

Page 24: "The fact that the Indians painted their faces and bodies is well-known. In war they did it with the idea of making themselves look ferocious." In fact, their skin painting was of a religious and traditional character, depicting the beliefs of their clans or tribes.

Page 28: Here the details of Indian "strange" customs are given. As to certain tribal burial customs, the author says, ". . . the more settled tribes recovered the bones later and buried them or preserved them in grisly piety." What is grisly to this author, and what is grisly to the American Indian might be two different things, perhaps representing two different cultures, and each should be respected. On the same page, reference is made to the "Digger Indians," a term of insult. There was no such tribe. Again, on page 29, the author continues to make such improper comparison when he states, "There were some dreadful concoctions made."

A statement made by this writer on page 29, which requires no great intellectual evaluation in order to uncover its grossly inhumane standards, is this: "The white man, in spite of his golden rule, was the aggressor and the thief. His cruelties are not to be condoned, and yet—suppose we—you and I—had just found this continent today, rich and untouched. What would we do about it? Sail away and leave the Indians in peace? We would not! We'd take it away from them."

Page 76, referring to the war in the Southeast, when the Choctaw, Creeks, Seminoles and Cherokees fought a war of defense of land and life, the author explains: "Nowhere was the war game played with more enthusiasm than in the Southeast. And it was a game; it wasn't real war. No tribe wanted to conquer another tribe or exterminate it. They just wanted excitement and scalps."

Page 78: "No women ever entered the Hot House, and in view of its probable stench, they were lucky." Is the author implying that Indians had more "stench" than whites? In fact, the sweat house uses were more religious than anything else.

Page 85: "All of these Indians lived along rivers, hence they had boats. Since these were used chiefly as ferries, any old kind of boat would do. What they had was, indeed, any old kind of boat!" These boats were inventive, showed superb uses of native materials, and were more convenient than watercraft utilized by the Europeans. As a matter of fact, the Europeans soon copied the watercraft made by the Natives.

Page 87: A fortuitous insult is handed the Indian Americans with this description: "The buffalo stampeded toward the cliff, running ever faster as noise and terror built up behind them. Over they went, falling into the corral, and the rest of the story was slaughter and waste." Such falsification can only be met with a direction to the writer to work over his source materials more carefully: his ignorance is showing. It is a well known fact that the buffalo was utilized in the economy of the tribes, with so little waste, that descriptions of the Native's unique and economical usage fills the pages of anthropological accounts.

The most arrogant misinformation is contained in these statements: Page 90, "Now the buffalo hunt that had been so arduous became a magnificent sport (for Indians)." Untrue, it was always a way of life, a part of the economy, and continued to be so, even more intensively, with the acquisition of the horse. Page 91, "Ordinarily the covers (of the tipi) were renewed each spring with skins from animals that had shed their winter coats and whose hides were thin." The skins were taken from the animals after the kill, were most meticulously dressed, tanned, and decorated.

Page 107: Describing the life of the Indians of the area west of the Rockies, which the author terms The Basin Indians, he states, "These people were bone-poor; they were primitive; they were dirty (who would waste water on washing?) and they lacked all color and dash." The writer adds, as an afterthought, "they were bright enough to survive in a land where a white man would, and did, starve to death." He is describing the Paiutes, the Bannocks and Goshutes, as typical of these tribes. He is maligning a whole people, whose economy had developed in harmony with their natural environment, whose inventions and cultures gave them a richness and spiritual fullness unknown to modern man. Information of a more ludicrous type is contained on page 108: in which the writer has drawn a picture of a Piñon nut (presumably about twice the actual size). This is a picture of a piñon cone, about half the actual size.

Page 108: "Once in a great while, these Indians might come upon a herd of pronghorn antelope, and this was a glorious find." Untrue. The Indian people knew just where the game was. They knew where the antelope and other game animals ranged. When the time was ready, they hunted them. Page 110: The scrabble for food left the Basin Indians too scattered to organize for raiding other people . . . There were no clans in the Basin and no marriage taboos." This writer is not familiar with the literature or the living evidence to the contrary.

Page 113: Description of the California tribes is oversimplified, generalized, inaccurate and inadequate. "The leaching was done (of acorns) in porous baskets over sand pits. Ultimately the meal was boiled as mush and was nutritious though practically tasteless." Leaching was seldom if ever done in porous baskets over sand pits. The meal was made into a wide variety of foods, including a bread, part of a stew, a pancake, and a gelatinous side dish to be eaten with meat. On the same page still describing California Indians, "Because of their diversity, these Indians are an ethnologist's delight; but because of their sedentary dullness they aren't very interesting to the rest of us . . ." In the first instance, referring to the acorn food, if it was tasteless to the author, he might concede that it was certainly delicious to the Natives (and today even to many others); and in the second instance, referring to these people being "not very interesting to the rest of us," this type of gratuitous snobbery and patronizing attitude ill becomes a writer of books offered to schoolchildren as a teaching tool.

On page 151 the competitive potlatch is described, with much intellectual superiority and gusto. That it is not true, and has been admitted to be untrue by anthropologists who have done continuing research on this aspect of Northwest Indian life, is apparently unknown to this writer. Few authors whose books have been evaluated in this volume have shown so much ignorance of Indian life, so much outright racial prejudice, so much fortuitous distortion and misrepresentation of Native life, as Mr. Tunis has done in this textbook. In another type of society, with even a minimum of sensitivity to the spiritual and moral rights of its peoples, this book would never have been permitted inside a classroom. It certainly has no place in a school which has for its special purpose the teaching of Indian youth.

†THE AMERICAN INDIAN. *By Oliver La Farge*. Golden Press, Inc., 1960, 215 pp. Special edition for young readers. Bureau of Indian Affairs schools. Institute of American Indian Arts, Santa Fe, New Mexico.

Oliver La Farge spent a good share of his life studying the American Indian. Born in 1901 in New York City, he was the son of an illustrious architect, a member of a cultured, well educated family. As a participant in archaeological expeditions to Mexico, Guatemala and Arizona, he very early became interested in aboriginal cultures. Soon (1933) he had helped found the Association on American Indian Affairs, and was its president for some time. He was a humanitarian noted for his interest in the American Indian.

The book under review properly opens with "They Discovered America." A good deal of general information is contained in the book. There are illustrations, with maps, drawings, reproductions of paintings, and reproductions of the work of Indian artists as well. Exception is taken, however, to paintings done by certain French and English artists, which are awful.

There is a very disturbing element in this book, more disturbing because it comes from a self-appointed friend of the Indian, than if it had come from a self-confessed supremacist. This element is the undercurrent of facetious superiority, which appears in so many areas that it cannot properly be ignored. At the risk of committing heresy in the eyes of some of our nonIndian friends, THE AMERICAN INDIAN is evaluated herein as a book marred by undercurrents of superiority, containing the same misconceptions held by many others, today as always, as they view the American Indian.

The first criticism pertains to the use of words having derogatory connotations, such as "barbarian, primitive, and prehistoric" in relation to the human beings native to this land before and during the first white-Indian contacts. If this book were a scholarly treatise, or intended for college students, the terms would have been explained in scientific context and would have been properly understood. In a popular book such as this, without further explanation, the connotation is degrading. Since Mr. La Farge does not give his sources, and there is no bibliography, a discussion of ideas is not possible. Quite obviously, the source for his description of Iroquois life is taken from the Jesuit Relations, which have been under critical scrutiny for some time. Much of the material accumulated by the Jesuit fathers was a result of misinterpretation and misunderstanding—phonied up for adaptation to the original Catholic concept of the Indian as a subhuman being, since the Bible does not mention this representative of the human species. Thus, La Farge deals with fervent enthusiasm upon aspects of torture, and ritual human sacrifice said to have been practiced by the Iroquoian people. The use of a certain type of torture in ritual practices is not explained, nor is the reader made aware that most captives were adopted into the tribe. One might ask, furthermore, why the highly exotic and "peculiar" characteristics of a people who are unknown to a writer are described with such meticulous detail. There are some writers who apparently take a masochistic pleasure in relating practices that were supposed to be used, practices for which there is no accurate authentication. Certainly the noble, humane, generous, liberty-loving aspects of the Iroquois character have not been explained nor described by La Farge with equal gusto. Nor do we find that the enormous contributions of these unique people are described in the La Farge book with the same enthusiasm as are the blow-by-blow accounts of alleged tortures. Until such time as the whole truth may become known about this phase of some Indian cultures, it would appear to be the better part of decency to discuss the matter objectively, which has not been done by La Farge.

Error exists in the estimate of population, which is given as approximately one million before European contact. There were that many Native inhabitants in the California region alone. Still another error, which has been refuted time and again both by Indian historians as well as scholars, is the use of the term "king" in connection with Native leadership. There were no kings, no nobility, no queens, and no princesses. This was a figment of the imagination of a few French, English and Spanish aristocrats, who used such propaganda to obtain support for their expeditions. The use of the word "chief" is also a white man's invention. There were no chiefs, only Indian leaders and teachers of the people, who held their position subject to the will of the people. Hereditary leadership existed, but if the man was unsatisfactory, or incapable of leadership, he was replaced by another. In any case, there was considerable variety in forms of social structure, and such designations are so superficial as to cause harmful misconceptions to flourish. If we consider Indian society as a dynamic part of their history and government, all sorts of human elements must not be overlooked, and generalizations should be carefully avoided (within the general frame of the society as a whole). A great many pages are devoted to intertribal warfare. Many authorities now believe that warfare was minimal before white contact.

Some facetious statements alluded to earlier in this evaluation are these: "The French allied themselves with the Choctaws — and the Natchez, while they lasted." "The Iroquoians took religion seriously, worked hard at it, and wove it into every moment of their lives." (pages 32, 44). This is just "precious" enough not to be outrightly insulting. That the Natchez were exterminated is a tragedy, not to be so fatuously described. What is so difficult to understand and to exclaim over, that these people "took religion seriously." Was there ever a people on earth (except those of today), who did NOT take religions seriously? On page 47, it is said, "The Iroquoian customs with respect to captives showed Southeastern influence and involved revolting cruelty." The statements that follow ape the Jesuit Relations. The type of cruelty described by La Farge is not authenticated. And when mentioning religious practices, an explanation is due in the proper context of tribal culture and religion.

Error is committed by omission on page 51: "After the Revolution, the British offered the Iroquois a reservation in Canada, to which many of them moved." There is no mention that the British, no less than the

Americans, were not noted for keeping their word. The reservation allowed the Iroquois was so much less land than they had been promised, that many refused to leave for Canada. Another error occurs on the same page: "During the nineteenth century, the Iroquois were talked into ceding a good deal of their land in the Northeast, and some of them were moved to Oklahoma and Wisconsin." This statement implies agreement. On the contrary, they were forced to leave.

Outright mockery is expressed on page 53: "Among some tribes, these shamans developed into remarkable magicians. They had such tricks as making the hut shake as if a terrible storm were blowing, making animal spirits talk out of the darkness, or plunging a knife into the air and bringing it back covered with blood."

Page 68: "The Shawnees also came out,of the east, but before the time of the white men. They seem to have been a nation that liked to travel." All the tribes traveled: to trade, to see how other tribesmen lived, to exchange ideas, and to bring home new articles of use or decoration. The Sioux, page 69, who were "later so great, were simply a group of closely related Woodland Hunters living west of the Chippewas. Some of them did a little farming, and from time to time they went into the High Plains to kill a few buffalo." A people do not develop leadership, courage, and greatness, overnight. And the Sioux had all of these qualities. This statement diminishes their culture, development and history. They had peaceful pursuits, but when it became necessary to defend themselves they used their leadership qualities and great independence in the direction of combat.

Describing the Indians of California, La Farge shows an extraordinary lack of knowledge. The information in this section is meager, and the author covers his ignorance with a great deal of generalization and some smart remarks. "Where rituals are few," he says, "a good deal of attention is likely to be paid to the strange things that happen when a girl becomes a woman, and similar attention may be extended to a boy's becoming a man." No strangeness was attached to the natural cycle of life, only respect. His description of the desert people as "very poor," (page 159), is another evidence of this author's lack of knowledge. What is it to be "poor" in a land where nobody starves, all have homes and land, clothing, and are in good health. To say "poor" is to make a comparison. And to make a comparison with modern technological poverty (as this author does by implication) is like comparing oranges and atomic bombs. Outrageous derogation exists in this description: "The Californians were not so much warlike as quarrelsome. Each little tribe guarded its pocket of territory jealously, and acted immediately against trespassers . . . Often, when there was serious trouble, two tribes would line up, then each would pick a champion to fight it out for the tribe." There is no serious answer to such a description as "quarrel-some." This writer is attempting to justify his lack of knowledge with a facetious remark. He has given a demeaning description of the traditional and peace-loving tribal mock battles which avoided wars and prevented hostilities. "After the fight, there was long consulting and haggling," (p. 160). If Mr. La Farge's cultured relatives were engaged in negotiations to end a disagreement, they would be "conferring." When Indians did it, they were "haggling."

Describing burial customs of the California tribes, on page 160, he states: "Often the moiety to which the deceased did not belong handled the funeral arrangements, so that the bereaved moiety was not contaminated." This was done out of love, to help the people, to serve them, and to give them aid in a time of deep distress. Consideration should also be given, in addition to this statement being derogatory in any event, that an attempt has been made to generalize all the burial customs of all the people, when in fact such customs varied among many of the tribes. Continuing this type of description, the author says: "After the funeral rites, or a year later when a second ceremony was held, the taboo on mentioning the dead person's name was lifted. That taboo was far more troublesome for primitive tribes who named people after objects than it would be for us. If the deceased's name was "White Deer" or "Oak Leaf" for instance, a couple of words in constant use had to be dropped until in some way the taboo could be gotten around." This picture of a stupid, dull people, with a language so vapid that such a problem could exist, is the result of sheer ignorance, of which La Farge was guilty in more than one way, and throughout the book.

"The priests gathered the roving Indians," into the missions, according to La Farge. He mentions the use of force, true, but the frame in which this is put, involves the reader in an image of roaming, childish people who could be "gathered in." They were not rovers in any case. As to the potlatch, the author makes the usual error, which is discussed by Drucker in his book "To Make My Name Good." Another glib remark is made in connection with slaves in the Northwest, page 173: "There was not much need for slaves in that economy, but having a few around the house showed that a chief was either a successful war leader, or rich enough to buy an expensive article."

There is so much misinformation, distortion of fact, and implication of a low order of mankind, that the book can be judged improper for

use in Indian schools, and incapable of use in nonIndian schools, because of the thin scholarship it displays and the misconceptions about
Indian life which are built into every part of it. Notwithstanding this
author's considerable reputation with some individuals, La Farge has
not understood Indian life, culture, or history. Finally, the book as a
whole is poorly organized, made by a man who had humane ideas, accumulated some information about some American Indian groups, and
did a whole lot of talking about it.

†AMERICAN INDIANS. *By William T. Hagan.* University of Chicago Press, 1961, 190 pp. Bureau of Indian Affairs, Fort Sill Indian
School, Lawton, Oklahoma.

The relationship between white man and Indian forms the framework of this book, the premise being that the Indian was "doomed at
the start by the conflict of cultures and attitudes." The conflict of cultures and attitudes is still with us, unhappily. It is not confined to governmental agencies, nor the ignorant and unlettered, the self-interested,
or even the average person.

The author explains the cultural variety existing among the Natives
quite clearly, but in making his point, he engages in generalizations of
personal characteristics supposedly held in common by whole tribes.
Such generalizations are misleading.

Page 3: Discussing the great variety of Indian physical characteristics,
material cultures, etc., the author says: "Did the average Indian take
his foe's head for a trophy, or did he content himself with just the scalp,
and did the scalp include the ears? . . . Was boiled puppy a delicacy or
a last resort to stave off famine?" These are connotations of personality
traits which are improperly imputed to a whole tribe. The relish displayed in the exotic, the "strange," and the descriptions of fashions of
taking scalps, without at the same time treating this in its historical
sense, leads to subjective conclusions and derogatory connotations. The
author continues, "The Choctaws and Chickasaws lived side by side,
yet the Choctaws were noted for their agricultural skills, the Chickasaws for their belligerency. The Sac and Fox tribes were even more
closely allied, but the Sacs were more stable and dependable in political
matters." A discussion of political stability, economic competency and
belligerency is suspect. One might ask, by whose standards are such
characterizations made? Or, for an example, in what context were the
Sacs more stable and dependable, for whose benefit? To whom were

the Chickasaws belligerent? One can hardly analyze the characteristics of any people in such a subjective way without leaving the door open to criticism of the author's own culture and attitudes.

Page 4: "When these people became mobile, they abandoned their garden patches to follow the buffalo herds." Untrue. They retained their lands, kept on producing the foods they needed, gathering the rest. Some hunted buffalo. Others remained and planted. Thus a new and more complex division of labor was one of the results of acquisition of the horse, which made buffalo hunting into a mass enterprise. Page 8: The Spanish missions "did preserve his (the Indian's) life and provide a rude plenty." This implies that the missions were good for the Indians. They were forced labor camps, resulting in disruption of whole families. The birth rate declined, the death rate being abnormally high.

Page 8: Referring to English colonization and the "nuisance and menace" in the very existence of the Indian, it is explained that the Indian "style of warfare, braining infants against trees and torturing captives, horrified Englishmen." This statement judges and condemns a whole race of people. It takes the exception for the rule. Further, why should Englishmen be horrified, considering the horrors of the Inquisition, the witch-burning in which they engaged, the massacres, criminal land-thefts and betrayal of trust, in which they excelled. The author himself cites such instances.

Page 10: When Powhatan died ". . . the Indians united under his successor, Opechancanough, "to avenge themselves for the petty slights inflicted by the whites and to eliminate this growing menace to their territory." They united in a general war to drive the invaders from their lands. The "petty slights" were massive thefts of their land.

Page 66: "Between 1816 and 1848 twelve states entered the Union, scores of treaties were negotiated by which the tribes relinquished the bulk of their holdings east of the Mississippi and consented to removal west . . ." These were forced removals, and the language of the author in saying they "consented," distorts a historic fact. The treaties were signed by unrecognized, unauthorized persons, and this in itself would make for some important historical observations, but the author does not address himself to these facts of history. In short, what the author has done, through semantic distortion, is to falsify history.

Page 156: The evaluation of the Wheeler-Howard Act, which presumably gave the rights of self-government to the tribes, is inaccurate. It is a fact, known to many Indian leaders who were directly involved during that era of Indian affairs, that this legislation was rammed down the throats of the people, was resisted by most of the tribes, and that the federal government sent enforcers into Indian country to get acceptance of the terms of the Act. This they accomplished in many cases; but in other cases, they were defeated. The matter discussed by this author is outside his field of expertise. In fact, the entire section on current affairs, the economic and political situation, contains many serious inaccuracies, and lacks objectivity.

Page 175: The author is correct concerning the difficulties of evaluating sources in Indian history, which are "almost exclusively the work of white men. Even the handful of Indian accounts usually has been compiled with the assistance of white interpreters and editors so that their validity is open to question." It is to be hoped that with the emergence of qualified Indian scholars who have the authority of their own heritage, the knowledge of their language, and the ability to work with objective scholars of whatever race, the educational materials presented will be of a sounder, more accurate, and more useful character than those used in the schools today.

AMERICAN INDIANS presents some useful information. If one is aware of the misconceptions existing in the book, the distortions and omissions of historic fact, it can be utilized within these limitations.

ACCULTURATIONAL PSYCHOLOGY, or, MODERN INDIAN PSYCHOLOGY. *By John F. Bryde, S.J., Ph.D.* Bureau of Indian Affairs textbook. Indian schools in the Sioux country.

This textbook was first published in an experimental form in 1967. It has since been adopted as a textbook by the Bureau of Indian Affairs. The writer is a long-time friend of the Sioux people, speaks their language and has witnessed their joys and sorrows, the good times and the bad, over a period of many long years. It is therefore with some reticence that this adverse evaluation is written.

Objectives of the textbook are to explore "what is wrong with the young Sioux student, "who, it has been said, has the highest dropout rate in the country, the lowest economic conditions, the highest unemployment, and "shows the least amount of motivation." The quotations are not ours. They are the phraseology of scholars who are generally not Indian. The book has been studied by several scholars, one of whom is a psychology teacher. In each case, the reader has expressed dissatisfaction with the book, for many different reasons. Considering this textbook, as a scholar and as an Indian, this evaluation finds it not only unsatisfactory as an aid to the young Sioux, but a dangerous tool in the wrong hands and an unreliable tool in the right hands.

The textbook attempts to relate the beliefs and philosophy of the Sioux people to the needs of the young person in the world of today. This is certainly a laudable goal. But the answers given to spiritual and material questions are entirely too puerile in the complex world of today, as well as in the complex society of the Sioux as they are today.

The burden of the instructional material in the first part of the book has to do with the problem of "how to be happy." How to be happy in two cultures. How to be happy and PROUD about being an Indian. How to act happily. It appears to this reviewer that Man himself (including the Sioux, who, it is said, had a deep belief in the idea of happiness), has had and still has a profound need to be NOT happy, if accomplishment in the deepest sense of the word is to be a goal. This does not necessarily mean financial, pragmatic accomplishment. But accomplishment in the humane and spiritual sense, in the sense of being one with nature, of being one with your people, knowing that one is making a contribution however little, to society and life, the family and the tribe. This type of accomplishment is filled with UNhappiness. For this, one needs "that blessed discontent" which belonged to the great poets, as well as to Jesus, Mohammed, Buddha, and the legendary Deganowida. There is nothing reprehensible about this, and that teacher who attempts to by-pass such an intensity of desire—which is the hallmark of the young (and when we cease having it we are old)—is short-changing mankind as well as the Sioux.

The second objection to this book is the patronizing tone within it—the "talking down" to the student. The manner in which, as an instance, the role of the social scientist is explained, is done in such a way as to diminish the intelligence of the student. Dr. Bryde says, "There is a certain kind of person today who is trained to find out the hidden and unconscious thoughts (values) of other people. This type of person is usually from a college or university and is called a social scientist." This would make some of the Sioux elders extremely unhappy. For years, they have been trying to instill into their youth the great philosophy of the Indian people. Their lack of success is probably one of the things wrong with today's youth, to speak very generally. The author compares the social scientist with the medical doctor, "who is trained to take out tonsils." He is described in such a way that the next time a young Sioux meets a social scientist, he will expect to be cured of his spiritual ills, just as the doctor is expected to cure him of his sick tonsils. This is an extremely crude and incorrect comparison. Further, "the way that the social scientist gets at the truth is by asking questions."

This type of omnipotence is truly praiseworthy, but it just isn't so. Social scientists have been asking the Sioux people "questions" for many years, and haven't "got at the truth" yet. Dr. Bryde sets the social scientist up as a kind of demi-God, capable of getting at truth, solving problems, and helping the Sioux to be happy, by asking questions. "It takes a lot of training to know a) what questions to ask, and b) how to interpret and see what the answers mean. They have to be able to look into the hidden meaning in the answer," the author explains.

The inescapable conclusion as a result of all this weary talk, is that no one is so infallible as the social scientist, whose canny interpretation of the "answers" is just like "they had put an x-ray to the heads of the people," according to the words of Dr. Bryde. The Sioux student surely cannot believe this, if he has intelligence, which he certainly has. Another element of judging character, and developing the happy life, according to this scholar, is to develop values of "good" and "bad." Examples are given of persons who have big cars, who are not necessarily "good," or that having possessions doesn't make one "good." Examples are drawn from the tourists who come to the reservations and have big cars; or from gangsters who have lots of money, but are "bad." What is good or bad has troubled philosophers for thousands of years. To attempt answering such a question with this type of overwhelming generalization and vulgarization is "bad," in and of itself.

The author's explanation of the peopling of this continent is highly speculative, and does not aid the student in developing a scholarly approach to scientific questions. If speculation is wanted, then other points of view should be given. Attempting to answer the question of Indian possession of land, he says on page 88: "Another similarity that ran throughout the various, widely separated tribes was that all of them considered the world and everything in it to be common property, or that it belonged to everybody." This is untrue. Each tribe claimed and held an area that could be used by members of the tribe. Other tribes were not allowed to encroach. It is certain that the Sioux themselves would know this. For, when the Chippewas attempted to possess Sioux property, there was conflict. Only the whites prevented a peaceful solution to the situation, when they encouraged the Chippewas to remain on Sioux property, to the end that the original inhabitants, the Sioux, were made to give it up. On the other hand, the Chippewas themselves were driven out of their eastern lands by the white men, so that they were pushed on and on, into the property of other tribes.

There is considerable history in this textbook, interspersed with the teaching of psychology. The treatment of history goes as far back as the

Olmecs, Incas, Mayas, and Aztecs, but there is no relation developed
between these ancient peoples and the Sioux themselves. Certainly some
good information could come of this whole chapter if the civilizations
of these people could have been related as a developmental process,
in which the Sioux themselves were a part, but this is not done. Derogatory statements are made about the Iroquois people, on page 140:
"They were the largest in number and they were very fierce and blood-
thirsty at times." The author then considers the theory that the Sioux,
who were anciently from the east, decided to "move away" from the
Iroquois, who were raiding the coast and taking captives. "This is only
a theory," the writer states. If this is a textbook, then such "theories"
ought not to be promulgated without discussion as to the pros and
cons of the matter. The derogatory statement about the Iroquois should
not have been made.

One cannot avoid questioning Dr. Bryde's ability as a historian,
when such statements as these are made: " . . . during the years 1822-23,
the Arikaras did a surprising thing. They started attacking the traders
who were bringing the very things they needed to hold out against their
enemies." The rest of the page (183) is devoted to a blood-curdling
review of how the Teton Sioux licked the Arikaras and how in doing
this they aided the American soldiery, but "showed them up" by best-
ing their old Arikara enemies with the army standing by in stupified
amazement. In the first place, the delight with which this yarn is related, is obviously to impress the Sioux with the idea that the author
appreciates the bravery of their ancestors. In the second place, Dr.
Bryde forfeits his position as an objective scholar, in thus relating a tale
without explaining the whole truth, which is this: What was at stake
in the Arikara attack upon the traders was the struggle for the control
of trade, the struggle against the avarice of the traders and their profit-
eering, fraudulent practices. After long years of suffering such conditions, the Arikaras finally decided to sweep their enemies out of the
trading business.

If Dr. Bryde intended to "upgrade the pride" of the Sioux with his
bloodcurdling story of how the Tetons licked the Arikaras while the
admiring Army stood by, he may have succeeded. But it is a high
price to pay for the psychological luxury of the wrong kind of "pride,"
and as a psychologist, the Father should have known better. Another
example is his story on page 186 about the Oglalas. It goes like this:
". . . the Oglalas being good Tetons, and the best fighters on the Plains,
were always sniffing the breeze for the possibility of new enemies to
try out . . ." Page after page of intertribal warfare is then described,

with enormous enthusiasm and gusto. There is not one word of explanation as to the causes for such fratricidal struggle, the economic
basis for it, or the cultural upheaval that was then taking place in
which brother was pitted against brother by the greed of white men
who wanted Indian lands. This desciption of the Oglalas may instill
"pride" in the Oglala Tetons, but it is the pride of brute animals, and
this they did not possess.

The author relates another story on page 190, in which the Plains
tribes met, in 1851, at Horse Creek near the Upper Platte. The purpose
of the meeting was to hold a peace council, but this is the way Dr.
Bryde describes what ensued: "The government hailed this peace
council as a great success and went back to St. Louis. The tribes broke
up and went home, fighting contentedly on the way with one another."
This evaluator feels reasonably.certain that the author is seriously attempting to depict the life and culture of the Sioux at this time in
their history, or at least their customs and mores. However, it is an
old wives' tale he is relating and he knows it.

A ridiculous note is struck on page 193, when, in describing Red
Cloud, the writer says that this Sioux leader was probably born in
1822, although Red Cloud himself stated he was born in 1821. But,
says Dr. Bryde, "It is easy to see how an old man, in the days when
strict calendars were not kept, could miss a year or two in trying to
recall an exact year." Who is to say whether Red Cloud was born in
1822, or 1821. He SAID he was born in 1821, and this should have been
enough.

The truth about the Sioux removal from the ancient lands in Minnesota, and their treatment by the whites, is falsified; whether deliberately or accidentally is beside the point. The fraud practiced against
the Sioux by the traders, by Governor Ramsey, and BIA Commissioner
Lea is glossed over. This book makes an apologia for the whites, of
the whole event, when there should have been scornful condemnation.
Relating the massacre of Indians, including women and children, at
Wounded Knee, which took place December 29, 1890, Dr. Bryde's
telling of this outrage differs markedly from that of official record.
According to Bryde's version, the massacre was a "mistake," and *all*
shared in the blame. According to the governmental investigation,
however, it was reported: "The terrible effect may be judged from
the fact that one woman survivor, Blue Whirlwind, with whom the
author conversed, received 14 wounds, while each of her two little boys
were also wounded by her side. In a few minutes two hundred Indians,
men, women, and children, with 60 soldiers, were lying dead and

wounded on the ground, the tepees had been torn down by the shells and four of them were burning above the helpless wounded, and the surviving handful of Indians were flying in wild panic to the shelter of the ravine, pursued by hundreds of maddened soldiers and followed up by a raking fire from the Hotchkiss guns, which had been moved into position to sweep the ravine. There can be no question that the pursuit was a massacre, in which fleeing women, with infants in their arms, were shot down after resistance had ceased and when almost every warrior was stretched dead or dying on the ground."

This is the official government report. But, according to Bryde, the women, children and men alike were covered with blankets, so that the soldiers could not distinguish between the warriors and others. Other descriptions given by Dr. Bryde of this infamous event, do not agree with the official and authenticated reports, but rather tend to efface the responsibility of the white soldiers. A general conclusion may be drawn from a reading of this book: It should not be used as a textbook for teaching Indian children about Sioux history. It should not be used as a social studies, or psychology textbook. Despite the many qualities of this work, which was obviously done with energy and care, it is psychologically ineffective and unprofessional in the context of the Sioux culture as well as in general scholarly terms. The continuous tone of superiority which the author adopts, when discussing values, cultures, and modes of behavior, would be insupportable and insufferable to any intelligent child or youth. It is only when Dr. Bryde engages in the telling of the tales of war, conflict, and of Sioux bravery on the battlefield that he excels.

John Bryde is a superlative storyteller. In truth, he has missed his vocation, and this evaluator would rather sit and listen to his tales of derring-do, the brave and bold stories of the legendary Sioux heroes, than hear him prate about behavioral patterns and advices, or interpret historical events.

† RED MAN'S AMERICA. *By Ruth M. Underhill.* University of Chicago Press, 1951, 400 pp. Bureau of Indian Affairs, Institute of American Indian Arts.

As Dr. Underhill herself states in the first chapter, ". . . there are hopes that, within a few years, the fog which covers the Indians' prehistory will clear away, and then, perhaps, the whole story must be rewritten." This is true not only as the prehistory is concerned, but equally true in connection with many other aspects of the history, especially since white contact.

It is in certain areas of established concepts that this book may be best evaluated. Source materials are profuse; there is a good bibliography; and the author makes every effort to authenticate her findings. However, although the painstaking efforts of the writer may be without criticism, there is always the crucial matter of choice. And choice will depend upon developed concepts, cultural attitudes based upon the instincts of one's own cultural heritage, as well as the influence of opinions developed by those whose sources are being utilized. In order to evaluate the book according to concepts which it supports or declines to support, therefore, these are the areas discussed:

The concept of origins: The theory held by most scientists is that man on this continent arrived over the Bering Sea, probably on foot, pursuing animals hunting food. More modern scientific researches, however, point to the strong probability of early arrivals from several directions: across the sea by way of small islands, or from South America by way of the many natural ports where boatmen could anchor on their way north, to name only two. At the same time, it would appear that since man himself evolved in only a few places on this earth; since the natives of most if not all countries of the modern world are not actually the first arrivals and may therefore be considered "immigrants"; hence that the question of man's origins on this continent has received more attention than it deserves in the elementary and high school textbooks. Considering the latest and most conservative estimates of the length of time that man has been here, which is roughly twenty to twenty five thousands of years, then even the most meticulous scientist should agree that this is indeed a far distance in man's antiquity. All other considerations notwithstanding, this dating would place early man — in a state of continuing development — upon this part of the earth long before the birth of Christ, probably the longest continuous race in one place, on the face of the earth. We think this should be enough to guarantee us our permanent place in America as the first, and only true Natives.

Far more to the point, and of greater importance in the history of our world, is the question of the peopling of this continent. In this area, there is a great deal of scientific work still to be done.

The second concept with which this evaluation deals, is that of warfare as part of the cultural life of the Natives before white contact. There is a growing acknowledgement on the part of many scholars that warfare, in the form described by most historians (as a major part of the culture) did not exist before white contact. That it did indeed become entrenched in the tribes, with organized soldier societies, and that it became part of the culture after white contact, is not disputed. Even in this regard, distinctions must be made as to degree and extent of warfare. Too, recognition must be given to areas of tribal life where warfare was negligible even after white contact. It is practically impossible today, utilizing available sources (including the Native historians still living), to develop a clear description of this, however. Written materials which have been utilized are of the same type as that of the Jesuit Relations, which are suspect. One source given by this author, for example, is John P. Brown, "Old Frontiers," 1938, page 6, in which he quotes the Cherokee as saying: "We cannot live without war. Should we make peace with the Tuscarora . . . we must immediately look out for some other nation with whom we can be engaged in our beloved occupation." Such a statement is questionable. However, it has come down through the years as hard evidence that the Cherokee delighted in war for its own sake.

Another aspect of this question, is the wide difference in the practice of warfare — and we are considering the period AFTER white contact — between the tribes, the areas, and the confederacies, as to sophistication of warfare types and practices. Still another question is one of consideration of causes of warfare. In this connection, a question of logic might be considered. If we eliminate the evidence of hearsay, or that of self-interested persons, or persons seeking to establish savagery as a universal Indian characteristic, we are compelled to the use of logic, until such time that other evidence is available. The one important cause of warfare was trespass, and in this sense the protection of the land which was life itself, was of paramount importance. Among the Yuma, who lived along the Colorado river, for some time there was continuous conflict with neighboring tribes. Both the Yuma and their neighbors depended upon the Colorado river for their economy. This ever-shifting, frivolous body of water constantly changed its course in the area of these tribes. With every change in the course of the Colorado, differences arose as to whose land was on which side of the river. Necessarily, there were disputes. Now consider the extent of dispute that arose upon white contact, when whole tribes were moved from their original home grounds, to the lands owned by other tribes. Consider the difficulties of ascertaining land ownership and possession, and use, when the federal government moved various tribes to land already in the possession of other tribes, which had been moved in a similar forced removal, to the same land. Let the reader evaluate such

conditions as to the cultures of the various tribes, their various traditions and economies. Let the reader then add to such an evaluation
the further fact of white empire-building and expropriation of the
Indian from his land. The whole picture of a country torn by conflict
and war then emerges. In this conflict the Indian was the crucial and
often the decisive factor until the end of the nineteenth century. Now
consider the manner in which textbooks in general, and this textbook
in particular, handle this vital phase of the country's history. The one-
sided, slanted, dominant-society element becomes clear, as an ideology
which forces its way through the fabric of every book, into the classroom, and into the minds of the students.

For the sake of discussion, another question might be posed: Is it
logical to assume that where the population is sparse, life should be
so casually handled? This was the case before white contact: Is it logical
to believe that war for the sake of war alone would be the fun and
games enjoyed by a people whose whole time on earth was, and had
to be, taken up in the business of living, developing an economy,
keeping the people together, maintaining instruction to the youth,
manufacturing their articles of material culture? All these considerations should be carefully weighed before believing what the textbooks state: that war was a fundamental part of the culture, part of
the economy, of ALL the tribes, during ALL the time including the
eras before white contact, and that the warfare ideology was part of
the very character and philosophy of ALL the people. In the same
sense, the description of the Natchez as having a "king" is wrong. There
was no monarchy in existence. There was no autocratic ruler holding sway over the people. There was, without doubt, a strong form
of government among them, and what the actual leadership of that
government consisted of, is a matter of continuing research.

A third concept involves the description of cultures of any group
of tribes or individual tribes. The modern concepts of area development or boundary lines, are unequal to the task of understanding
Indian culture before such political boundaries were set. The Native
boundaries were based on the economy, the environment, the natural
geography of the land. The author is tied to the strings of political
geography, and this becomes obvious when she discusses the cultures
of the California Indian groups. This State defies treatment of its
native population unless political boundaries are set aside for purposes
of analyses of the cultures and economy. To make a detailed analysis
of this subject would be the same as writing a book on the matter,

and such a book will be in print by early 1970 (American Indians in California History).

A fourth concept is that of the use of torture as part of the culture of many tribes. With few exceptions, such books as the one now under discussion, make a big thing out of the practice of torture. Abundant detail is given attesting to atrocities, and to torture as a way of life, as well as the practice of slavery. Are these descriptions entirely true? Examing the original sources, we find again that they are usually dependent upon the Jesuit Relations. Other sources are those of whites. There appears to be little doubt that torture did exist in certain tribes as part of religious ritual and ceremony. In this regard, we of the modern age, with all of our more refined wars and nuclear bomb tortures, are ill prepared to take the posture of the plaintiff in the case. But in the light of the conquering race which strives even today, to find justification for over-running the native lands and destroying its peoples, it would appear more practical and certainly more fair to describe the contributions made by the Indians to society at large. And, when dealing with evidences of practices which seem strange to us today — it might also be more just to mention the fact that all civilizations had practices at one time, in one form or another, which seem strange to us today. The facts, in any case, are not all in, the data has not yet been completely assembled, and may never be. It appears to us, therefore, that the descriptions of the strange, the exotic, the unusual in the eyes of modern man, and the endless tales of human sacrifice and torture, should be handled more objectively. Further, that if described, it should not be in an unsubstantiated form, but should be treated in the historic context. Man has been known to engage in such practices since the world began. For more specific criticisms of incorrect judgment and improper conjecture, these are listed:

Page 271: About the Yuma of the Colorado River country. "They have the appearance of people who found themselves by chance in marvelous planting country and were practically forced to take advantage of it." This is a highly speculative statement, specious in connotation. When were the Yuma seen to have this appearance that this determination could be made? We know that the Yuma people were farmers, planting and enjoying the activity, protecting and defending this "marvelous planting country."

Page 276: Discussing the Indians of southern California, it is said: "Like the Paiute, they wandered in small groups in the summer and congregated in villages for the winter." Why the use of the word "wandered" to describe a people who, in an organized manner, went from their winter homes to their summer homes, for century upon century, each band knowing the bounds of their lands, their work apportioned with simple technological method so that food could be harvested, stored, and protected throughout the year. The author also uses the terminology "Mission Indians." There were no such tribes, and if this is meant to describe Indian groups and tribes during the mission period and immediately thereafter, then another description should have followed. Not all of the Indians of southern California were "Mission Indians." It may be understood.why the Bureau of Indian Affairs so designates the tribes and tribal groups; but for a scholar it is not admissible.

Page 283: About the gold rush, and the Indians in gold rush territory: "These Indians, at least in an organizational sense, were among those who had little to lose." This statement was read over and over again, before the full and shocking impact of its meaning was absorbed by the evaluators. They had everything to lose, in the cultural, economic, and survival sense, and anything said to the contrary is adding insult to injury.

Page 292: Here is described the potlatch and the competitive potlatch givers. This description is more inaccurate than most and should be corrected, especially in the light of more recent knowledge, which confirms what the Native people have been saying ever since white contact. Page 302: The Northwest Indians are discussed here, and the following is stated: "Only slaves could not hope to improve their position." Untrue. Many slaves became members of the tribes, married into the tribes, and some even became leaders.

Page 339: An improper comparison is made between the native people and the Japanese. "Granted that the land given them was poor and equipment almost nonexistent, we can still imagine groups of Japanese in the same area as making a good showing. The Indians, with entirely different experience, scarcely made a beginning." Since Dr. Underhill does not explain "slightly different experience," the reader is free to assume the experience was one of more "civilized" society. But no effort is made to explain that the Japanese have had for some hundreds of years, an entirely different culture. The lack of ordinary hoes, shovels, instruments of any kind (let alone "equipment") certainly had something to do with the so-called failure. The lack of water had much more to do with it. Even the genius of the Japanese people and their famed husbandry, would not produce water where there was none. Data has been examined, moreover, which proves the contrary to Dr. Underhill's assertion. The Tejon Reserve in California is one example, and not an isolated one, in which the Indian people were extraordinarily successful as farmers, in most difficult conditions.

*THE FIRST AMERICANS. By Daniel Jacobson. Ginn & Co., 1969, 240 pp. Public school supplementary text.

Since this book is written in a semi-story manner, it is quite difficult to separate the fanciful from the factual. The story form is particularly difficult to handle when dealing with Indian history, and the author suffers from the results of his unfortunate choice of style. Use of this format requires a most intimate knowledge of the people, the most personal connection between writer and the people, and in fact a body of information which is not expressed in this book.

An attempt is made to characterize the Indian peoples, both by tribe and as they developed from those who were the earliest arrivals to this continent. The story depicts Indian people as imagined individuals, with names presumably as close to authentic as possible, but with descriptions both in words and illustrations that are generally far from reality. For example, in the introduction, the author describes those early explorers who crossed the land bridge following the game, and who settled in various parts of the country. These people are said to have arrived in this region approximately twenty or twenty-five thousand years ago, by most scientists. At that time, Homo Sapiens was well developed, but what the illustration shows is a Neanderthal man, who is supposed to have lived approximately 100,000 years ago, according to scientific investigation. Other illustrations are similarly crude, the whole effect being that of nearly human people. Certainly the man sitting in front of his cave, low-browed, long-armed, squatting and stoop-shouldered, is not the well developed Homo Sapiens who opened up twenty thousand years of exploration and settlement of a New World upon his arrival in North America.

The author takes it for granted as gospel truth, that the point of entry into North America was across the land bridge connecting Asia and America — a body of ice at that time of the earth's history, and that this is a unanimously accepted scientific fact. Recent scientific thought considers that man could have come from several directions. This possibility should have been indicated in the textbook. The Indians of southern California are described as living "mainly on acorn." They would have starved, or been continually sick, if this were

so. Depicted also as mainly seed gatherers, this too is inaccurate. From
the beginning of their occupation of this country, they hunted, fished,
gathered seeds and nuts, made tools, built shelters and homes, practiced
their religions, and lived well in that lush, rich country.

The time element in the book is often so nebulous, that one is hard
pressed to understand what period of history the author is discussing,
when he describes the culture, economy, and customs of a tribe or group.
This is one of the principal failures of the book. The reader is free to
make his own assumptions as to the time period being discussed. And
so, this reader decided that when describing the Indians of southern
California (The Old Millers), the author was discussing Indians of a
period perhaps ten thousand years ago. However, lo and behold, an
earth lodge is mentioned "circular in shape, and a portion of it was
underground." Now this type of semi-subterranean home was not built
until a new religious sect swept the region. Even then, its followers
were not many in southern California. The sect arose in the 1800's,
certainly not the time the reader is led to believe when the Old Millers
lived. Part one, which describes The Old Bison Hunters, The Old
Basket Makers, and The Old Millers, is inaccurate and over-generalizes
in these very names of the culture presumably existing during the early
periods of man on this continent. Their culture and economy was far
more complex and many-sided, to be described in such simplistic terminology.

The Gatherers are described on page 24. These early people are supposed to have subsisted entirely on seeds, roots, nuts, bulbs, and berries,
according to the writer. Had this been their diet, then no game would
have been available, and certainly both game and fish were available.
The description is inaccurate. The Gatherers are said to have "roamed
the semi-arid lands and forests in large bands." They are also said to
have "sometimes" gone to war "with other groups." This is a most
general description. With whom were they supposed to have gone to
war, and why? Information such as this deserves an explanation, and
no explanation is forthcoming in this book. They did not in fact,
"roam" over the land. They had settled habitations, and went from
one place to another much as other peoples do, either to trade with
another group, to visit friends, to hunt and fish, or to get into a warmer
climate in the winter.

The Paiute people are inaccurately described, the names of their
bands inaccurately translated, and the designation of their house-types
is inaccurately given. No Paiute bands were called by such names
as "Chokecherries, Rye Seeds, or The Crickets." Paiute houses were

not named "wickiups," only the whites used this improper term. The names figuratively given for individuals who are made to "talk out loud" in this book, are inaccurate as Paiute names.

Describing the Iroquois, the author appears to agree with the Jesuit Relations as to their torture practices, but manages to transform this questionable custom into some sort of benevolent test for bravery. It is so incongruous that the reaction is to ask the writer to get on with it, if he believes that torture was part of the Iroquois way of life, instead of attempting to sugar it up.

Throughout the book, various segments of Indian groups are depicted, both in story form and a form presumably factual. The facts are not bolstered with recognizable information. Here and there, some light comes through, but it would take one who has knowledge in his own right to uncover the information. Furthermore, the Native groups are treated in an isolated manner; nowhere is the impact of another culture seen in the lives of these people. Only in the Epilogue does this conflict occur. Generally, the textbook has many inaccuracies, not the least of which is the map of Indian reservations at the end of the book. Some of the most populous, those of California for example, do not exist in the map. The New England states show no reserves. The Indian Reorganization Act is described as a Godsend to the Natives, and this is inaccurate. The story of the Native in America is a static one in this book.

* HAPPY HUNTING GROUNDS. *By Stanley Vestal.* Lyons & Carnahan, 1963, 214 pp. Offered as supplementary book in various school districts.

The life and history of the American Indians has long been a source of inspiration to English-speaking writers. The close link with nature, the sense of freedom, and the romance of open space has formed the spirit and background for fiction, articles, nostalgic poetry, and sentimental nonsense about the Native Americans. Few if any have captured the true life of the Indian. This book is no exception.

Beautifully illustrated, Mr. Vestal's book was first published in 1928. Its subject, according to the author's introduction, is "to present a comprehensive picture of Plains Indian life — the Indian seen against his proper background, as he was a century or more ago, without admixture of civilized conceptions." One hundred years ago, the Plains Indian had been subjected to "civilized conceptions" for at least a half century. It would be impossible to treat the first Plainsmen without considering the influence of white invasion, white technology, and white ideological pressures. But this, nevertheless, is what Mr. Vestal has attempted to do. The story has to do with inter-tribal conflict and competition for control of the buffalo and the areas where the animal roamed. Here and there, some feeling of Plains life comes through. But largely, the book is filled with sweet sentiment, nature-worship, and a treatment of the Native peoples which does not promote understanding.

In story form, the conflict among the tribes is described. The inaccurate picture that emerges is due largely to the fact that there is no attempt to give the reasons for anything that happens in the book. Exception is taken to these lines on page 19: "Like all Plains Indians, Killer loved the horse. Without it, his ancestors had been starving skulkers in the woods, following the deer on foot, laboriously digging pits to entrap antelope, or grubbing with a hoe about the roots of corn and bean plants." This is an inaccurate picture of Plains Indian life before the time of the horse. No conditions such as these existed.

On page 209, Note 3, a brief description of the Sun Dance is given. The description is inaccurate, and exception is taken to the words "their savage gods," as a derogatory statement. Exception is also taken to the phrase "primitive religion," on page 213. Their religion was no more primitive than some of those practiced today.

The book cannot be recommended for a true picture of the Plains Indians. At best, it can be said to be a sentimental account of certain tribes, but without the flavor of truth. The word "flavor" is used, because the book is largely fanciful from start to finish.

†A HISTORY OF THE DAKOTA OR SIOUX INDIANS. *By Doane Robinson, Secretary of the South Dakota Department of History.* Ross & Haines, 1967, 523 pp. Bureau of Indian Affairs school at Flandreau, South Dakota.

Reprinted from the book of the same name and author, originally published in 1904, this History has been resurrected for classroom use by the Bureau of Indian Affairs. It contains a great deal of information aboue Sioux-white relations, and in this sense is an excellent source book concerning treaties, behind-the-scenes intrigue, and exposures of conditions leading up to events in Sioux history, through the early part of the twentieth century.

The textbook, however, fails completely as a source of information about the culture, history of the Sioux, and the economy. The author's attitudes are well expressed in his preface, which declares: ". . . while he (the Sioux) is in his present stage of transition which marks the revolution in his customs from those of the barbarian to those of civilization . . ." Another statement, that the Sioux, or Dakota, are "the most powerful of all the Indian races," does not conform to scientific determination that the Indian peoples are one race. In the same preface, the author says, "The course of the Sioux as a tribe is now completed." This will be news to the Sioux, who still exist as a tribe. Sioux parents will also be a little chagrined to know that their children are being taught their people are finished as a race and a tribe.

In chapter 1, it is explained: "Most of their so-called traditions are mere inventions," the author says, "varying from the prosaic to the fancifully poetic, according to the genius and inspiration of the inventor . . . Naturally, these conflicting stories have no ethnological value, and they have corrupted and ruined all of the older traditions." The writer does not say how he knows all this, and by what superior relationship to the Sioux Native historians he has managed to acquire story-telling, and the information which is still in the possession of Native historians.

Page 29: "Of course the squaw was always available as a beast of burden, but manifestly a great skin tipi was beyond even her extraordinary power to transport for a day's journey." The footnote indicates this statement was taken from the Lewis and Clark journal, which makes it not the less a bit of foolishness, and derogatory.

Robinson relates many of the dishonest maneuvers practiced against the Sioux, but this does not deter him from describing their defensive efforts to rid themselves of an unbearable situation, as "massacres." Thus, on page 269, the Sioux action at Acton was a "massacre." On page 271, he says: "Thus began the great massacre." On page 273, it is stated: "It is not the part of this paper to relate all of the horrors pertaining to this massacre." An attempt is made to whitewash the historic record, when the Sioux were tried for defending their hereditary lands in Minnesota, in which three hundred Sioux were convicted with such indecent speed by the Army personnel, that the efforts of General Sibley to execute them on the spot were halted and the trials resumed at another place, through the direct intervention of President Lincoln. Describing this incident, the author says: ". . . military courts do not as a rule stand upon technicalities in testimony, nor is there the difficulty in obtaining testimony to convict Indians of murder that there would be to convict white men. They are given to boasting of their crimes, and very few of them were inclined to deny their guilt when charged." The writer ignores the facts, in which the Siuox were engaged in a war, and would be the last to deny their advantages over the enemy.

During the time before and after these trials, the people of Minnesota, led by the military, broke out again and again in an effort to exterminate more than 1,500 Sioux prisoners. These facts are dealt with in such a way by the author, however, that the Sioux are made to appear like brutes and murderers, when in fact they were defending their homes, lives and property.

Page 400: "The heathen Indians under Gall, Crazy Horse, and Sitting Bull." Page 430: The author leaves no doubt about his loyalties to General Custer in the great battle wherein the Sioux were victorious. This too is described as a "massacre," by the author. Page 468: Red Cloud and Sitting Bull are dubbed "Old Heathen Indians."

This history of the Sioux people, although certain important facts are given, is so twisted as to become the story of a people completely brutish. All the while, as the author is forced again and again to reveal the justice of their cause, he turns about to brand the Sioux as murderers, heathen, creatures of the lowest order. Perhaps the background of this writer may help to explain this. In his own words, (see footnote, page 268 of the textbook), he states: "The childhood of the writer was spent among the Wisconsin volunteers who took part in the suppression of the outbreak. In 1877 he came to Minnesota and carefully examined the localities of the fights at New Ulm and the Lower agency, and in 1883 went over the situation at Birch Coulee and Fort Ridgely. From childhood he has been in almost daily association with men who were in some capacity or other connected with the outbreak and the suppression." This statement indicates that his sources were army personnel, settlers, and those who were themselves responsible for the actions which forced the Sioux to defend themselves.

That such a book, written in the heat of racism, still bearing the marks of the settlers' hate of the Sioux people, should be made required reading for children of those Sioux who are being insulted and villified therein, is little more than obscene.

American Indians

(Summary of Evaluations (eight books evaluated)
What distinguishes the condition of education in America today, is the dearth of good books about the history and culture of the Amer-

ican Indians. These eight books are now in use in Bureau of Indian Affairs-directed schools. Some high schools also utilize them. Consequently, they present a fair picture of current textbook use in connection with the specific subject of the American Indian.

1: All books were found to contain derogatory statements about the American Indians. In addition, most of the books contained derogatory statements by implication or invidious comparison.

2: None of the books described the Indian history and culture in a developmental form.

3: All of the books treated the history of the Native American entirely in the context of the white society, the relationship with the white society. None of the books treated the history and culture of the Indian within his own society.

4: Contributions of the American Indians were described in only two books: Dr. Hagan's book, THE AMERICAN INDIANS, and Dr. Underhill's book, RED MAN'S AMERICA. Neither of these two adequately deal with the impact on national and world economy of the contributions of the Indian.

5: None of the books described the period of the gold rush accurately.

6: None of the books deal with the American Indian in the world of today, his current contributions, progress, and development of leadership. The Hagan book attempts to describe and analyze the current political situation of the American Indian internally, but this fails because of the author's own preconceived opinions, and his failure to take cognizance of Indian opinions and knowledge, so that a one-sided description is given.

7: In the field of primary readers, which have not been evaluated, there are some which are worthy of use, even though they generally idealize Indian people and Indian life, which is a distasteful quality. Nevertheless, the Melmont books on various Indian tribes are useful until better ones come along.

VIII

World History and Geography

Criteria

1: The history and culture of the American Indian should be treated as part of the history of the races of man.

2: The story of mankind on this continent, his explorations and settlement of the land, as its discoverer, should be treated when ancient races are treated. The American Indian is one of the oldest races of man in the world, and has inhabited the same area of the earth for a longer time than most other peoples.

3: Social problems of the American Indian should be treated as part of the social problems of the world at large when discussing this subject in a textbook such as this subject encompasses.

4: When discussing the cultural and economic development of the New World, also discussed should be the effect upon the Old World, of the economy and cultures of the New World and its Native population, together with their contributions to national and world economy and thought.

5: All textbooks in world history and geography deal with the subject entirely from the white viewpoint, as one of colonial conquest. The complete history of the world and its peoples should be given, together with the story of their struggles against colonialism and conquest. The various stages of society that evolved through time, the beliefs and religions of the people, their political systems and their effect on the masses of people, should be discussed.

6: When describing the culture of the Old World, an accurate comparison should be made with that of the Native New World. Invidious comparisons should be avoided. The questions of colonialism and conquest should be handled as a study of the facts of history, not as an apologia for the European invaders who came to this country.

7: When treating of the American nation today, it should be recognized that the Indian is a part of American life today, the original and basic foundation upon which the American Nation was capable of coming into existence, of continuing to survive, and whose contributions made possible the economic advance of this nation. The propaganda of how "great, powerful, and rich" America is, should be avoided. This type of self-satisfaction ill becomes a nation with the problems of today, and has nothing to do with the efforts of the majority of the people—the so-called "little people" to improve their lives, educate their children, and create a world free from wars.

*†THE STORY OF NATIONS. By *Rodgers, Adams* & *Brown.* Holt, Rinehart & Winston, 1965, 800 pp. Bureau of Indian Affairs schools. Public school text.

A classic example of the failure of textbooks in world history to create any identification between the development of man and his governments in America, and that of the rest of the world, is shown in this book.

The history of man is described in the early chapters of this text, from the very beginning so far as archaeological research has been able to add to modern knowledge about this subject. But not one statement or mention is made of the early comers, or the early inhabitants of North America. The story of the conquest of Latin America is told on page 668, but the Spaniards are described as "The most daring adventurers of all history." The authors relate the history of the infamous conquests, but in describing the current situation, in which "native arts are blended with the European" importation, descendants of the first people of the Central and South American countries are ignored. A further criticism of this text is that the story of modern countries in South America is told without regard for the conditions of the peoples as they are today, told realistically and without glossing over the problems. Everything is honey and roses in Argentina, Peru and Bolivia, according to this text. Most informed people know better.

The failure to describe the contributions of the Native Americans to world economy exists in this textbook, as in most others. The failure

to relate the contacts between the American Indians with the development of Europe, particularly England, is evident here too. Contributions in philosophy and thought of any of the Native peoples is ignored. While two artists, Diego Rivera and Orozco, are highly praised
for their mural paintings, many of which depict the life of Native
Indian peoples, the people themselves are not discussed, as to where
they are today, and what their situation is. A world history dealing
with the story of nations would have treated some fundamental characteristics of the nations existing in the New World when Europeans
first came to divide and conquer.

*†LIVING AS WORLD NEIGHBORS. *By Cutright & Jarolimek.*
   Macmillan, 1966, 536 pp. Bureau of Indian Affairs schools. Public
   schools text.

It seems incredible, that in a world history and geography, the beginnings of the human race would not be discussed. In this sense, early
Man is discussed, but in extremely general terms, and not at all concerned with the development of the races of Man.

By the time this textbook gets to the Natives of the North and South
American continents, he has discussed China, the Nile, and Ireland.
Describing Indians of the Great Plains, they are said to have been
"nomads or wanderers." This is inaccurate. All the tribes, upon white
contact, had definite land boundaries, land use, and their own technology and economic system, in addition to their hunting and fishing
pursuits. Extreme generalization and oversimplification is shown on
page 15, in which the authors state: "When Europeans first came to
North America, they found that the woodland Indians were deer
hunters, Indians who roamed the Great Plains were buffalo hunters. On
the Pacific Coast, many Indians were salmon fishermen." To describe a
whole complex culture in these terms is at the least, ludicrous. Certainly
their cultures included farming in many cases, hunting other animals
than deer or buffalo, fishing other than salmon, gathering plants of all
kinds, and converting other vegetable, nut and seed foods into edible
items for their economy.

Inaccuracy exists on page 16, when the authors deal with the population of the continent in 1492, which is said to have been about 300,000.
The very least number is given at 600,000, some give it as one million.
Other scholars today consider the figure of three million is closer to
truth. An improper comparison is made between the "standard of living

of early man" which is described as low — and the modern standard of living, which is said to be "high." The standards of living, however, in many parts of the world, are described as "poverty." Nothing is said of the poverty in the United States. To compare the standard of living of early man, or in more descriptive terms, the Natives of North America at the time of white contact, as a "low" standard is entirely inaccurate and scientifically incorrect. The same standards of judgment cannot be applied to both stages of society in the first place.

Food, shelter, and clothing are described as man's most simple needs by scientists. That the Natives of America had these in abundance is a definite standard of "living." The two stages of society cannot be described according to the same standards. Indians of America are described in the context of "yesterday," that is to say before white European contact, and among other simplistic statements made in one short paragraph, it is said that "the Iroquois were constantly on the warpath, as they moved from one hunting ground to another." This is untrue. Before white contact, the Iroquois were not a warring people. They were not nomads wandering from one hunting ground to another. They were settled people growing corn and other agricultural products for their own use, and often for trade, which raises their social system to a different level also.

The textbook fails to deal with the contributions of the Indians to national and world economy. It fails also to deal with the cultural contributions of the Indians, in democratic thought and ideals. While this is not the major purpose of the book, it nevertheless constitutes a failure. However, this criticism is one which can be made in connection with the way other cultures are handled, which is entirely in the context of their material cultures. A good beginning is made, and the first such treatment seen in the many books evaluated in this Study, on pages 431 and 432. In ten short chapters, the authors compare the economy of the early Indians with that of the early settlers, describing the needs of each culture as represented by the people at that specific stage of the nation's development. Nevertheless, the tendency to generalize impairs the contribution that could have been made by the writers, for Indian culture is taken in large lumps as to their economy, and this, of course does not develop a full understanding of the subject. Still further, the differences and the conflicts between the two social systems (that of the Native and that of the European) are treated entirely in the context of the material culture, while the question of customs and traditions, culture and religions, has no place in the comparison.

The American Indian is not treated in the world of today. There is no discussion of the Native and the Constitution or his place in the structure of the government, which is complex but nonetheless a matter of extreme importance not only to the Indian but to the country as a whole. A general criticism can be made of this textbook: it is extremely uneven in the quality of its scholarship, and is quite obviously the work of several minds, each of them varying sharply from the others as to ability and expertise.

OUR BEGINNINGS IN THE OLD WORLD. By Eibling, King & Harlow. Laidlaw Brothers, 1961. 384 pp. Public school text.

"What are prehistoric times?" is the question asked on page 23. The answer given is guaranteed to place the American Indian in the so-called stone age. The authors divide history into two areas: Prehistoric and historic. While it is true that the designation "prehistoric" may imply pre-literate, or history before modern writing took place, if left with this sophomoric definition, the excuse is given ideologically to ignore the Native Americans as intelligent contributors to this nation.

This is what has happened in the textbook under evaluation. None of the contributions of America's original inhabitants are mentioned. According to this book "One colonist discovered how to raise tobacco, cure it, and ship it," (p. 362). The tobacco plant and its use was an Indian discovery, not a white man's. Again, "The colonists brought ideas of freedom they could not have in Europe. These ideas became part of American customs and laws. They have come to you as your heritage. These hard won freedoms have helped make our country a great world power." The ideas of freedom brought by the colonists were contradicted by their actions, not only against the Indian people, but against their own as well. No word is mentioned about the ideas and the philosophy of freedom which is a common heritage of the American people, brought by the American Indian. And for another note, to question a certain ideology: what is so splendid in being "a great world power?" It implies domination of smaller nations, control where the freedoms of others in their own way should be allowed to exist.

†MEN AND NATIONS, A WORLD HISTORY. By Mazour & Peoples. Harcourt, Brace & World, 1961, 790 pp. Bureau of Indian Af-

fairs schools. Riverside Indian school, Anadarko, Oklahoma. Public
schools text.

In its 800 pages of text, this book fails completely to develop a clear
and basic understanding of Man's beginnings. The approach, though
an attempt is made to explain early man and his works, is such as to
divide "civilization" arbitrarily from what is termed "prehistoric" man.
This is a superficial approach, and does not result in the development
of understanding of man's inventions, arts, cultures, and progress
through the ages.

Most scientists now have developed other methods of noting man's
historic periods of change. Certain types of writing not known to historians have been found. Because they cannot now be deciphered does
not mean that they do not exist. In fact, the record of man's achievements through the ages are known and have been known to scientists of
various disciplines through such techniques as that of the archaeologist.
The record shows many innovations, inventions, development of the
cultures, all of which have perhaps not been found in a known type of
writing. Modern archaeological methods have been capable of recon-
structing a whole technology, culture, lifeways of a people. This textbook also divides prehistoric time and historic time into a Stone Age of
Man and Civilization. This too, is so shallow as to impair understanding. Such terms as Stone Age, or Primitive are misnomers. More descriptive, is the term "preliterate" to describe a stage of society in which
writing such as it is known today, was not used.

It follows from this basic philosophy as shown in the text under consideration, that "civilized man" when he conquered the lands of "stone
age man" was bringing progress, no matter that he destroyed a whole
people. It does not occur to most textbook writers that "progress" may
be made available without wholesale destruction of a people and their
traditions or cultures. The ideology of progress through conquest per-
mits acceptance of the predatory conquest of the American continent
by Europeans. It is unacceptable. It is the ideology of Hitler and Franco.
That the philosophy exemplified in the book leaves its impression on
the rest of the volume is seen when it is noted that the only arts and inventions of the American Indian which the textbook recognizes are to
be found on page 378: "It was during the 1830's that the modern rubber
industry became possible . . . (Columbus) had found Indians playing
with balls made of the gum of a certain tree." No other recognition of
Indian arts and inventions is described.

Considerable attention is given to the attacks by Indians upon the settlers, and their need to build stockades to protect themselves. The Spanish missionaries "converted the Indians," but no mention is made of the forced labor system employed by them. Dealing with the Indian resistance to invasion of their country, the authors say: ". . . the Indians resented having their hunting grounds taken way." Resentment is hardly the word for the wars that broke out in defense of their homeland on the part of the Indian people. The use of "hunting grounds" in this context implies that the Native people were only interested in hunting, and since progress demanded that large areas of land be converted to farming and cattle raising, the Indians were a bar to progress. However, the Indians very early learned new ways of farming, established towns and villages, improved their government, and in all ways showed a desire to develop a higher and more progressive culture, and better technology.

No mention of the Indian in federal governmental structure, development, or relations, or in the development of the west, in the gold rush, in the general progress of the nation. This is one of the many books that has undergone revision since 1961. But the revision has not corrected this wrong approach, nor the deficiencies of the book.

†MAN'S ACHIEVEMENTS THROUGH THE AGES. *By Habberton & Roth.* Laidlaw, 1958, 800 pp. Bureau of Indian Affairs schools. Chilocco Indian School.

According to this textbook, Man's ancient achievements took place in Europe, Africa and Asia. Lacking is any description of man's achievements in America before contact with the Europeans. Even references to the Indian people of this continent are rare, and no reference whatever is made to their important contributions to mankind the world over. The Native Americans are ignored altogether, except in connection with Spanish colonization. In this case, on page 375, the "priests established schools for the Indians, and taught them many practical arts, including agriculture. The attitude of the clergy was a fatherly one. They thought of the natives as simple people whom it was their duty to look after and defend." Where is the information as to what the Natives taught the priests? Too, no one who has studied the history of the Spanish missionary period could fail to learn that the priests were defenders of the Spanish imperial aristocracy, that the Indians were in a state of forced labor, and that the principal reason for concern was the protection of the only labor force available at that time in history and in these places.

Contributions of the Native peoples prior to white contact included the development of the leaching process, by which the nut of the oak tree was made available as a source of a most nutritious and staple food, just as bread is today. Indian potatoes saved Ireland from starvation. Indian corn has traveled the world over and become one of the main and most lucrative commodities in the world. Indian canoes, travois, hammocks, conservation, snowshoes, irrigation, democratic thought and philosophy, arts, knowledge of nature and the uses of natural plants— all these are only a few of the contributions of the American Indians to this land and to the world at large.

Finally, the white-dominant approach of the authors is reflected in this statement on page 450, which, standing alone without further explanation, can lead to a further deepening of ideas of racial superiority. "There are many important thoughts to be gained from a study of this chapter. One of these is that democracy developed with the westward expansion of the United States." The development of democracy at the expense of the genocide of Native peoples, forced removal of thousands of American Indians, leaving them without rights or democratic privileges, can hardly be explained in this way without some sort of accompanying statement indicating that not all is wine and roses with "democracy."

*†MAN'S STORY. *By T. Walter Wallbank.* Scott, Foresman, 1956, 767 pp. Bureau of Indian Affairs schools. Albuquerque Indian School. Public schools text.

The subject matter is best described by the sub-title: "World History in its Geographic Setting." From the description of the author's intentions, one would expect that man's rise to civilization might have been dealt with in some historical sense. Yet, from the beginning, Europe and the Far East receive the greatest degree of attention. It seems clear that the author is more at home in this area. The author states (page 20): "Only history can acquaint you with the traditions, ideals, and goals which have brought about the American way of life." Yet, the traditions and ideals of the American Indian are left out of account. A chapter is devoted to "Achievements of the American Indian," but this is largely about the Native peoples of Mexico, Central America, and South America, who are credited quite correctly for the development of agriculture, unique arts and achitecture, and the beginnings of a written language.

Even here, the influence of environment and geography is not dealt with, and the book suffers from this defect. As to the Indians of North America, these Natives are deemed infinitely inferior to those of the Southern continent. It is debatable whether the author's judgment as to what constitutes "civilization" may be accepted. Among those qualities which he finds consistent with civilization (as opposed to barbarism) are "well organized group action, pleasing social manners, and challenging thoughts," (p. 44). The arts and inventions of the North American Natives are either not understood, or ignored by this writer. Their social structure is not described. Nor is their unique ecological situation brought to bear upon any analysis of their way of life.

In such a book, the young Indian student, particularly, could have been made to relate to his history. But the opportunity was not taken by the author to do this.

†THE WORLD AROUND US. *By Zoe A. Thralls.* Harcourt, Brace & World, 1961, 480 pp. Bureau of Indian Affairs Schools, Phoenix Area Indian School, Arizona.

Designed to teach geography and knowledge of the world, this book is static in treatment, handles the American Indian in certain areas as though they are still living in ancient ways with no modern knowledge. An opportunity has been missed here to compare technological and cultural advances, especially as they have affected the lives of the Native Americans. Indians of South America, in text and photograph, are described as primitive, pre-historic people, lurking behind jungle trees. No differentiation is made as to whether they are being described in the life of today, one hundred years ago, or thousands of years ago.

†PAST TO PRESENT: A WORLD HISTORY. *By Zebel & Schwartz.* The Macmillan Co., 1963, 708 pp. Bureau of Indian Affairs schools. Navajo Indian School.

Use of "New Stone Age Man" to describe Indians improper and leads to misconceptions. On page 17, this definition of civilization is inaccurate: "... that advanced stage of culture in which men, living together in large communities, enjoy such prosperity and well-being that they are free to concern themselves with intellectual and artistic activities." Some civilizations did not live in large communities. Some civilizations did not enjoy "prosperity and well-being," because a few in the higher social strata lived on the backs of the multitudes. Some were not precisely free to concern themselves with intellectual pursuits but did so despite the pressures of feeding, clothing, and housing themselves. Page 260: "The early Indians lived much like other primitive peoples." Description of "primitive" is incorrect. Page 260: "They supported themselves by hunting and fishing, wore clothing made of animal skins, and lived in simple tents." Many Indians wore clothing made of cotton and vegetable fibres. Most Native Americans did not live in tents. No American Indians supported themselves by hunting and fishing alone. The book develops the story of America from the European viewpoint.

†A WORLD HISTORY: A CULTURAL APPROACH. *By Daniel Roselle,* Ginn & Co., 1966, 791 pp. Bureau of Indian Affairs schools. Fort Sill Indian School, Lawton, Oklahoma.

Pages 385-386: "The English in North America . . . The French in North America." In these sections, no mention is made of the existence of the American Indians, their ownership of the land which was colonized by the Europeans. Page 391: "Americans now could settle on the western lands that had been under the restrictive control of the British government." This reference is to the English Proclamation of 1763, which recognized Indian ownership of the lands in question, and stated that they would not be taken from them by force. This is not made clear in the quoted passage. Page 380-393: The chapter titled "England wins an empire and loses her American colonies." Nowhere in this chapter are the relations between the colonists and the native inhabitants discussed. Page 429: "Long before Columbus came to the new world, man had developed various societies in Mexico, Central America, and South America." No mention of Indian societies in Canada and the United States. Inaccuracies, misconceptions and omissions occur in this book.

*OUR BIG WORLD: Geography for Today's World. *By Barrows, Parker, & Sorenson.* Silver, Burdette, 1961, 190 pp. Public School Text.

Native culture and ways of life are entirely absent from this textbook. Even when discussing Alaska, the Eskimo people are dealt with in such a generalized way that no one can derive any knowledge as to just how these people live, what they think and feel, what their culture was and is. Without such material, this book turns out to be a propaganda vehicle for a Chamber of Commerce and little more. There is only one mention of Indians in this entire book. On page 166, when "painted poles" are referred to.

*†LIVING WORLD HISTORY. *By Wallbank & Schrier.* Scott, Foresman, 1964, 768 pp. Bureau of Indian Affairs schools at Billings and Busby, Montana. Public schools, senior high school level.

The American Indian is treated in a section starting on page 253. While recognition is given to the development of a Native culture in North and South America, this is so fragmented and so obviously set aside from the rest of the book, that there is no relationship between this section and the study of world history as a whole.

By inference, the definition of a "true civilization" is given as that of a culture that built cities and had writing. The conclusion drawn by these writers, therefore, is that the Indians of the Northeast had no civilization, and were "less" developed than others. Thus, the Iroquois of the Five Nations are by implication accorded a lower place in the civilized world than (for example) that of the Pueblos. As to the Cheyennes and the Sioux, they are described as "the best fighters in the world. Before the 1600's, most of them made a meager living as farmers, but after the Spanish brought horses to America, these Indians became buffalo hunters."

The Plains people always hunted the buffalo, in addition to their agricultural, hunting, and gathering pursuits. After the horse was acquired, their economy naturally became enlarged and enriched. But this description of their complex social system is a generalization which does not lead to understanding. There is no attempt made to describe the cultures in a stage of development. The treatment is static. There is no mention of the American Indian in the world of today. There is no mention of a single American Indian who contributed to the history of this nation. Even in the chapters on Spanish, English, French and Portuguese colonial development, there is no mention whatever of the existence of the American Indian in colonial life. The fact that the Native Americans constituted the entire labor force in the Spanish missions is overlooked. The history is therefore static and fragmented.

*†EXPLORING AMERICAN NEIGHBORS, IN LATIN AMERICA
AND CANADA. *By Gray, Hancock, Gross, Hamilton, & Meyers.* Follett Publishing Co., 1966. Bureau of Indian Affairs school at Tesuque
Day School, Santa Fe, New Mexico. Public schools Text.

European approach, with consequent ignoring of the Native peoples
who discovered Latin America and Canada. Inaccurate information
exists on page 24, in which it is stated: The Central and South American tribes are said to have been "governed by emperors or by a ruling
class of warrior nobles and priests. There were armies and police to enforce the laws, and judges to settle disputes . . ." This description is incorrect. There was no system involving a nobility, or an emperor. There
was indeed, extensive division of labor, and a class of leaders, but this
description is suited for European political organization, not for that
of the Indian people of Central and South America.

On the same page, it is explained, most painstakingly, that the Native
peoples—even though they knew farming—were PRIMITIVE peoples,
wild, nomads. Cortez and the other Spanish conquistadores who invaded Indian lands and mercilessly crushed their governments and took
their property, are described as "bold adventurers." To make a more
modern analogy, it could be assumed, therefore, that in years to come,
when history books are written, perhaps the North Vietnamese will be
described as "bold adventurers." This two-edged sword must be considered when dealing with world history!

The aura of bold adventuring and pioneering spirit is also lent to the
invaders of South America. The period of history, from 1538 to 1541,
when de Orellano went from east to west of South America, is filled with
danger for the intrepid invaders, who "had to fight for their lives against
hostile Indians they met." No notice is taken of the fact that these
people were trespassing upon land owned by the Indian people, that
they were breaking the law, that they had not even the courtesy to announce themselves or to ask for permission to travel in the Indian
country.

Treating the early settlement of Canada, the same ideology is shown,
and the poor settlers are said to have had to surround their farmhouses
with stockades, ". . . because Indians often attacked the more isolated
farms." World history is treated from the viewpoint of a conquering
and invading European people, and it is taken for granted that their

depredations upon the Native people were all in the interests of progress and scientific exploration.

*†EXPLORING THE OLD WORLD. *By Hamer, Follett, Gross, Yohe, Ahlschwede, & Stephenson.* Follett, 1964, 480 pp. Bureau of Indian Affairs, Albuquerque Indian School. Public schools text.

While this book deals with the origins of man, the approach and viewpoint is European. Too, the authors display an ignorance of scholarly research. In discussing the Stone Age, page 21, "The Indians of our country, for example, were still living in the Stone Age when the first white settlers came to America. Even if the authors are granted the privilege of using an outworn and improper description such as "Stone Age," the culture, economy, and lifeways of the Natives upon white contact, are still not understood by means of this description. The book is concerned generally with the "Old World,"—Europe, Asia and Africa, and this evaluation need not deal with this aspect of the book. However, considering the approach which has been criticized above, and inaccuracies existing in the text, one wishes there was time and occasion to critically examine other aspects of the textbook, and with greater thoroughness.

†OUR WORLD HISTORY. *By C. E. Black.* Ginn & Co., 1962, 710 pp. Bureau of Indian Affairs schools. Institute of American Indian Arts, Santa Fe, N.M.

Old world civilizations, Old World prehistory, and Old World contributions are dealt with extensively. But the contributions of the Native peoples of America, both South and North, are not treated. Even in the chapter on the French and English colonies, there is no mention made, and no notice taken whatever, of the Native peoples and their role in colonial history.

*†EXPLORING REGIONS NEAR AND FAR. *By Gross, Follett, Gabler & McIntire.* Follett, 1964, 288 pp. Bureau of Indian Affairs schools. Public schools text.

Page 41, "the forest gave the Indians many things they needed. They made good use of the forest, but sometimes they destroyed part of it. They didn't think it was wrong to burn the trees. They wanted to make open places where grass and berries would grow. Then they could kill the deer and bears and other animals that came there to feed." This criticism displays a lack of knowledge about land use by the Native people. Forests were kept clear enough to prevent fires, to allow the big trees ample room for growth, and to create natural gardens. Their use of the forests protected the animal life, created food supplies, and prevented fires.

"All the Navajo families on this plateau grew corn and squashes. But none of them really owned the land which they farmed. All this region was part of an Indian reservation." Without explaining the various types of land "ownership," this sentence leads to one of the most basic misconceptions concerning the Indian use of land. It is true, that the federal government can take away Indian reservation land by congressional action. But so also can local, state and federal government take the land away from any citizen by condemnation proceedings. The two forms of ownership require a more basic explanation than that given in this textbook.

The book is based on the usual European "discovery" approach. "Then a little over a hundred years ago white men came to this region. They killed the buffalo and put the Indians on reservations." This part of history, related on page 120, deserves more than such generalization.

*†THE HISTORY OF OUR WORLD. *By Boak, Slosson, Anderson, & Bartlett.* Houghton Mifflin, 1963, 794 pp. Bureau of Indian Affairs schools. Albuquerque Indian School, New Mexico. Public school text.

In 794 pages dealing with the history of our world from man's beginning to the present, the authors fail to describe the culture and economy of the Natives of the United States or of North America generally. On page 7, it is stated: "The Indians who inhabited North America when the first European settlers came here had the same natural surroundings as we do today, yet their way of life was quite different from ours. They hunted bison on the plains where we raise cattle, and they huddled around campfires in the winter's cold, leaving untouched the coal they had not learned to use." Such invidious comparison is improper in a school text.

Page 46: "To prove that Indians could have made the trip (across the ocean), he (Heyerdahl) and his friends risked their lives on a primitive raft, which was the only kind of boat that the Indians knew how to build . . . Of course, this journey did not prove that the Indians really made such a trip . . . " Such statements degrade the Native people. Perhaps the Indians had indeed made such a trip. The supposition is as good one way as another, and the comparison is improper (the only kind of a boat that the Indians knew how to build).

On page 285: "The New World had been peopled long before the appearance of Europeans. Many of the natives whom Columbus called Indians still followed Stone Age ways of living. But remains which archaeologists have studied, as well as the stories of early European explorers, indicate that some groups had developed a high level of culture." The authors should describe what is meant by "Stone Age" culture, as well as "high level."

The use of the potato is mentioned, but not the Natives who developed it. Generally, treatment of the Native Americans in this textbook is entirely inadequate, marred by distortions of fact, and develops no picture of the culture and life found here by the Europeans. Thus, the history of man is lacking one of its most important aspects, and the authors have failed to describe the whole of mankind's development. The impact of the New World upon European civilization is not considered, and that impact was indeed vital, considering that it affected world economy, customs, political theories, and religious ideas.

*†BEYOND THE AMERICAS. *By Hanna, Jacks, Kohn & Lively.* Scott, Foresman & Co., 504 pp. Bureau of Indian Affairs schools. Public schools text.

World history and geography is the subject of this textbook. The approach is entirely European, "Europeans brought their way of living to the New World." Page 36 describes the "Lands of Our Ancestors," and all of these American ancestors are from one or another country of Europe. There is no mention of the fact that these early Europeans who came to the New World met a whole population of Native peoples. The subject of this book, of course, deals with the countries "beyond" the Americas, consequently there is no specific treatment of Native peoples of the North American continent. Nevertheless, some treatment should have been given of the contributions of the Natives of North and South America to the world at large. Trade, economy and political events in all of Europe underwent some very serious changes as a result of European colonization in America.

These are some of the basic factors to consider when discussing any of the countries of Europe. Without some type of discussion in a historic context of this nature, the subject is not understood, but becomes a static study of maps, directions, and locations.

†*OUR WORLD THROUGH THE AGES. By *Platt & Drummond.* Prentice-Hall, 1961 rev., 707 pp. Bureau of Indian Affairs schools. Public school text.

In the first chapter, when the authors describe the contributions of America to the world and the contributions of the world to America, there is an opportunity to describe what the Native American has contributed both to America and the world at large. This is not done. On page 4, objection is taken to the word "savage" in describing early man. Unless this word is used in a scientific connotation, as part of a nomenclature describing various stages of society, it is improper and insulting, both to the American Indian and to mankind as a whole. On page 13, the discussion of race is inadequate and because it is entirely from the biological point of view, is inaccurate. People belonging to a certain "race" need not have the physical characteristics mentioned by these authors.

There is also a question of social acceptance, community acceptance, acceptance of a dominant majority of any group of people. Thus, we see American Indians who may be not more than half a mixture of white and Indian, who are not accepted as "white" by the dominant white society. The same is true of the Negro, who, although he may be only a small part Negro, is not accepted by the whites as more white than Negro. The question of race is much more involved than this highly simplistic treatment of it. The historic division of man's development into Old Stone Age and New Stone Age, as well as the term "primitive man" is not utilized by scholars. Pre-literate man might be a better description than primitive man. New and Old Stone Age do not describe the technology nor social stage of society in which early people lived. On page 18, it is stated that European civilization was introduced into the Americas about 1500 A. D. More accurate would have been the statement that European colonization and conquest began in the Americas at that time.

There is no substantiation for the description of Mayan, Aztec, and Inca civilization, when these are discussed on page 66. The authors state that these peoples had emperors and a nobility. The description of Mayan "emperors," as well as the judgment that they were in decline, is not authenticated. The whole treatment of the subject of ancient American civilizations and their contributions to the world, is treated in two pages. This is so entirely inadequate that one has the right to question the usefulness of the book as a whole.

Nowhere in this textbook is there treatment, or even mention, of the contributions of the American Indian to the modern world. The Native Americans, when found by the early voyagers, exerted a strong and critical influence upon European economy, philosophy and religion, as well as upon customs and even styles. This is completely ignored, and such a failure is enough to refuse acceptance of the textbook for classroom use.

As the authors themselves state in the very first chapter, a careful study of world history "should help to wipe out prejudice and to increase toleration." If the contributions of a whole people are completely ignored in a study of world history, how can prejudice be wiped out? If improper descriptions of mankind in his march to a better life are given, how can prejudice be wiped out? Objection, finally, is taken to the word "toleration," even though it has become an accepted term to describe man's relationship to man. What is needed is not toleration particularly. Who wants to be "tolerated?" What is needed is full acceptance, understanding, recognition of rights not only to citizenship and voting, but to leadership as well. This is not "toleration." It is complete recognition and acceptance of man everywhere, by men everywhere.

*†THE CHANGING OLD WORLD: MANKIND IN TIME AND PLACE. *By Cooper, Sorensen,* & *Todd.* Silver Burdett, 1964, 470 pp. Bureau of Indian Affairs schools. Public school text.

While it is accepted that this textbook is confined to a description of the Old World and primarily with Europe, Asia, Africa, and the Middle East, objection is taken to its limitations and its usefulness in describing the subject chosen by the authors. While this exception is not enough to refuse acceptance of the book, its limitations and omissions in other areas is serious enough for this. There is not one word said about the effect of the emergence and contact with the Native Americans upon the history of England. This was profound enough to cause considerable change in Europe's economy, politics, and social values. The contributions of the Native American to world economy and thought is not dealt with. Neither are the races of man described, and this is certainly an important factor in the study of "Mankind in Time and Place." In describing the three great religions of the world (Jewish, Christian and Moslem) mention should have also been made that there are also other religions which should be understood and studied. Discussing the feudal systems of Europe (page 140), some mention should have been made of the fact that in colonizing America, this system was the one in use at the missions.

*†WORLD GEOGRAPHY. *By John Hodgson Bradley.* Ginn & Co., 1960, 583 pp. Bureau of Indian Affairs school. Public School text.

The study of geography provides an unusual opportunity to deal with the Native world, its traditions, cultures, and variety, in an ecological frame. If the scholar is competent and imaginative, this can provide an objective basis for understanding the history of the people.

This has been done, although in a limited way, in the textbook written by Dr. Bradley. Sections on the southwest, which deal with the ecology of the country and what the Native people did in order to create a life and an economy for themselves, is well handled. The Pueblo people, the Hopi and the Navajo are described objectively and with scholarly insight into their way of life.

That the author has not followed this pattern in other areas is to be deplored. For example, describing the Great Plains, he fails to explain how the Native people lived on the land; in comparison, the present situation in that region after white people had been overexploiting the earth, is deplorable. Such a comparison of ecological uses would have been instructional, and of historic value to the student. In dealing with the "ancient culture" on the Intermountain steppes, the author states that the cliff dwellers who occupied that land originally might have been the ancestors of those Indians who live there now (page 125), but that the Indians who live there now can tell us "practically nothing about them." The descendants of those "cliff dwellers" are still around us, and if properly interpreted, their oral literature reveals much information about the earliest people of the Intermountain steppes.

It would appear to this evaluator, that some discussion of conservation, comparatively treated, might have been a valuable asset in such a book. The natural conservation methods utilized by the Natives provide an area for judgment in comparison with those methods utilized today.

*†HOMELANDS OF THE WORLD. *By Thurston, Hankins & Haaby.* Charles E. Merrill Books, 1960. Wanblee Day School, South Dakota. Public School text.

An elementary school reader, the language is facetious, untrue to life, and highly strained in conversations which are part of the text. Discussing the Indians of one part of the "Homelands," the author makes free use of the derogatory word "savages," to which objection is taken. The brief historical references are from the European point of view, in which the Indians are viewed as interlopers whom the settlers had to protect themselves against. A most distasteful element appears in the text, when some children are made to express surprise, shock and "gasp" when they see Indians on horseback—today! The implication is that Indians are a curiosity, something strange and "different." While this may be quite a true reaction among some city children, it is nothing to be proud of, and certainly not an element to introduce into a textbook—especially when the textbook is used in an Indian school. The facetious, "precious," unreal is more the rule than anything else when this book deals with the American Indian. There is little if any hard information about the Indians. Describing the life of today, among the Navajos for example, the author leaves the impression that there are no problems, all is great and progressive, and everybody is happy. This is inaccurate.

*†THE WORLD STORY. *By Bruun & Haines.* D. C. Heath & Co., 1963, 707 pp. Bureau of Indian Affairs schools. Busby Indian School, Montana. Public school text.

The authors provide a fair introduction to the study of history, the emergence of man, and the developmental process of mankind and his societies. Nevertheless, in defining history itself, an error is made in this way: On page 18, it is stated that "The two most general and most striking trends in world history during the last five thousand years have been (1) the gradual linking up of widely scattered peoples, cultures, and continents, and (2) the advances in knowledge, in technology and in world population."

While the first of these trends might be considered as inclusive of the knowledge of the New World by travelers and conquerors of the Old World, it is not sufficiently clear that it was knowledge of the North and South American continents that changed man's life, added immeasurably to man's scientific knowledge of the world, and brought to bear, upon Europe particularly, great changes in economy, politics, and customs. Thus, not only is the linking up "of scattered peoples" a critical trend, but specifically the linking up of the North and South American continents and in that sense, the entrance upon the world scene of a new world population—the Native Peoples, or Indians, as Columbus improperly called them.

In the pages of this textbook, (29-32) there is the first clear and objective description of the entry of man into the North American continent. Other possibilities than the Bering land bridge are discussed. The student is treated as an intelligent person, and even the language reflects this approach. It is good to be able to make this positive evaluation, as concerns this aspect of the textbook.

Page 111: The estimated population of North America is given in the following words: "It is doubtful whether the seven million square miles that now comprise the United States and Canada ever supported more than a million Indians." This is inaccurate, as more recent scientific estimates show. The error in language, which has become an error in ideological concept, is repeated in this book only once, with the words that "Columbus discovered America."

The conquest of the Spaniards, Portuguese and other European nations are described with skill and interest. But the contributions of the Native peoples of these countries to the European nations are not dealt with at all. More importantly, is the fact that the effects of these conquests upon the conquering nations are not treated. The subject of English and other European colonization is told briefly and well. But it is related without any consideration of the Native American population, which played a critical part in the period of colonization, as well as in all other periods of American history.

The westward movement of the whites is handled in the same way, as though the Indians were no factor at all in the process. Only one brief statement is made in this connection, on page 418, in which it is explained that the frontiersmen from the thirteen colonies entered the expansionist movement from the east, and that "they drove back the scattered Indian tribes and occupied their hunting grounds." The implication in this statement is that the Indian tribes didn't amount to much anyhow, and what the frontiersmen were taking were only hunting grounds.

This is inaccurate, for what these white frontiersmen were taking was Indian homeland, hunting and fishing lands and coasts, rivers and streams, campsites and food gathering land, and areas then in possession of the Native peoples, either by aboriginal occupation, or by treaty with the United States government, and often by both. The entire section on the growth of America is written from the European point of view, and the Native is completely ignored, both as part of the population which was critical and important because of the conflict of the two cultures and economies, and as a political consideration in the influence on policy and the development of the nation.

*†THE WIDE WORLD: A Geography. *By James* & *Davis.* Macmillan Co., 1959, 536 pp. Bureau of Indian Affairs schools; Riverside Indian School, Anadarko, Oklahoma. Public school text.

Discussing the various developments that influence and control culture, the authors state, on page 159, that the second great step in mankind's cultural progress came with agriculture. Without agriculture, man could not develop culturally, could not develop communities, or have settled existence.

While this may be true in general terms, it cannot be taken as a measure of cultural development without reservation. For, when considering the cutural development of such regions as southern California, or northern California, the question is far more complex. Even though the Native peoples of these two regions knew agriculture and practiced it, yet the more abundant supply of food came from the natural environment. Therefore, the pursuits of hunting and fishing, gathering and transforming the gathered materials into foods, and in general utilizing the natural products of the earth, were of far more consequence in the culture than agriculture. The riches of the land were sufficient to support a very large population. Further in considering this question, is the development of the internal culture of the people, so far as knowledge and ability to organize themselves in such a way as to take the fullest advantage of the natural environment. There were some areas in the west without the use of agriculture at all. Yet, their culture was complex, of a highly developed nature for their time in the area and for that particular stage of society.

Thus, it does not necessarily follow, that culture develops extensively because of the existence of agriculture. The principle is too general. While these examples may be considered exceptions, yet there are enough such exceptions to make it necessary to qualify this determination. In the same vein, the statement on page 163 explains that "If any culture is to survive for long, ways of using the resource base without destroying it must be found." The authors do not take this concept to its conclusion; and this is, that modern society, for all of its highly developed culture, technology and civilization, is rapidly destroying its resource base.

An example of this change is shown on the same page, but without accepting the same inevitable conclusions. The authors state that people have the ability to rise over the physical limits of the habitat. And so, the story of the New England states is told, in which the Europeans, taking a land that was rich and filled with a surplus of resources, was transformed into a practical waste by the Europeans, who misused the resources. The authors distort the logic of this development, when they state that "New England as a region never had many natural resources after the forests were destroyed." They themselves destroyed the forests, however. But this is not stated. An opportunity is lost to explain the needs and techniques of conservation, which the Native Americans had developed to a high degree. Instead of telling the story as it actually happened, the authors by omission commit an inaccuracy, and in the very next page (165), they explain that the Europeans in New England "cleared the forests, built farms, roads, and fences." The treatment lacks logic.

That they did these things without consideration and without respect for the natural resources, is not expressed. Finally, in the discussion of political revolution and change, the authors fail to explain the influence made upon Europe by the colonization of North and South America. As a more positive evaluation, the short column on page 176, which gives a limited list of crops taken to Europe, Asia, and Africa from America; and an accompanying column showing the crops of Europe, Asia, and Africa taken to the Americas is certainly a step forward in treatment of contributions of people to one another.

*OUR WORLD AND ITS PEOPLES. *By Kolevzon & Heine.*
Allyn & Bacon, Inc., 1964, 544 pp. Public school text.

Americans have helped to make their country great, it is stated in a chapter devoted to the United States as a world leader. Among the Americans who have performed this outstanding task, are mentioned the European immigrants and all of those who came here as foreigners to make up the "great melting pot."

Indians are mentioned only in this sentence: "They came from Europe across three thousand miles of stormy seas to land on the shores of a little-known continent. Threatened by hostile Indians, they cleared thick forests for farming and built towns. . . " (p. 89). It should also have been stated that these settlers took Indian lands, and that when they began to clear the forests they didn't know when to stop and destroyed the natural resources of the New England country. On page 97, the corn belt of the United States is mentioned, and is described very well, including all the ways in which it is used, and also informing the reader that corn is now America's most lucrative product. Only one thing is not mentioned, that corn was a contribution of the American Indian to the United States and world economy.

When, on page 147, the people of the west are discussed, it is stated that "By 1800 millions of acres of the Great Plains were being used for grazing." It is then recounted how the United States government "gave away" at first "160 acres" to anyone who would settle and farm on the Great Plains, which amount was later raised "to 640 acres." An error by omission is made here, when it is not stated that the largesse of the United States government was by virtue of the taking of Indian lands for the purpose of giving it "away" to the settlers and ranchers.

Describing the people of the Pacific coast, on page 164, it is stated that in 1845 California "had fewer than 8,000 people. This is inaccurate. There were at least 23,000 people in California at that time. Not to count the Indian population is not only an error, but an inhuman insult. Although the United States is described according to various regions, and although the people of each region are dealt with in this textbook, there is no mention or treatment of the American Indian, not even during the gold rush. Error by gross omission is the failure of this textbook.

WORLD GEOGRAPHY TODAY. By Israel, Roemer, & Durand Jr. Holt, Rinehart & Winston, 1966, 568 pp. Public school text.

The inference is made on page 442 that the American Indians were just as much immigrants to this land as Europeans and others, in this statement: "The population of the United States originated in many parts of the earth. The American Indians are thought to have come from Asia. Over 40 million immigrants came to our shores from Europe . . . "

It is scientifically proven that man did not originate on this continent. It is, therefore, a tautology to explain that the American Indian came from some other place. But to put the matter in the light which these authors have done, is to imply that the Natives of this nation stand on the same footing as all other immigrants. To make this inference is to deny the Native his rightful place as the original American, and this leads to the assumption that there is nothing special about his position in relation to either the federal government, or his place historically as one who possessed and occupied this land, when in fact there is.

Chapter 45, dealing with New England: Birthplace of American Industry, the authors by omission draw an inaccurate picture of the development of this part of the country. This is done with every region of the United States. It is as though the Native did not exist, and did nothing to contribute to the land and its people. In the same way, chapter 47 discusses the midwest, and the corn belt takes prominence as producing America's most important crop. But no credit is given the American Indian for this contribution. Discussing the Southwestern part of the country, the only mention of the Indians appears in this section. In this case, the treatment is so generalized that there is very little understanding developed. According to information given on page 498, the Eskimos live in the north, and live chiefly by "fishing, trapping, and tending herds of reindeer." Many Eskimos cannot make a living in their old ways any longer, and are found in the cities now, working in factories, fisheries, canning enterprises. There are quite a few who are extraordinarily fine artists. There is no mention of the Indians or Aleuts of Alaska.

Dealing with Canada, the Indians do not even exist there, according to these authors, because all other peoples are mentioned, except the Natives. Discussing the Native peoples of Latin America, the writers of this textbook give them the derogatory term "primitive," though their only claim to this description is that they are in poverty, are forgotten, and are clinging to their racial heritage despite the hardships involved therein. The Inca are mentioned only in connection with their treasure, found and taken by the Spanish conquerers. Error by omission is the greatest failure of this textbook. Derogatory statements and descriptions occur when the Indians are mentioned.

*†AT HOME AROUND THE WORLD. *By Delia Goetz.* Ginn & Co., 1965, 335 pp. Bureau of Indian Affairs schools. Public school text.

Fourth grade students who study from this textbook will be able to view various homelands of the world only through the eyes of a typical middle-class family. The desires, interests, and learning habits of middle-class people are worked into the structure of the book. An attempt to describe the people of the ten areas which are discussed as "homes" around the world is unsuccessful. People come through to the student like stick-dolls. For example, what is an Eskimo, or who is an Eskimo? This textbook says: "Eskimos are people who live in the far northern lands of North America." The question might just as well have been left at "what," is an Eskimo. These are not people, they are places on a piece of paper called a map. It is to be hoped that soon the school system will cease using books such as this, which insult the intelligence, and have no relation to life, or even to places. This book would not have been evaluated at all, because there is nothing to evaluate in a book that is as vapid as this one. But it is being used in the Indian schools, and this makes it all the more reprehensible.

*†GLOBAL GEOGRAPHY. *By Val Cleef & Finney.* Allyn & Bacon, Inc., 1966, 520 pp. Bureau of Indian Affairs schools. Choctaw Indian School, Mississippi. Public school text.

In their preface, the authors state that this book is "basically a text in living geography. It emphasizes people and places, time and space." This, however, embodies merely good intentions, for the textbook does not give the student a sense of "living" geography; neither does it deal with people. Certainly there is no indication of time and space.

If this indeed had been incorporated into the textbook, the information would have been given that the American Indian's corn was a most profitable contribution to the world. Instead, the industry, harvesting, and growth of this most lucrative product is treated in the most static way. On page 79, it is stated that "For many years people have thought of desert lands as wastelands. We know this is wrong, for many Arabs, Berbers, and other peoples have long populated the deserts of North Africa and Asia." Why ignore the American Indians, who lived well for centuries in the deserts and wastelands of this continent.

Similarly, there are no "people" in Canada — the only information being that the Canadian people are "proud," etc. Mere platitudes hide the arid content of this textbook. The same may be said of the treatment of Latin American countries. There are no people, and the large Indian population is handled in a single sentence: "The government is trying to improve the conditions of the Indians."

*†A WORLD VIEW. *By Sorensen, with McIntyre & Branley.* Silver,

Burdette, 1961. Bureau of Indian Affairs, Roosevelt School, Fort Apache, Arizona.

Page 49: Eskimos are described as a people who "make most of their living directly from natural resources." Untrue for today. Even the Eskimos today use canned foods, synthetic products, meat imported from the lower Forty-eight, and dairy products not found among their natural resources.

On the same page, it is stated that among the wildlife hunted by the Eskimos are seals and other "birds." We are assuming that it is all right to teach Native children that seals are birds. These authors should be instructed that a seal is a mammal.

Serious omissions occur when the textbook deals with various areas of the world, especially the North American continent. Apparently there was no life along the northwest coast, or the eastern coast, for these people are not mentioned. On page 237, there is reference to "unexplored Indian lands in the western and northwestern regions." This is inaccurate. These lands were explored and occupied by Indians.

Discussing the peoples of Canada, the Native is allowed "a few thousand Indians" in the great forests, and along the Arctic coast "the Eskimos continue their endless search for fish and wild game." This picture of a sparse and accidental people, aimlessly searching for fish and wild game, is hardly a true description of the Native peoples of Canada. Certainly there are many more than 3,000 Indians, and not only in the "great forests," either.

Dealing with the products of the world, and especially those of Canada, South America and the United States, this book says nothing of the native foods, medicines, and other world-known, world-utilized products of today, which were the contributions of the Native peoples. Their arts and inventions received no recognition. The contributions of these people are not dealt with.

World History and Geography

SUMMARY OF EVALUATIONS (28 BOOKS EVALUATED)

1: Not one book treats the history and culture of the American Indian as part of the history of the races of man.

2: The ancient Indian races of the North and South American

continent are ignored in 24 of the books, and with considerable generalization in the others.

3: The contributions of the Native Americans to the Old World are not treated in any of the 28 books evaluated.

4: All the textbooks deal with world history from the standpoint and approach of the white peoples of this world.

5: Invidious and improper comparisons of the Native Americans with other cultures, primarily white, are made in all the books.

6: Those books discussing America in the world of nations today, ignore the Indian completely.

7: Whenever the Native Americans are discussed, the treatment is spliced in here and there, fragmented, not made a part of the whole. Some of the books, however, deal with Mayan, Inca, and Aztec civilizations as background for Spanish conquest and colonization.

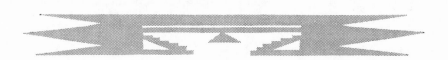

IX

Curriculum Related Miscellany and

A Sampling of Readers

THE GENERAL CRITERIA: Human decency, respect for other Peoples, and acknowledgement of the existence of the Native American in the History of this Nation and the World of Today.

These twenty-one books which are presented here as evaluations do not fit into any ready category.

Two are supplementary books on the Negro Americans.

Some are primary readers; a few are biographies of "Great Americans," stories of important American historical documents, and elementary school social studies books in special areas.

Not one of these books deals with the Native American accurately. Every one of these books mentions the Indian in one way or another — always incorrectly, filled with inaccuracy and misconception.

Among the Heroes of America, in the many books which have recently been published, only one of OURS is mentioned, Sequoyah. Pretending that the Native American does not exist is the game men play today. That this should not be allowed to continue, is the reason for the publication of TEXTBOOKS AND THE AMERICAN INDIANS.

THE HEROES OF AMERICA

TRAIL BLAZERS OF AMERICAN HISTORY. *By Mason & Cartwright*. Ginn & Co., 1961, 336 pp. Public schools text.

GREAT NAMES IN OUR COUNTRY'S STORY. *By Eibling, Gil-*

martin, & Skehan, Laidlaw, 1961, 312 pp. Wahpeton Indian School text, North Dakota.

40 AMERICAN BIOGRAPHIES. *By Helen Miller Bailey,* Harcourt, Brace & World, 1964, 250 pp. Public school textbook.

GREAT AMERICANS. *By Fowler & Fisher,* The Fideler Company, 1966, 128 pp. Public schools textbook.

"Trailblazers of American History," treats of Columbus, John Smith, William Bradford, Paul Revere, Benjamin Franklin, George Washington, Daniel Boone, Father Serra, George Washington Carver, Henry Ford, and the Wright Brothers, among the 25 listed as "trail blazers." But there is not one American Indian so honored.

"Great Names in Our Country's Story," contains the biographies of Christopher Columbus, Miles Standish, Haym Salomon, Thomas Jefferson, Daniel Boone, Lewis and Clark, Andrew Jackson, Thomas Edison, Henry Ford, George Washington Carver, Herbert Hoover, Woodrow Wilson, Franklin Roosevelt, and others. But not one American Indian "great name" is treated.

"40 American Biographies" deals with Leif Ericson, Magellan, Serra, Paul Revere, Haym Salomon, Dorothea Dix, Frederick Douglass, Harriet Tubman, Luther Burbank, Samuel Gompers, Grandma Moses, Albert Einstein and George Marshall among others. Two American Indians are described: Sequoia and Will Rogers. Sequoia's place in the hearts of his people and in their history is assured, an incontrovertible fact. Will Rogers was beloved by all, but he was not a leader of the Cherokee people.

"Great Americans" deals with 17 Americans, including six presidents, Thomas Edison, Henry Ford, and Richard E. Byrd. There is not one American Indian mentioned.

It is in this realm of recognition: leadership, accomplishment and contribution to the people, that the continuing conflicts are seen between the white-dominated world and that of the Native American. The sad fact is, (from the point of view of today's world and its problems) that this nation's heroes are not our heroes. In fact, even those heroes from the Indian world who have been publicized by the dominant society are our traitors; heroes from the white world have in great part been and still are the betrayers of our trust and faith, the destroyers of our people and their culture, the marauders upon our land, who are historically responsible for our present situation.

Take Pocahontas. She was no hero of the people. The fact that she was acceptable to the English aristocracy does not entitle her to a place in our Hall of Fame. Take Squanto, he who was captured and sent to England and who, upon his return, became a friend of the white man to the detriment of his own people. Also take Elias Boudinot, he who did so much to advance the knowledge of his Cherokee people, only to betray them with the signing of an unlawful treaty, so that he was executed by his own Cherokee friends of the past.

Andrew Jackson occupies a high place in all listings of the heroes of our country. He, it is said, was a "man of the people." His simple origins alone, however, do not entitle him to a place in this country's hall of heroes. He was the worst enemy the Indian people ever had. He was responsible for the removal of the tribes from their homes, for the Trail of Tears, for turning on his friends the Cherokees, who helped him in war. He was an enemy, triple grade A.

Shall we Indians mention our own heroes and leaders? To name a mere handful out of the hundreds who justly deserve this honor: Joseph Brant, Mohawk; Red Cloud, Sioux; Roman Nose, Cheyenne; Geronimo, Apache; Black Hawk, Sac and Fox; Sitting Bull, Sioux; Logan, Mingo; Popé, Pueblo; Red Jacket, Seneca; Little Turtle, Miami; Sequoia, Cherokee; Joseph, Nez Percé; Sacajawea, Shoshone; Tecumseh, Shawnee; William Fuller, Mi Wuk; John Ross, Cherokee; Seattle, Dwamish; Palma, Quechan; Massasoit, Wampanoag; Osceola, Seminole; Cochise, Apache; Ganado Mucho, Navajo; Cornplanter, Seneca; High Wolf, Sioux; Captain Jack, Modoc. George Conway was a Chippewa (1818-1863), who wrote many histories and essays, among them Traditional History and Characteristic Sketches of the Ojibway; Indian Life and History, Organization of a New Indian Territory, European Sketches. Cornplanter was the first prohibitionist in this nation.

Their numbers are legion. Their true stories remain untold.

It is said in the history books again and again, that this country is great, powerful, influential, rich, democratic; that it is the best, the most, the biggest and the greatest in all ways. According to these books no nation compares with us in all the virtues. Modesty is certainly not a national characteristic as displayed in the textbooks, and mere patriotism cannot account for the continuous bombardment of self-satisfaction and self-congratulation. In such a Nation, we poor and humble Indians might ask, is it not possible to allow recognition for the greatness of some of the men and women who lived and died for us ... who defended us, led us, fought the invaders of our land, displayed a profound depth of mind and spirit, and contributed so much to the history of OUR people?

The Native American understands the difficulty encountered by the white society in accepting the heroes of the American Indian. After all, this country was wrested from the Indians by virtue of the defeat of our great heroes and their untrained, ill-equipped armies of individuals who fought with one purpose; the defense of their land and their way of life. The Negro Americans have been able to gain recognition. But there is no danger here. For, after all, the Negro Americans worked as part of the white society, within the white society, became one with the white society so far as this society permitted it. And so, with the gracious consent of this white-dominated nation, the Negro has at last gained his place in the country's hall of fame. To grant such a place to the American Indian requires a largeness of spirit and an acceptance of the place of the Redman in our history that this country is apparently not yet ready to allow. Until this recognition is given, however, all talk of a *united* nation remains idle chatter.

*AMERICAN BIOGRAPHIES, Teachers Edition. *By Eva Knox Witte.* Holt, Rinehart, & Winston, 288 pp. Fourth grade public schools supplementary textbook.

There are no Indian biographies in this book. There is no mention of the Supreme Court decisions regarding Indians. There is no mention of Civil Rights and the American Indian, nor of Title 25, which controls reservation property and development. There is no mention of the Indian and his voting rights. There are a few statements regarding Roger Williams and his friendship with the Indians. There is no mention of Indian in education, art, and industry; and there is no mention of the present world as to the role of the American Indians. There is also no mention of any Mexican-Americans.

†IN ALL OUR STATES. *By Hanna, Jacks, Kohn, & Lively.* Scott, Foresman & Co., Bureau of Indian Affairs Schools, Juneau, Alaska.

"Alaska became part of the United States about one hundred years ago. At that time, the only people living there were Indians and a few fur traders." This statement, on page 218, will certainly surprise the Eskimo and Aleut children who are making use of the textbook. The book is lacking in information about Indians in the states being studied. The areas of the country's Northeast, North Central states, the south, west, Alaska and Hawaii are treated in the textbook. The words "Indian, Apache, Seminole, Blackfoot," are interspersed here and there, but only in the sense that they were there when the whites came. Other than the maps used as illustrations, the information about PEOPLE is generalized, oversimplified: no information whatever exists about the Native people of the land.

†YOUR TOWNS AND CITIES. *By Eleanor Thomas.* Ginn & Co., 1967, 238 pp. Elementary School text, Bureau of Indian Affairs, Fort Yates Indian School, North Dakota.

A very nice, antiseptic, middle-class life is shown in this book for children. Some information exists as to how ideal markets operate, the use of steel, the fire and safety department, and how cities are in general planned and grow. Ideal situations are used as examples. The chapter dealing with the history of this sample town in America, is so general and so idealized that no life whatever comes out of it. The Indians "lived in West Bend long before the white men came here." Then one settler comes, he brings his family, others come and take up land near the Indian homes. Apparently the Indians are happy to have people steal their land and usurp their property. At least this is what happens in "YOUR TOWNS AND CITIES". The same generalizations and idealizations occur in discussing other places such as Washington, D.C.

*JANET AND MARK. *By Mabel O'Donnell.* Harper & Row, publishers. Printed by California State Department of Education, 1969.

A first grade reader done in the look-see method, this book makes use of the cowboy and Indians theme on pages 26, 27, and 28. The text is to be utilized together with watching a television program, in which cowboys and Indians are chasing each other. In time to the television show, the child is required to read: "Go, cowboy!" Or, "Go, go, Indians." Thus, the children are obliged to take sides in the conflict, as a sort of game; the last scene shows the Indians fading out of the picture, as they are chased into oblivion by the "cowboys."

It is the opinion of the evaluators that the stereotyped cowboy-Indian theme is bad enough. Featuring general conflict, fighting, and chasing of the cowboys by the Indians or vice versa should not be made the subject for a child's first grade reader. It does not help develop any standards in the learning process. In fact, this game which is being played with the help of the school reader, is not a game at all. It should be understood that such things happened, and that they were real; they were not games to be hallooed at, or shouted about or ballyhooed.

Outside of our own evaluation, by the way, it is strange indeed that the few Black children in the book are "just there;" somehow they don't talk. It is almost as though they were just stuck into the book to satisfy some criteria.

†WORKING TOGETHER. *McIntire & Hill.* Follett Publishing Co., 1965, 256 pp. Bureau of Indian Affairs, Eagle Butte, South Dakota, Indian Elementary School.

Studying about the atlas, how we get foods, clothing, and how we travel and receive messages make up the greatest part of the elementary school book. One chapter is devoted to "Indians and Pioneers." General information is given about the Native people of various regions. Very few names of the tribes are mentioned, but indication is given that there were many tribes, speaking many languages and living in a variety of ways.

It is questionable, whether this type of "goody-goody" book is right and proper for young students. The idea seems to be, among many teachers and reflected in textbooks such as these, that mention of conflict and controversy should be avoided. Whether this is a good learning process or not, is now being considered seriously by many educators. Some of them hold to the view that merely positive information should be given, and elements of conflict be avoided. Others believe that the truth should be told the pupil, thus preparing the child for life, facing him with facts as they were and are today. But, in such a way that positive thinking results.

Educators who are members of the American Indian Historical Society believe in the latter course, and are confirmed in the idea that ways can be found indeed to tell the children how land was taken from the Indians, how settlers squatted illegally on Indian land, and what happened in our country's history as a result.

Some inaccuracies exist, page 200 concerning reservations; page 203 concerning chieftainship; page 225 regarding totem poles. Improper comparison is made on page 208 when plains Indian villages are compared to modern schools with electric lights and trains.

†LEARNING ABOUT OUR NEIGHBORS. By Wann, Wann &

Sheehy. Allyn & Bacon, 1966. 192 pp. Bureau of Indian Affairs schools. Miccosukee Agency, Homestead, Florida. Also used by Public Schools, State of Florida.

All-white, middle-class, cleanly antiseptic—the above elementary grade level textbook is completely unsatisfactory, and irrelevant both to the lives of Indian children and those of other racial groups who go to the public schools of the State of Florida. Shown are beautiful new station wagons, new fire department equipment without a blemish, supermarkets, fine modern bicycles, and people who exist only in upper class suburbia. Completely ignored are the Native people of the state, the Negro, the Spanish descendants. Everybody is white. The history is also entirely white. There is no mention made of the rich and fascinating history of this state, even though the opportunity is taken for full page maps to show where cacao comes from.

†GOING PLACES: A GUIDE TO DIRECTIONS. *By William D. Pattison.* Rand McNally & Co., 1965, 90 pp. Miccosukee Day School, Florida. Primary reader.

This is a primary reader in geography. Most of the book is good and of course requires an excellent teacher for adequate instruction. However, the first part, which deals with the finding of direction, and orientation as to direction in daily life, is completely irrelevant to the Indian child. These are middle class children, in middle class surroundings, eating hot dogs and ice cream sandwiches, surrounded by parks, flower gardens, picket fences, and suburban homes. Some way must be found to relate the child to his normal surroundings. Only white children exist in this book, moreover. There are no other races in the world of this text.

†HOMELANDS OF THE WORLD: Geography-Centered Social Studies. *By Thurston, Hankins, Haaby.* Charles E. Merrill Books, 1960, 280 pp. Wanblee Indian Day School, South Dakota.

Indians are called "savages," their homeland considered as the particular property and concern of the European alone. Like this, on page 56, "There were savage Indian tribes that hunted the buffaloes for food. They made clothes of the hides, and skins to cover their tents. The Indians often attacked the covered-wagon trains. My great-grandfather was attacked at the Platte River." "Gee! I wish I'd been there," cried Jack. Meeting a Navajo mother, the family which forms the center of this story, gives the mother's baby some candy, watches as she purchases food at the trading center, admires her blankets—and this is the end of our contact with the Indian world through this textbook.

*A NEW HOMETOWN. By *Preston, Cox & Wavle*. Heath & Co., 1964, 64 pp.

GREENFIELD, U.S.A. By *Preston, McIntosh & Cameron*. Heath & Co., 1964, 175 pp.

Both these books are for primary grades, and are utilized in the Indian school at Busby, Montana. They suffer from the same ailment, malnutrition of the intellect. They are strictly for middle-class children, because only middle-class life is shown, middle-class people are pictured, and middle-class homes described.

Only whites exist in the worlds of these two books. There are no others. It is extremely doubtful if any Indian child could relate his own life to that shown in the pages of these two readers for children.

If examples are needed, here they are: Father drives a new car. Stores which "sell things" in the Greenfield, U.S.A. book include a flower store, a drug store, and a book store. None of these bear any resemblance to what the children at Busby, Montana see in their daily lives. In the same book, a modern fire station is seen, a traffic policeman on the corner, trees around a house with a picket fence. In the history of the town, only pioneers and settlers are shown. In the plan of the town, there are neat little houses on little square plots of neat little lands. And so on. That such absurdities which pose as primary books still exist, is a travesty upon the educational system.

*CANADA. By *Theo L. Hills & Sarah Jane Hills*, 1966, 160 pp. Book 5 of the series.

This book could be a Chamber of Commerce tract. It is so bland that little or no understanding is derived about this vast part of the continent or its people. Description of rivers, lakes, terrain, and so on are given, but when historical background is attempted, the book is a failure. There is mention of the first people, the Eskimos, Indians, and

Aleuts, but nothing more is said about them. There is mention of Eskimo and Indian crafts, but the description is a mere token of the real thing; they are treated as simply products which could attract tourists. There is no description of their current situation, education, poverty, or encroachment of whites through the federal and provincial governments, which is still in evidence.

*NEGROES WHO HELPED BUILD AMERICA. *By Madeline Robinson Stratton with a Preface by Joseph E. Penn.* Ginn & Co., 1965, 163 pp., Eighth grade public school supplementary text.

While the purpose of this book is "to provide basic information about the contribution of Negro Americans to the development of our nation," the historical background given in the preface displays the same misconceptions, lack of knowledge, and historical inaccuracies that exist in almost all other books used in the schools.

Indeed, the preface is written from the white man's point of view, and from the viewpoint of the Negro who longs for a place in the white-dominated society. The truth is not told here about the Nation's history. Regardless of the accomplishments of the Negro Americans treated in the biographical content of the book itself, the story of our history should be told as it is, as it was.

On the first page of the preface, it is stated, "Negroes assisted in the conquest and exploration of parts of North and South America which are now the countries of Mexico, Guatemala, Chile, Peru, and Venezuela. Negroes accompanied Balboa to the Pacific Ocean in 1513. In 1526, they accompanied the Spanish exporer Ayllon, on his expedition from the Florida Peninsula to what is now Virginia. There they helped to establish the town of San Miguel near present day Jamestown. Negroes were in many parties which explored the southwestern part of the United States; parties led by Cabeza DeVaca, Coronado, and DeSoto." Lacking in this information is the fact that many Negroes helped the Indians in their struggle against the white settlers, in defending the land against invasion. Lacking also is the fact of Negro refugees in the Seminole Nation, and their blending into the Indian tribal structure as leaders, workers, farmers, and participants in the struggle for survival of the Indian people. Too, it is questionable as to whether any glory attaches to those who were with Coronado, or who participated in the wars against the Indian people, as this preface implies. Only history and man's future progress in democratic thought and attainment of ideals can make this verdict. We Indians believe the verdict of history is ultimately with us. We will have historic justice in the end, even though we have suffered the loss of our country and consequent injustices without number, throughout the history of white domination of this land.

In all the current outpouring of textbook literature about the American Negro, wherever the historic background is touched, the same errors, misconceptions, and distortions of fact exist, as are shown in books displaying all-white ideology. It may well be that in correcting one historic injustice in our books, the publishers and authors will continue to perpetuate another.

The preface states that "Negro families later sought freedom in the frontier of the west; in the nineteenth century, many moved west where racial prejudice did not exist." In that day, racial prejudice was rampant, violent, with definite attempts and many successes in genocide. This was directed specifically and relentlessly against the American Indian.

In this evaluative statement, we do not credit the writer of the preface with racial prejudice, for we believe that there is no racial prejudice of the American Blackman against the American Indian—not yet. Rather we would evaluate this preface as one displaying historic ignorance. It is a fact of current American ideology that the Negro American shares with other Americans who are not Indian, the general lack of knowledge and understanding of Indian affairs, our history, culture, and current needs and desires. The task is therefore even more pressing, to educate the whole public concerning the Native Americans and their place in the history and culture of this country. In this preface, the Black Americans are made to align themselves with the white invaders. This historic fact is not one to be proud of, at the same time, it must be stated also, that there were some Indians who played Benedict Arnold to their own people. These will be handled in textbooks and instructional materials written by Indians who are faithful to the demand for historic justice and truth which is now opening up a new horizon for the American Native. Information that the Negro played a part in the defense of the Indian homeland should be incorporated in the general process of education now going on.

NEGRO AMERICAN HERITAGE. By Lawrence, Randall, Endo, McStay. Century Schoolbook Press, 1965, 196 pp. Public schools text, Fifth or eighth grade.

It is an odd commentary on current education, that even when attempted corrections are being made in the history and culture of one "minority" group, the errors about Indians and the approach to Indian history is just as wrong as it has always been. This book is no exception. Since the Indian appears only seldom, a specific observation can be made in one instance, of improper handling of Indian history as related to the life and history of the Black man.

On page 44 it is stated, "Of the many events that occurred in America's march westward, one of the most dramatic was when General Custer . . made his last stand . . Negro Isaiah Dorman had spent many years in this part of the United States. He acquired much experience in dealing with Indians and learned their language and customs. The war department assigned him to serve as an interpreter for General Custer, who was fighting to end attacks on white settlers by such Indians leaders as Sitting Bull, Crazy Horse and Rain-in-the Face. The Battle of Little Big Horn . . lasted only twenty minutes with General Custer and his army being massacred by Sioux Indians under Crazy Horse."

Whether his service under Custer was a glorious event of which to be proud, is debatable, but Mr. Dorman is placed in the unenviable position of being on the wrong side in the efforts of the Native Americans to protect themselves against invaders. The Sioux and other Plains Indians were waging a defensive war to save their land, their culture and their homes. They defeated Custer in a fair fight. In this book, the Sioux victory is called a "massacre." In truth, it was a signal victory for the Indian people, and history would have been better served if it had been followed by other similar victories. It is not too much to expect that this country might have been more peace-loving, more tolerant of the views and cultures of others, and just as proficient in technology as it is today.

Treating of slavery, and the long struggle of the Black people against this evil, many of whom became runaways attempting to find a haven in the North, the book fails to mention that in many cases the Indian tribes gave asylum and became a refuge for the runaway slaves. The Seminoles particularly, were made the victims of bitter attacks by the United States Army and the southern states, because they organized a refuge for the Black people. Many Negroes married into Indian tribes and participated in the affairs of the people. The protection of Black slaves occurred not only in Florida, but elsewhere in the country including California, according to documented evidence in the hands of authors of this evaluation.

STORY OF AMERICAN TRANSPORTATION. By Wilma Wilson Cain. The Fideler Company, 1966, 128 pp. Public schools text, elementary levels.

This textbook opens the story of transportation with the Indian use of the canoe in water transportation. There is no mention made of the tribes using this type of transportation. Nor is there mention of the many types of boats used by the Natives—which varied in different parts of the country as did their languages. Many canoes were not made of birchbark. Other types of transportation, such as the travois used in transporting goods, are not mentioned. The methods of navigating Indian watercraft, even in the strong currents of great rivers and oceans, might have made reading of considerable interest and information for the student. A statement might have been made, also, that these methods of transportation such as the canoe and the dugout were a considerable contribution to the world, and are utilized even today. Facts such as these are omitted.

LIVING AMERICAN DOCUMENTS. Selected and edited by Starr, Todd and Curti. Harcourt, Brace & World, 1961, 358 pp. Eighth grade textbook, public schools.

The authors define the word "document" as an "original or official statement which stands as a bench mark in the story of American progress, and in a larger sense, in mankind's upward march toward freedom." The eighty documents chosen, which are given in chronological order, include the Magna Carta, the Habeas Corpus Act of the English Parliament, Patrick Henry's speech before the Virginia Convention in 1775, Thomas Paine's The Crisis, 1776, The Clayton Anti-trust Act of 1914, The Homestead Act of 1862, and finally John F. Kennedy's Inaugural address of 1961.

Describing the uses of such documents, as they relate to the development of American democratic thought and processes, the authors very correctly state, "Documents also provide the opportunity to practice and develop skills essential to critical thinking . . . The importance of these skills cannot be overemphasized in a world that is so desperately in need of the guiding hand of intelligence." Why, then, since there is such a world of profound thought and philosophy in documents relating to the American Indian, have these not been considered at all! One might mention the first Treaty drawn between the United States and an Indian Nation, the Delawares. Or, the words of Brant, Seattle, Joseph, at important moments in our history. Or, the decisions of Chief Justice Marshall in connection with important cases of Indian-federal relationships. More currently, Chief Justice Tobriner rendered a decision in the peyote case of Jack Woody, (1964), which was a declaration of human rights, and a document of immense human and literary value. These are "living documents" of our country's history, blazing trails of personal freedom for the nation as a whole.

However, the Dawes Act of 1887, which was supposed to grant "personal liberty" to the Indian people by allotting them individual parcels of land, and which nearly destroyed Indian landholdings, as well as impoverishing thousands of the Native people, and which was a failure from the start, is mentioned. The Homestead Act of 1862 is mentioned, which opened up large parcels of Indian land to the greed of so-called "settlers"— thereby violating treaties with the Natives which were supposed to last "forever." These two documents are "living documents" of human degradation, autocracy in government, evidences of a self-destructive society bent on acquisition for its own sake. That they were couched in high-flown terms of "liberty, independence, and freedom" does not alter their true purpose, which was to destroy Indian life and culture.

THE MISSISSIPPI: GIANT AT WORK. By Patricia Lauber. Garrard Publishing Co., 95 pp.

THE COLORADO: MOVER OF MOUNTAINS. By Alexander L. Crosby. Garrard, 96 pp.

These two books are evaluated together because they show an interesting difference in approach. Both were published in 1961. Both are well written. The language is clear and expressive. But here the likeness ends.

The COLORADO book has incorporated the Native peoples, describing them in the most natural way, making them a part of the history of this great river, showing them as they were, and while failing to indicate how they are today, yet creating a desire for further study.

The Mississippi book completely ignores the Indians, only mentioning the fact that the Native people were the first who lived with the river. The author states that the Indians did not know "how long it was. They did not know where its source was. They may not have known where the river ended. They could not know, as we do, that the river was one of the greatest in the world," (p. 11). Such poppycock can only be excused by the ignorance of the author. The Indians called the river "Mississippi"—Fathers of Waters. They certainly knew the extent and importance of this great body of water. Had this writer done her homework, she would have known that there were five attempts to find the source of the Mississippi river. The first was by Zebulon Pike in 1806, who went as far as what is now known as Cass Lake in Minnesota. The second attempt was made by Lewis Cass in 1820, who reached Cass Lake, and named it. The third attempt was made by an Italian, Count Beltrami, who reached a small lake between Red Lake and Cass Lake. The fourth attempt was made in 1823 by Stephen H. Long, whose purpose was to determine the correct boundary line between America and Canada. He reached Pembina, determined this was the correct boundary between the two countries, and named a lake which he thought was the source of the Mississippi, Lake Julia. When Henry Rowe Schoolcraft went into the Minnesota country in 1832, he was accompanied by an Indian guide, a Chippewa named Yellow Head. He guided the party south to cross a portage to Elk Lake, and this, he told Schoolcraft, "is the source of the Father of Waters." Schoolcraft was unimpressed by the name of this lake, so he re-named it Lake Itasca.

The Indians had explored this country long before white contact. They knew every river, stream, mountain and pass. They knew not only the source and termination of the Mississippi, but more important, they knew its uses. The author has missed telling one of the most fascinating stories of our history—the uses and knowledge of this great river by the Indians themselves.

X

Three Classics of Criticism

The historic Memorial to the Mayor of Chicago by the Grand Council Fire of American Indians in 1927, which opens the story of TEXT-BOOKS AND THE AMERICAN INDIANS, resulted in a brief flurry of interest and concern. The enormous depth of ignorance and ideological prejudice then existing in the schools was well known at the time. But the tremendous extent of educational bureaucracy was not realized.

Today the situation is even worse. Inaccuracy of data persists. Those who write the textbooks, and the publishers who print them, have little or no understanding of American Indian history, cultures, or philosophy. Scholarly preparation is lacking, and this is perhaps the worst of all the criticisms described throughout this study. The efforts to remedy the situation are met with resistance from many sources. Besides, the current state of the educational system is one of monstrous bureaucracy engendered by the massive growth of classroom population and the inadequacy of educational administration to deal with this problem. Attempts to cope with classroom growth, curriculum defects, and administrative failures have so far proved ineffective.

Within this framework, the attempts to clean up the textbooks, as they relate the role of the American Indian in the history of our country, present great difficulties. It is, therefore, of general value to consider three books which have been subjected to intensive criticism. These three examples also offer some indication of the routes that may be taken to remedy the situation. In two cases, the books have been withdrawn from classroom use. In one case, the textbook was finally rejected by the State Curriculum Commission on November 6, 1969. In all three cases, the books have been in classroom use for more than ten years. Considerable harm has been done, and it will be the duty of the educational system to correct it. Indian scholars have already begun the task, and our help is offered to secure an accurate and scholarly body of literature about the role of the Native American in the history of our land.

*THE CASE OF THE FOURTH GRADE TEXTBOOK
"California Indian Days."
By Helen Bauer. Published by Doubleday & Co., 1963

In 1966, the American Indian Historical Society evaluated eighty-one textbooks, all of which were being proposed for adoption in the state of California. The Society found not one book which it could approve. In one instance, a fourth grade supplementary book was proposed. The continuing struggle against the use of this book in the classrooms is told herewith.

This book was judged to be so filled with errors, that a complete revision would have been required in order to meet the Criteria. In 1966, the book was not adopted. Such adoption, in the state of California, requires the districts to use the book. However, the publishers managed to have this book accepted by some districts. It is practically impossible, in conditions where there are not less than one thousand, four hundred or more school districts in a state, to combat the acceptance of a book for classroom use, when the approach is made directly to each individual district.

In 1969, the publishers again proposed this book for required use in the schools of the state, indicating that revisions had been made. A foreword in the new edition even attempted to place the Indian Historical Society in a position of having "helped" in the revision. This was untrue. Upon examination, the book was found to be practically the same as the earlier edition. Consequently, the Society published, in its quarterly journal, THE INDIAN HISTORIAN, a comprehensive evaluation by Lowell John Bean, professor in anthropology at California State College at Hayward. That part of his article describing inaccuracies, distortions, and misconceptions in "California Indian Days" is reprinted here:

This text contains frequent errors in data, as well as omissions of significant fact, despite the easily accessible data on the native peoples of the region. Since the author provides no indication of her sources of information, it is assumed from the nature of the data presented, that several have been used, some ethnographical and others from governmental agencies.

Most of the data presented are generally in error. A statement suggesting that the planting of crops was unknown, is incorrect, (Forbes, 1963). Another gross error is the statement that there are only "about seventy sites where pictographs have been found" in California. There are more than that many sites recorded in the Cahuilla area of southern California alone. The Chumash area is even more dramatic with its representations of aboriginal art, (Grant, 1966). Numerous errors of fact occur in the recording of plant names and plant uses. The rendering of Indian words into English is upon occasion incorrect. Words from a single language are used as representative of all; thus by implication the word is construed as having been used by all California language groups.

Some notable examples of omission are: while yucca species are discussed, the most important of this species in California aboriginal subsistence—the yucca whipplei—is not mentioned at all, although its use is described but without indicating the species itself (Barrows, 1900; Kroeber, 1924). When yucca Schidigera is discussed as a food source, the blossom, which was a prime source of food, is entirely overlooked. It is as though it were explained that the Greek people utilized the leaf of the grape in cooking, but failed to mention that the grape itself was used as food, for wine, and many other purposes. When game animals are mentioned, it is significant that antelope, elk, and mountain sheep, three big-game animals commonly hunted in the California region, are not mentioned; nor is the list of other animals, insects and birds at all representative of the vast variety of fauna used by the people of this region for food. Other omissions occur when house types are discussed. The significant ceremonial-community house, for example, is not discussed at all, nor is the variation of housing adequately treated.

A particular image of the Indian of California emerges when the choice of words selected to describe the cultures is examined. In "California Indian Days," homes and houses become "huts"; culture is always "custom"; and homes are always "simple." When native California's finest aboriginal pottery is described, it is classified as being "rather well made" (page 32). A sacred, beautifully-choreographed dance is performed "wildly" (page 126). Throughout Mrs. Bauer's book, the Indian receives somewhat less than equal comparison with the currently dominant culture. The Indian "roams" in his territory. Consequently his relation to land would seem to be physical rather than social. (Reference is here made in the article, to a quotation from an article by Felix S. Cohen, which is reprinted elsewhere in this book.)

This type of insidious prejudice, implicit stereotyping and patronizing racial self-importance continues throughout the book. Such phrases as "they took food from places" (page 11), rather than that they collected and gathered, with utmost care, and the most sophisticated knowledge of their environment, exemplifies an insistence that aboriginal culture was "simple" in the "primitive" connotation. In "California Indian Days" the author says "they lived their simple way of life . . ." (page 3). Referring to archaeological data, "what they left behind were things that told of their simple but useful way of life . . ." (page 23). The use of the word "simple" in these contexts does not suggest an attempt at legitimate cross-cultural comparison, but rather indicates a categorical denial that anything complex or sophisticated could have existed in native California. This constant reference to a diminutive, diminished status of Indian culture is carried through to other aspects of the California aboriginal cultures; their homes are little, their stories are characterized as a "sort of sing-song story" (page 68). "Each tribe," says Bauer, "had some kind of music. Music to them was not a tune, but more a humming or low, slow chanting in time to the stomping of feet or the clapping of hands (page 90). The fact that musicologists and mythographers have addressed many scholarly articles to the California Indians' oral literature and music; and that these aesthetic expressions are ranked as complex, unique, and highly important cultural contributions, is totally ignored. (See Dockstadter, 1957.)

Rather than seek answers to questions in the available scholarly literature, the author indulges in conjecture, often gratuitous, and frequently imputing doubt upon the ability of the Indians to reason effectively. Upon the arrival of the Spanish the California Indian "perhaps thought of them as gods from the 'spirit world' " (page 20). Regarding their land the Indians knew so well, and with which they identified so very intensely, Bauer says "they must have loved their beautiful California home." If it is argued that this type of language exemplifies the "discovery" method of the learning process, then the argument is a specious excuse for language that is actually patronizing and inept—the semantics of the self-important dominant culture.

In art and literature, the unnecessary conjecture reaches another level of gratuity. Body paintings are "perhaps there to frighten bad spirits . . ." (page 35). Pictographs and petrographs of the area "appear to be a kind of Indian art . . ." (page 94). And the rich oral literature of the California Indian was developed "because they could not understand all these things, they made up stories about them" (page 128). In this vein the author continues, and the implication to most readers will be that European culture doesn't make things up, and European culture DOES understand "these things." The false-face image is further enlarged when Bauer says, "these stories were told from father to son and from one tribe to another, until they seemed to be true . . ." (page 128). The rationality and intelligence of the Indian is further denied because of a series of "lucky" circumstances. And so the reader is told that Indians were "lucky" to find so many oak trees in California, and some were "lucky" to have strong soapstone jars (page 61). More, "when they were lucky every family in the village had a feast" (page 61). The fact that acorns were useful because of skillful and demanding processing techniques, one of the greatest inventions of early man, and that the soapstone jars were quarried, shaped, polished and decorated, and that feasts were the consequence of careful planning and arduous hunting, gathering and storage techniques, is not brought to the attention of the reader.

In addition to the unnecessary conjectures already mentioned, invidious comparisons as well contribute to the distorted Indian "image," comparisons which place the Indian in a negative position. For example, California Indians are said to have "left behind no famous ruins of cities, no temple, or great works of art as some other people," (page 23), and "The Indians of the Colorado River make the poorest (!) examples of baskets in California." Any positive purpose of these statements escapes this reader. A positive statement regarding the densely populated coastal villages of the Gabrieleno Indians and the Chumash Indians might be appropriate, but at the very least a rational cause might be offered to the reader for the comparison of California Indians with those of other traditions and circumstances. Nor is it acknowledged that the Colorado River Indians did not need to emphasize basketry as an aesthetic or utilitarian form because they had a well developed pottery industry. In fact, the opportunity for pointing out to the student reader the relationship between developments of material culture and ecological need and potential, might have been taken successfully with these same examples.

Oversimplification can produce distortion and a negative view of a cultural situation as effectively as incorrect data. Bauer's book manages this in several areas of Indian life: child training and care, division of labor, marriage, ritual and religion are some examples. It is said that "in cold weather, a rabbit skin was thrown over the cradle," to protect the infant; (page 119); boys were "given many harmless tests to prove their bravery" (page 68); dancing is characterized as being done for fun, or "wild" in character. The purpose of dancing in one instance is because "they wanted luck in hunting or to find something that would make them rich or to be cured of an illness" (page 49). Marriage arrangements are also seen as rather simple affairs: "the young man who gave the most gifts (to the bride's parents) was almost always able to get the girl he wanted for his wife" (page 124).

The author's characterization of the division of labor denies what is a particularly obvious factor of aboriginal California life; that the sexual dichotomization of roles was not as rigidly defined as it was with some other American Indian groups. Thus, to Bauer, "women were the gatherers and men the hunters." This oversimplification prevents the reader from appreciating the orderly and well integrated nature of social organization involved in subsistence, which included the young and the old, men and women, in cooperative units, the goal of which was an efficient exploitation of complex environments. Furthermore, the social organizational aspects of the labor process is attributed to a wish to make work a happy occasion rather than a desire for efficient exploitation. The reader is told, "in the fall, when the oaks had ripe acorns, women left their homes in the village, usually in a group to make the harvest task happier" (page 49). This is analogous to saying that workers in an automobile factory go to a factory to work together because it makes the work a happier occasion.

The art and religion of California's Indian culture receive interpretative distortion when the artistically innovative Colorado River pottery industry is ignored and their pottery is reduced to that which "was good enough for their daily needs: cooking and family baskets and pots and water and storage jars . . ." (page 88). The elaborate effigies and painted ware which museums and private collectors are so anxious to acquire today, is ignored. In religion too, the Indian is not allowed total humanness. They do not "exactly pray for what they wanted . . . they danced and sang about their needs . . ." nor did anyone "teach the Indians about religion . . ." (page 115). The style absurdly enough continues: "No one taught Indians about religion . . . where they came from or where they were going. Even though it was a mystery, Indians had their own ideas about things . . ." (page 115). One has the right to conclude that Indians had no religion, but merely "ideas about things." A total ignorance regarding the sophistication and pervasiveness of religion among California Indians is demonstrated here. But more to the point is that it is not permitted the Indian to have a systematic and recognized religion in this book! Would it be incorrect to read in such a passage, the meaning that "they did not have a CHRISTIAN religion, therefore they did not have one at all?"

Other distortions appear with regularity. The personality characteristics of the California Indians are reduced to an absurd stereotype. The technique of stereotyping by categorical adjectives which we see applied to various ethnic groups is present here too. The Indian becomes "easy-going," "free," and "happy," "patient," "never worrying." Such behavioral characteristics would have guaranteed starvation and death to California aboriginal populations. Quite the contrary is true, however. Rigidly structured social relationships, technological innovations, trade systems, rituals and philosophy, which aided in the management of Indian resources, were usual in California cultures; but explanations given in this book reflect the very opposite. The data in "California Indian Days" then, appears to be contorted to support definite prejudices. Bauer sees food gathering times as "vacations," and the use of steatite for bowls and jars and arrows as "factors of luck." She says, "a supply of acorns can be found with little work . . ." (page 48), and the Indians are a patient people, who "never hurried or worried very much . . . what they couldn't find one day they found at another time and another place . . ." (page 49).

Life at the mission is described as "secure . . ." (page 136). The author asks "Is this what the Indian really wanted? They had been used to a free life. How hard it must have been for them to stay in one place when they had been so used to roaming, to be farmers instead of food gatherers and hunters. So many kinds of work and living had to be learned . . ." (page 136). While the intention of the author may quite possibly have been to describe the Indian plight in the missions with some sympathy, it is hardly a true statement.

The discovery of gold is correlated with America's interest in California, whereas gold had been discovered long before this time. We are told that the Indian at this time had difficulty understanding a European economic system. They could not understand "the mad scramble for the shiny gold . . ." (page 139). This, despite the fact that a large number of Indians were well integrated into the economy of Mexican California and some were even important rancho owners and officials, in Spanish and Mexican California. The American period is inaccurately credited with protecting Indians. Bauer says that nothing was done to protect the Indians until the 1850's (page 140). A study of the history with the opening of the American period in the 1850's will adequately disprove this statement.

The increasing loss of Indian lands is noted in this way: "Year after year the Indians lost more and more of their land . . ." (page 141). This is a rather passive explanation. It might more accurately have read "more and more land was taken until . . ."

Following several generations of contact with European cultures, Bauer says the Indian is "in a condition of bewilderment . . . Everything

is strange to him, life is very different and very fast . . ." (page 143).
While this may very well be true in certain instances, it fails to account
for the successful adaptation of thousands of California Indians into
every phase of contemporary American culture; or for the many educated Indian people in the arts, education, social science and welfare,
and the hundreds of college students who are Indian.

Finally, there is addenda to the book, including a chart indicating
the locations and main differences among tribes. This, instead of pro-
viding additional data, provides instead increased confusion. The charts
are set up to compare several aspects of Indian culture: tribal names
and languages, territories, clothing and ornaments, houses, foods, baskets, boats, customs, and other information. The categories themselves
preclude the possibility of placing emphasis on many significant factors
of aboriginal culture. The charts, by omission, would appear to indicate
many facets of culture are nonexistent; for example, under the category
"houses," they are described for the Yahi but not for the Karok. Is the
reader to conclude that the Karok did not have houses? The tribes are
not compared, nor are they contrasted, although the format would lend
itself to that task. More to the point, is the fact that the selected data is
often trivial in nature, adding little understanding or appreciation of
the cultures. Sometimes, in fact, the information is incorrect.

In conclusion, we must judge this book as being condescending and
patronizing to people of another culture. It is stereotypic in its conception of the people it strives to describe, and inaccurate historically and
ethnographically. Furthermore, it deliberately obscures facts of historic
importance, such as occurs in the omission of the facts of brutality and
exploitation occurring throughout the European occupation.

Since publication in THE INDIAN HISTORIAN, Lowell Bean's
article has raised a great deal of discussion among teachers, and has
brought to the forefront some of the most important ideological problems in education. Teachers have begun to use the article on the college
level for instructional purposes in education courses. The California
State Curriculum Commission was scheduled to consider textbooks for
adoption in fourth grade, and the *California Indian Days* book, one of
the four to which the Society had objected, was submitted for use in
classrooms of the state. (The other three books have been evaluated
elsewhere in this Study.) When the publisher, Doubleday & Co., received a copy of THE INDIAN HISTORIAN and read the Bean article,
the vice president himself responded by sending a special delivery letter
to all members of the Curriculum Commission, attempting to refute

the critique made in the article. He also attacked Mr. Bean as a "self-styled teacher." (Bean has a life teaching credential from the State of California, and is an assistant professor at California State College, Hayward). The document also attacked the Indian Historical Society, both by implication and outright falsehoods. This gentleman stated that the criticisms were "trivial, frivolous and petty," and that "Most minority groups are sensitive nowadays (and this is not to be disparaged), and any slight differences of wording that ordinarily would be overlooked, may be picked up and given undue emphasis," he stated. Further, said he, "Are we not dealing with a matter of ethnic sensitivity and social protest here rather than accuracy per se?" The Society was accused of rendering "personal feelings, opinions and interpretations." The publisher's letter also stated that the "language" of this textbook was of "fourth grade level," acceptable for that level of teaching (!).

This letter, sent five days before the meeting of the Curriculum Commission, was not intended for the eyes of Society members. It came to the attention of its officers only two days before the meeting of the Commission. A delegation was immediately selected, Indian leaders of the area were asked to be present at the meeting of the Commission, and three members of the Society appeared before the Commission at its meeting: Rupert Costo, president; Jane Penn, one of the founders and Honored Indian Historian; and Lowell John Bean, an associate. These three, flanked by other anthropologists, and many Indian leaders, appeared before the Commission to defend the Society's position and request rejection of all four of the Doubleday books.

Attention was called to the Statutes of the State of California, which forbid the adoption of books prejudicial and demeaning to minority groups, and arrangements were made through the California Indian Legal Services Association to institute legal action should the books be adopted. The State Curriculum Commission, after reading the Bean article, and listening to the evidence presented at the meeting, rejected all four books presented by Doubleday. A further step has already been taken by the Indian Historical Society, and that is to publish a book which will portray the role of the Indian in that state with truth and objectivity. This book, THE AMERICAN INDIANS IN CALIFORNIA HISTORY, will be off the press early in 1970. The Indian Historical Society feels that responsibility does not end with rejection of a bad book. It is also necessary to replace the poor materials with others of a scholarly, objective nature.

Sections of the State Statute which refer to the adoption of books, applicable to the Doubleday issue, are these: — *"Number 8553 —*

Instruction in social sciences shall include the early history of California and a study of the role and contributions of American Negroes, American Indians, Mexicans, and other ethnic groups in the economic, political, and social development of California and the United States of America. *Number 9001* — No teacher shall give instruction nor shall a school district sponsor any activity which reflects adversely upon persons because of their race, color, creed, national origin or ancestry. *Number 9002* — No textbook, or other instructional materials shall be adopted by the state board or by any governing board for use in the public schools which contains any matter reflecting adversely upon persons because of their race, color, creed, national origin or ancestry. *Number 9305* — The board shall, when adopting textbooks and teachers' manuals for use in elementary schools for the teaching of courses in civics and history of the United States and the State of California, include only such textbooks which correctly portray the role and contribution of the American Negro and members of other ethnic groups in the total development of the United States and of the State of Colifornia."

*THE CASE OF THE STATE TEXTBOOK
"Minnesota, Star Of The North"

By Ford & Johnson. Lyons & Carnahan, Sixth grade text book, Minnesota schools.

Attention to this book was first drawn by Mrs. Ruth Myers, a Chippewa woman of Duluth, Minnesota. Mrs. Myers is a member of the American Indian Historical Society, and called upon the Society for sample materials and experiences in the field of textbook evaluation when she first became aware of the book. Rosemary Christianson, an Indian woman of Minneapolis, Minnesota, was in contact with the Society at the same time.

Working through the Duluth Human Rights Committee, Mrs. Myers secured their help in obtaining a critical evaluation of the book; they then presented their findings and recommendations to the State's school administrators. The recommendation was for withdrawal of the book from use in the state schools. Another aspect of the committee's findings included criticism of the publishers, who, it was stated, committed "irregularities" in that the textbook had been published three times under different titles with substantial sections of the work remaining unchanged, and no notification having been given that there had been previous publication.

The Minnesota State Board of Education finally agreed to withdraw the book from use. Some of the complaints against this textbook involved charges of specific bias against the Indian community. These included terms depicting Indians as "lazy," "savages," and "dependent." Also objected to was a description of "wasteful slaughter" of buffalo and a characterization of Dred Scott, the subject of a United States Supreme Court decision on the disposition of runaway slaves, a "humble colored man."

A complete evaluation of this textbook, however, reveals much more than degrading descriptions of the Native people and a Negro man. It reveals inaccuracies, distortion of history, falsification of history in important areas, and a whole body of misinterpretation of Native life. Scholars of the Indian Historical Society have, therefore, done a thorough evaluation of the book, and present it herewith as an example of what is probably still being written about the American Indian in other State and United States history textbooks.

In the first case, objection is taken to the Minnesota State Seal, which is reproduced on page viii of the introduction. It is described thus: "The seal shows a pioneer farmer plowing on the banks of the Mississippi River, his gun and powder horn within reach on a near-by stump. He is looking back at an Indian on horseback who gallops away toward the setting sun." The American Indian in the State of Minnesota is part of the history. Conflict occurred because the settlers took Indian land, generally with the approval of the United States government, and such conflict was defensive on the part of the Indian. The connotation in the Seal is that the Indian had to go, was in the way of progress, and is now a part of the dead past. The Native Minnesotan is still very much alive, has made and continues to make great contributions to the people and the state. Unless the leaders of this state wish ancient animosities to continue, ancient differences to flourish, and old wounds to remain open, it is recommended that the Seal be changed. It is an insult to the Native American of Minnesota.

Page 1: Minnesota is eulogized as a state with enormous natural resources, whose gifts were taken by the settlers and upon the basis of which a great country flourished. "Since Mother Nature has given much help, earning a living in this great state has been made easier." Perhaps even the greater gift was that of the American Indian, who preserved the land, treasured its forests and streams, and showed the settlers its uses. This is error by omission.

Page 4: "However, the most important of Minnesota's resources is not the rich farm land, the minerals, or the forests. It is the people themselves... Her people have come from many lands." European immigrants are mentioned; the Old World as a whole is mentioned. But the Native Minnesotan is not mentioned at all. Continuing on page 6: "Happily some of the Old World folk songs, dances, games and holiday customs have been kept alive . . . " It should be stated that the only true Native customs, songs, and games have been kept alive by the Indian people, and that these should be made known, and treasured by all the people. This too, is gross error by omission.

Page 8: Improper comparison of personal characteristics and physical appearance is made. "The Sioux were expert horsemen, living largely on the prairies. They were taller and more graceful than the Chippewas and were quicker in their movements; but the Chippewas, living in the forests, were wonderful woodsmen and had greater strength and endurance." By whose standards are these comparisons made? Such generalizations are improper, are in poor taste, and cannot be justified.

Page 9: "There are many reminders of the red men still with us, the most common being the many beautiful Indian names." The best and most potent reminder is the fact that the Indians themselves are still with us. Page 11: "Before coming in contact with the white man, the Indian hunted to get a living and was content when he had enough food and clothing for himself and his family." This is an improper conjecture, certainly not based on fact. It does not explain the Indian's beautiful arts, his hide paintings, his inventive genius in bettering his life within the frame of his environment without destroying that environment, and his many technological inventions and discoveries.

Page 14: The Indian is blamed for the decimation of the buffalo on the Plains, in this statement: "The tongues were considered particularly choice, and, at this hunt 1375 tongues were brought into camp. Since such numbers were killed, it is no wonder that the buffalo is no longer found roaming our plains." This is a falsehood. The buffalo were slaughtered wholesale by white hunters. It is a well known fact that the Indians used every part of the buffalo.

Page 16: Describing the process of hulling rice, the author states: "Strange to say, this was always done by a man, and some say that this is the only kind of work which a male Indian was ever known to do." This is certainly an improper conjecture. And insulting as well. There is no evidence to support the misconception that Indian men were sluggards. An outrageous distortion is this: "Usually about a quarter of the hulls were still left on the grain, but neither these nor the dirt from the treading feet seemed to trouble the Indians, who never bothered to wash it before cooking it." This too is an insult.

Page 26: "The Indians held the Americans in greater respect than they held any other white people. Explorers tell us that when they referred to our warlike achievements, they said that the Americans were neither French nor Englishmen, but white Indians." There is no evidence for such a belief.

Page 140: One of the blackest cases of fraud ever perpetrated upon the Indian people is recounted, but with a disregard for the truth. The facts are these: When, in 1851, the Sisseton and Wahpeton bands of the Sioux people signed a treaty with the United States government, they were forced to cede all their lands in Iowa and Minnesota Territory to the federal government. For this, they were paid ten cents an acre. As part of this huge land grab, the government agreed to allow the sum of $275,000 for the two Bands, to permit them to remove to another area, to pay their expenses while awaiting removal (which was tentatively set at two years), and to allow them to subsist for the first year following removal. The $275,000 was to be paid to the chiefs, "Provided, that said sum shall be paid to the chiefs in such manner as they, hereafter, in open council shall request, and as soon after the removal of said Indians to the home set apart for them, as a necessary appropriation therefore shall be made by Congress." (Kappler's Treaties, page 589. Treaty of Traverse des Sioux) Representing the United States Government in negotiations and the signing of the treaty, were Luke Lea, Commissioner of Indian Affairs; and Alexander Ramsey, governor of the Territory and ex officio superintendent of Indian Affairs. At this time, the Sioux owned almost all of the State of Minnesota; whites owning only the merest fraction of these rich lands. Another treaty made with the Southern Sioux, took the remaining lands of the Indians, and for them an advance payment of $200,000 was to be made, in the same manner and for the same purpose as that paid to the Sisseton and Wahpetons.

According to an account given by Doane Robinson, in his "History of the Dakota or Sioux Indians, the following is what actually happened. We have little reason to doubt this highly prejudiced writer whose work is laced with degrading statements about the Indian people:

The amount for both sums was appropriated by Congress August 30, 1852, and the entire amount was paid over to Governor Ramsey. Since the beginning of white contact with the Sioux and the Chippewa, white traders had come in like beasts of prey, defrauding the Indian people in every way possible, selling them goods at exorbitant prices, and perfectly willing to wait for their money, certain that in some way at some time their money would come back to them tenfold. According to a statement by one writer, "Where so large a loaf was to be cut it may be depended upon that the traders were not idle. Members of these tribes owed the traders individual debts aggregating large amounts. Many of these debts were outlawed and many of the debtors were dead. But the traders held the tribe responsible for every one of these debts," and demanded that the entire tribe be penalized for the debts of a few.

The traders arrived at Traverse des Sioux, and at the time of the signing of the treaty, demanded that provision be made for payment of these sums in the treaties. The Indians refused, and requested that the government's advance payment be made to them "in open council," as above described. "Nevertheless," explains one writer, on the day when the Treaty was being signed, "one of the strangest occurrences of Indian-white relations took place. At the same time that the Indians were signing the treaty of Traverse des Sioux, in the same apartment where the treaty was signed and upon a board placed across the head of a barrel, but a yard or so distant from the table by which the commissioners sat, Major Joseph R. Brown presided over another paper. When the chiefs had signed the first (treaty) document, they were ushered to Brown. There they signed the other paper. Afterwards this second paper was known as the "Traders' Paper." It was an acknowledgement on the part of the Indians of the justice of the Traders' Claims, and agreement that these claims should be paid out of the money due them under the treaty." Upon learning of the existence of this paper, which they had signed believing it to be a copy of the treaty itself, the chiefs of the Sisseton and Wahpeton tribes made a formal protest to Governor Ramsey, stating in part that " . . . we did sign a paper which we supposed at the time to be a copy of the treaty or some other paper necessary to the carrying out of the agreement . . . in the sale of our lands. We have since learned with surprise and astonishment that we were deceived, misled, imposed upon and wronged by our pretended friends . . . We most solemnly protest that we never intended by any act of ours to set aside any such sum of money for the payment of assumed debts against our people, nor do we believe it possible for our people to owe one-fourth part the amount thus assumed to be due to our creditors aforesaid." (Senate Executive Document 29, 2nd session, 32nd Congress.)

By Act of August 30, 1852, Congress made the necessary appropriation of money to pay the Indians under the Treaties of Traverse des Sioux and Mendota. Commissioner Luke Lea's advice when he turned over the money, was to be "governed by sound discretion in its dispersion." These sums were then given over to Governor Ramsey. The law, however, was specific in its direction that the money due under the Treaties should be paid in the precise manner indicated therein, regardless of any other agreement. Ramsey then disbursed this money according to the schedule attached to the "Traders' Paper". But to settle his accounts with the department, he had to have a receipt from the Sisseton and the Wahpeton for the full amount of money due them. To obtain this receipt he visited the Indians and tried to get it from them. They were obstinate and would not sign the receipt. The money was distributed to the traders regardless, by Ramsey.

Time passed and the situation for the Indians became desperate. While waiting for their annuities they were poorly supplied with provisions and were soon at the point of starvation. Red Iron, a Wahpeton chief, in his desperation and conceiving that they were being imposed upon and cheated, organized a soldier's lodge among his young men, but Governor Ramsey promptly "broke him" of his chieftainship, appointed another chief in his stead, and had the old man arrested and imprisoned. Red Iron then signed a receipt, and eleven others followed, only two of whom were the signers of the Treaty and the Traders' Paper. Annuities were then distributed. Later, in reporting to Commissioner Lea on the disposition of the Indian funds, Ramsey stated that he had disbursed the greatest part of their funds to the traders, because, as he put it, the Indians were "notoriously fickle," and prone to come under the control of selfish persons.

Charges, containing many definite specifications, were later made against Governor Ramsey. A commission was appointed by the President to investigate. The findings stated that Governor Ramsey "was not warranted under the circumstances in paying over the money upon any authority derived from it, the Traders' Paper." The commissioners refused to justify the actions of Ramsey, and also refused to clear Governor Ramsey of the charges of maladministration made against him. Nevertheless, the Senate by resolution exonerated Ramsey. Reporting this matter some years later, Robinson noted the following:

"A bare recital of the facts set forth, which are the matters in the case, show Governor Ramsey, notwithstanding the exoneration by the Senate, morally reprehensible in his conduct. He was manifestly arbitrary, illegal and unjust in his action. In paying the traders from funds belonging to the Indians, Ramsey took no trouble to verify their claims, did not demand that their accounts be judicially examined (although the Indians insisted that this be done) and instead of attempting to protect the Indians, which they were officially bound to do, their whole action was based upon the protection of the traders at the Indians' expense. They must always bear a large share in the responsibility for the awful tragedy that followed."

Famine, starvation, the most inhuman sufferings beset these Native people as the result of delay in supplies being sent, Governor Ramsey holding up supplies in an attempt to "squeeze the Indians" into submission. There were delays in receipt of food supplies, refusals to pay the annuities on the basis of which the Indian lands had been taken. The most abject and dismal impoverishment resulted from the treatment accorded them by the Governor and officialdom of Minnesota. As a direct result of Ramsey's machinations, and in sheer desperation, because they had nothing to lose but their already destroyed lives, the American Indians took to arms, in a death-struggle to rid themselves of the incubus of such fraudulent inhuman Americans like Ramsey, who were speaking the highflown phrases of civilization and worship of their God, while stealing the food and funds, and defrauding the Indian people at every turn.

This in part, deleting the more specific instances of fraud practiced upon the Indians, is the story as it really happened. Now here following, is the manner in which this outrage is handled in the textbook under review:

"The traders took advantage of the fact that the Indians did not understand what they were doing and deceived the chiefs into signing another paper . . . (page 140). It has been said that Ramseys' life work was itself a cornerstone in the foundation of our great state. From the time when he was first appointed governor until his death in 1903, his life was one of whole-hearted intelligent service to Minnesota."

Indeed, in 1855, the Chippewa Indians were forced to give up their lands in northern Minnesota, and through this action, Chippewa valuable iron deposits, not yet known, came into possession of the white man. Too, the vast forest of America's finest pines came into white possession by this action. Another service rendered the whites of Minnesota was the treaty consummated by Ramsey with the Chippewas in 1863 (Old Crossing Treaty) by which millions of acres of the best wheat growing land in the world were acquired by the whites — Indian lands.

Page 157: Inaccurate data and the seeds of misconception are planted in a statement on this page, that, "When you remember, that for many years these savages had roamed the woods and plains wherever they wished, it is little wonder that the restraint of life on the reservations was very hard for them." These Indians were not nomads. They had settled lands, which included hunting grounds. The term "savage" is degrading. Page 157: "Always lazy, the Indians depended on the food and clothing, as well as money, supplied by the government according to the terms of the treaties." Page 460: The only reference to Indians of Minnesota today appears on this page. "Indians are increasing, at present there are about 13,000 in the state. Full citizenship is granted them, and they are free to live wherever they wish. Many leave the reservations for the cities, where it is easier to find employment."

This in part, is the story of the Minnesota state textbook, which for many years has inculcated a racist ideology in the schools of the state. During the process of discussing the recommendation to withdraw the book, an interesting observation was made by a member of a state educational committee, who said: "We must take considerable pains that we, as a committee, avoid being censors, telling teachers — professionals in their field — what they can teach and what textbooks to use." At first blush, this certainly sounds highly progressive, a defense of free speech, in fact. Upon closer examination, however, it is nothing but an apologists' creed, insisting that the racist and prejudicial instructional materials have a right to remain in the schools, to breed more racists and supremacists among the children of this country. The fact is, that the State Board of Education in Minnesota does indeed administer "approved lists" of books for use in the schools. This in itself is a form of choice, and if it be called censorship, then the whole fabric of our society ideologically ought to be examined, to see who is censoring whom. Another interesting feature of this issue was the position taken by the American Civil Liberties Union, which was that of opposing censorship in the interests of "free speech" on the case. There is no trouble in getting racist literature into the schools. The problem is in getting the truth into the school books, and into the minds of the school children.

*THE CASE OF THE SUPPLEMENTARY TEXTBOOK

"LAND OF THE OAKS"

Published in 1953 by the Oakland, California Unified School District. Reprinted 1955 and 1959. *By James Harlow.* 248 pp. Junior High School level.

The book was a local history. It had been in use for 11 years, and remained in use due to the fact that the city Board of Education required local history to be taught. The first step, upon receiving a complaint (from a teacher in this case), was to obtain the book, read and evaluate it. This was done.

Upon corroboration as to the degrading quality of the book, the Society sent the following letter to the Superintendent of the Oakland Unified School District —

Dear Sir:
Attached is a request for reconsideration of the book, "Land of the Oaks," which we submit according to the procedures set by the district. Please consider this as a formal complaint and protest against this book, and against its further use in the schools. Our attention was called to this junior high school supplementary textbook by several teachers in the Oakland district. Unfortunately while we have evaluated all the books submitted to the State Curriculum Commission, and have presented our evaluations, we have not yet had an opportunity to examine the books on the district level.

This would be an enormous task. We should be able to depend upon the general understanding of our educators NOT to allow prejudicial, uninformed, degrading materials to be accepted for classroom use. But in this case, we find to our dismay that such a book has indeed been in use in the Oakland school system for 11 years. This book misinterprets Indian history and customs. We believe it degrades the Indian people as to their history, culture, and traditions.

As you know, the book does not presume to be factual. It is a so-called "light" treatment of Oakland history. But we think it misses the mark in this direction as well. It is not good literature. It is not humor. It is a vulgarization of history and does not belong in the classroom. Of course, this is our opinion. But we ask you to note that this Society is comprised of Indian historians, schoolteachers, professors of history and anthropology, and Indian people in every trade and profession. This evaluation is a serious effort to correct an injustice. This book is an injustice against our people.

It is true, that we Indians are a little late in the task of preserving our history. But you educators certainly have a responsibility to ALL the people, to present the truth and not a distortion.

Yours sincerely,
RUPERT COSTO, a Cahuilla man, President

September 7, 1966   PHILIP GALVAN, an Ohlone man, Secretary

EVALUATION: "LAND OF THE OAKS"

Submitted by the American Indian Historical Society, an All-Indian educational, cultural, and historical organization, with National headquarters at The Chautauqua House, 1451 Masonic Avenue, San Fransisco, California, 94117.

GENERAL: This book contains no factual material concerning the

American Indians in the Oakland area. No sources are quoted. No references are given. No evidence is submitted to support the propaganda material contained therein. It purports to be a departure "to some extent, from the usual social studies textbook, in that it is light and conversational in approach; it deals with the anecdotal and humorous phases of local history, as well as the factual; and it is colored in places so as to secure more dramatic reading." (From the preface)

This statement appears to be a plea for the reader's indulgence as to any possible errors contained in the book. But the approach is not merely "light"; it is facetious as well as insulting. This approach is ill suited to such a subject as the Indians of America and their role in our history. Especially when it is tinctured with outright misinterpretation of Indian life and history. To display prejudice is bad enough. But to try and be funny about it adds insult to error.

SPECIFIC ERRORS: Page 16: "They (the Indians) liked the land for the same reason the animals had. The weather was warm and comfortable. There was plenty of food for everybody." The comparison between "Indians and animals" is degrading to the Indians as a people, as a race, and as individuals. All human beings have "animal" instincts and needs. Yet textbooks do not make such comparisons about other peoples.

"They built their village around a little creek they named Temescal. Today the creek is known as Lake Temescal." (Page 16) The word Temescal is not an Indian word of California linguistic origin. It is an Aztec word adopted by the Spanish.

Page 17: "These early Indians were often called Digger Indians. The were called "diggers" because the women and children were always digging around in the ground for seeds and bugs. The bugs were roasted and salted and eaten. They were very delicious, if you happen to like roasted bugs." It is assumed that this statement was designed to evoke indulgent laughter. But further consideration will reveal such a device engenders a supremacist psychosis in those who find it possible to laugh at such a display of arrogant provincialism. It is immaterial whether the author meant it to be taken in that manner. It suffices to damn it as an insidious display of innate prejudice and inexcusable ignorance, in the very image developed in readers. No one needs to be a gourmet to know about the so-called "bugs" eaten by the Indian people. One can get the special and rare variety of grasshoppers which the Indians enjoyed for $2 a one-ounce can today. Or snails, or certain insect larvae, highly prized by gourmets. When Americans saw the

Indians eating tripe, they were disgusted and called it "savagery," and made this term a formal description of the Native people in their diaries and books. When the Spaniards saw the East Bay Indians eating sturgeon roe, they were horrified and called it indelicate and uncivilized. Now we call it caviar and pay $5 a half pound for it. What is it to be "strange"? What is it to be acceptably "normal," on the other hand? WHO is strange? Our own Indian people, who lived well, simply, peacefully? Or the white Americans, who make sophisticated war and play the expert as to the mores of modern culture? What sort of a smirking, self-satisfied civilization has been made here in OUR country, that such insults may be put in print and fed to young people as instructional materials?

On the same page we find, "The Digger Indians liked to take life easy." There was no such tribe as Digger. This is a term of insult and ought not to be used. Indian life was not "easy" nor was the native lazy. He worked hard and well, and had a highly organized life, or he could not have survived in decency, in that type of society and in that environment. "Civilization develops only when people travel about and learn new things from other people. The Digger Indians were happy with things the way they were." The oversimplification as to how civilization develops is impermissible in school use. The Indians traveled as far as Lower California, Arizona, and Nevada. They learned new skills from different tribes. Yet they did not develop the particular type of civilization represented by the Spaniards and Americans. They didn't need it in their economy; when they were introduced to it, they didn't like its philosophy of greed and selfishness.

On Page 18: "When winter came and the cold winds started to blow, they covered their bodies with big gobs of mud. They left the mud on all winter, only replacing from time to time what had fallen off." This is a misinterpretation of Indian customs. The body was covered with mud in certain ceremonies, in certain rituals, in an effort to hide from the white man's depredations, and as a cleansing agent At no time was "mud" utilized to keep the body warm, nor was it ever left on the body for any length of time. Again, "His mud suit would just wash away and leave him all chilly." This is supposed to be funny. It probably does evoke titters among the students, who thereafter have left in their minds certain ideological elements of prejudice and racial superiority. But this type of humor, which degrades a whole people, is positively indecent in an educator and absolutely inadmissible. "The women soaked the acorn flour in water mixed with ashes. This took the bitter taste away." Ashes were not used in taking the bitter taste away. The process was LEACHING, one of the outstanding, unique achievements of Indians of California.

Page 20: "Every time you dig into the ground, you are likely to bump into something you could use to decorate your house on Hallowe'en." This refers to the multitude of shell mounds (refuse heaps) and Indian burial grounds existing in the Bay Area. It is an invitation to unqualified students to dig in archaeological sites. It is also an invitation to desecrate Indian burial grounds and cemeteries. Enough of this has been done already — to the sorrow of the Indian people and the loss of priceless objects of antiquity, without inviting a project in this direction. It is also in outrageously bad taste. "An Indian village was a rather strange looking thing. It looked like a bunch of bumps, about five feet high, in the ground. These 'bumps' were actually huts made of mud and branches. When the rains came, the branches kept the mud from sliding away altogether. Still, the houses must have become pretty soft and mushy. That didn't seem to bother the Indians. After all, they were covered with mud, so they probably felt very much at home." What is strange? To whom? The huts were ingeniously constructed of hard oak poles, tree branches and clay. It simply served their purposes. There is a wealth of information to be gained from a study of American Indian homes and shelters, information which educates the student as to the remarkable history of mankind. The tone of lightness and levity at the close of this statement is a literary achievement which should be accorded a major place in a handbook of defamation.

Page 21: "It seems like an awfully complicated way of taking a bath, but it was probably better than no bath at all." The steam bath is an Indian invention now utilized by the whole world. Indians had streams and lakes in which to bathe and they did, as often each day as time permitted. "If there was any trouble with a neighboring village, the men marched off to battle." This is another oversimplification of Indian history and culture. It is so simple it is wrong. Only as a last resort did the East Bay Indians engage in "battle." And then first of all, in the event of any trouble, they called a council and discussed the matter, considering possibilities of arbitration. "The women, on the other hand, had most of the hard work to do. Papa Indian would go out in the woods and kill a big deer. He would drag it home, drop it proudly at his wife's feet; then his work was done. Mama Indian had to skin the deer, cure it, cook it, and figure out some way of making a new pair of pants out of the buckskin for papa." This is another vulgarization of Indian life, degrading, insulting. It isn't even funny. "At the

same time she had to keep an eye on at least a half dozen little Indians
who were forever dropping off cliffs, getting lost, or catching whooping
cough. In her spare time, mama had to make enough acorn flour to last
through the winter." Indian children were disciplined, highly knowledgeable about the woods and their country. They never had whooping cough, which is a whiteman's disease. Cooked acorn is usually made
to last for the next meal. Only the acorn nuts were stored, and they
could be stored for as long as two years. Indian ingenuity in construct-
ing their storage bins might have been of far more interest to the
students than this silly attempt at humor.

"The Indians could neither read nor write." NO people in that
stage of society had writing. The word "could" leads to misconceptions.
Neither could 99% of the Spaniards read and write, and THEY had
the art of writing. The '49'ers are estimated to have been 75% illiterate.
"It might be that the Indians were so untidy that germs were afraid
of them. They seemed to keep healthy in spite of the lives they led.
But then their lives were such that they had plenty of good food, clean
water, exercise, fresh air, and sleep." Despite the modifying last part
of this paragraph, the introductory sentence is degrading. First, Indians
were not at all "untidy." No one who has seen an Indian oldtime hut
or shelter would believe that. The earth floor was kept fastidiously
clean. Every cooking and craft-making utensil was in its place and
ready for use. Does the author really believe that the porcelain bathtub
is the hallmark of culture?

On page 23: "If an Indian got sick, he was almost sure to die, since
little was known about the proper treatment of illness and injury."
The Indian knowledge of medicinal herbs and plants are too well
known to make comment on this inaccuracy. Indians had a longer life
span than the white man has today. They had few if any diseases. They
had a knowledge of treating the special conditions which might threaten
their health, such as accidents, fractures, eating improper foods, or
poisonous snake bite. They had a superb knowledge of botany. Diseases
introduced by the white man, however, were of such a virulent nature,
that natural immunity could not function, and Indian methods were incapable of treating them. "He would wear a horrible false face, sing
spooky songs, and do weird dances, all of which were guaranteed to scare
the wits out of any evil spirit." This description of shamanistic methods
is incorrect and degrading. It displays ignorance of an Indian religious
ritual. Too, what is weird? What is strange? Modern women's painted
faces are weird to Indians even today. A legend which the author attempts to palm off as authentically Indian, is not a legend of these

people. Titled "How Fire Came to Earth," it is some white man's phonied-up story as to what HE thinks the legend should be.

Page 25: "Communications and transportation. The Indians didn't bother much with either of these important things." The trade routes of the California and other Indian tribes are too well known to give citations confirming that they had long and well-established routes — taking them hundreds of miles to other tribal lands for trade, as well as for special observances. Settlers who stole Indian land and made war upon the people have good reason to know the Indian system of communication, which were superb for that day and under those conditions. Our superhighways of today are largely built upon the same routes as the Indian trails and roads. A misstatement is that "The chief would send out a boy with six small pebbles to give to each of the other chiefs." No pebbles were used. Knotted strings were generally taken, as well as other devices.

Page 26: A distortion of Indian life is contained in another statement. "If, for example, a house caught fire, all the Indians would run over to help people get out. Then they would all stand around chatting pleasantly and watching the house burn. After the fire, they would all help clean up the mess and start to build a new house." Fire was one thing under supreme control of the natives. Forests were scrupulously protected against spontaneous fires by controlled burning of brush. The accidental fires of Indian homes was practically unknown. They would hardly be likely to stand around in the event of such a fire. The entire village and all the surrounding villages would be out immediately, to control such a disaster. The same distortion is shown in this statement: "The men of the village were the policemen and the soldiers. It was their job to protect the village, women and children, from all dangers." There were no policemen, and no group or individual had that role to play in ancient Indian life of the California region.

Page 28: Demeaning statements about the Indians are made again and again, such as this — "They never tried to make their villages more beautiful. They never bothered to learn newer, better ways of doing things." In fact, they had the entire country filled with the beauty of God and nature. Their hills, clean and maintained by themselves, were lovely to behold. Their meadows, streams, valleys and forests, were works of art hanging upon the walls of their natural home. They lived and thrived in all this beauty. They appreciated it, loved it, preserved and cared for it; they cherished it, and enhanced it. Care of the forests, streams and meadows, is an Indian art only now acquiring the appreciation of others. Conservation was an Indian mode of life only now being considered the most effective method of preserving our remaining natural beauty. See what we have made possible for you to have, and look what you have done with it! The Indian people had an avid taste for knowledge. They continually developed their knowledge of the woods, shrubs, flowers, bushes, trees. They had a name for each plant, leaf, berry, flower, tree. And all the varieties of each of these received its own name in each Indian tongue. Their languages were complex, capable of a multitude of shades of meaning and inflection, rivaling the English tongue in many respects.

This book says, "They went further back into the wilderness where they could be by themselves," instead of telling the truth, that they were driven, and pushed, and hounded out of their lands and homes by the whites, Spaniard, Mexican, and American. This is a matter of record, which has resulted in litigation. Such cases at court have produced volumes of evidence proving exactly which areas the Indians lived in and possessed, according to tribe. Such men as Dr. A. L. Kroeber and Dr. Robert Heizer gave sworn evidence to this effect.

Page 29: An outrageously insulting remark is made in these words — "If the white man had not come to this part of the country, the Indians would have gone on living peacefully through the years, sitting alongside their mud houses, eating clams and throwing the shells on top of grandpa's grave." If the white man had not driven us out of our land and our homes, we would have developed, in the next hundred years, a unique and progressive society. Probably without procelain bathtubs, television sets, and sophisticated wars; but certainly a life well suited to the human being in the eyes of God and nature. This slanderous and degrading statement and image given of the Indian family, is inaccurate in every respect.

To summarize, the mass of materials readily available about the Indians of the Oakland-East Bay area had not even been touched in preparation for this textbook. Descendants of these tribes still live in this area, their ancient homeland. The secretary of this Indian Historical Society, who is a signer of this evaluation, is one such descendant, an Ohlone Indian whose people lived here until the white man drove them out. They still live here, the proud descendants of Oakland's only native people.

Adopted by the Executive Council,
American Indian Historical Society
December 6, 1968

XI

A Commentary on Curriculum

– I –

THE PUBLIC SCHOOL SYSTEM

TEXTBOOKS AND THE AMERICAN INDIAN has concentrated attention on the basic materials of instruction for a specific reason. At this point in the history of the American educational system, the most important question is one of content. Methodology, new concepts, the discovery or inquiry approach, and the new media are splendid assets for the use of the teacher, and will make the learning process a much more successful experience for the student — IF content exists which provides the materials of learning, forming the meat and bones around which the new methodolgy is structured.

It is the CONTENT of education which is at this time under fire. The content of education makes the dominant whites of our society the class which controls ideology, and slants history to their needs and goals. We are not talking about the average citizen of today. We are talking of those who control and dominate our society. They stand most to benefit from having history tilted in their direction. It is now too late to take back our lands, to bring back our dead, or to retrieve our culture. The dominant society, controlled by money-making king-pins of greed, have ruined it for ever.

We are interested in what shall be done now. And what we believe should be done now is to tell the whole truth in the books that are being used by children all over this land, as they study the history

of our country, state, city, and the world at large. You can work out
all kinds of innovative media, methodolgy, to put learning into the
brain of a student efficiently. But if you cannot be permitted to put
the whole TRUTH, all the information regarding the truth, into the
brain of the student, you will not cause profound understanding about
the past. And then there will be no understanding of how to deal with
the present.

Thus, it is in curriculum that the men are separated from the boys.
WHAT will be taught in the various grade levels, from kindergarten
up to high school and beyond? The question is not so much what will
be the structure of the courses, but WHAT the courses will be. Creative
teachers and professionals, and even the ordinary average Americans
can be trusted to come up with all sorts of innovative ideas as to methodology and media. The question is, who shall determine the CONTENT?

Five years ago, the American Indian Historical Society came forward
with a plan for the study of mankind, his history upon the earth. It
was suggested that this study should begin in the first grade. More
could be done to develop an understanding of the many races of man
in this way, than is being done today, certainly. To date, we have seen
one small book, which seems headed in this direction. Its title is "Looking at Man's Past," by Hart Stilwell. This is a good beginning, and we
wish the publishers would do more in this direction. But the books
will not be able to help the situation if they are not incorporated into
the curriculum.

Certainly, this Indian Society has not been the first, nor are we the
only ones to realize that curriculum changes must come, and quickly.
Committees, commissions, task forces, and special research projects have
been organized and funded with huge amounts of money to work out
some changes in curriculum. If you read these thousands of pages of
reports, you will find few if any concrete suggestions for curriculum
change. You will find high-flown platitudes, philosophy about methodology, conceptual approaches and multi-media. The researchers are
striving mightily to find some magic formula with which to transform
our current dead curriculum into something filled with life and blood.
We have read dozens of reports. Not one has any concrete suggestions.
A suggestion made by many scholars, has been the teaching of anthropology as a science in the early grades. In California, one such program
was funded, researched, and completed. A unit in anthropology was
developed. Studying the unit, one is forced to the conclusion that what
must result is to make avid pot hunters out of junior high school students, and nothing more.

A singularly fine example of new methodology as applied to the study of civics and citizenship has come from Ginn and Company, in two books which have been evaluated in this Study. The method is good, and it is to be expected that the students — provided they have a good instructor — will come out of such a class with a deeper knowledge of this subject. Only one thing is missing: the inclusion in this study, of the American Indian. So here again we come back to the matter of content. It is not our place to come forward here with a proposal for new curriculum. But this much we can say: whatever the curriculum may develop, the Native American must be a living part of the study of American history, social sciences, citizenship, and world history, from the first grade on.

For example, in the early grades, the study of the history of man would include the American Indian as the Native in his own land, his origins, his development, discovery of the land, and settlement of the land. Many schools have the study of "communities" in one of the early grades. It should be possible to include a developmental history of the community in America, including that of the Natives of this land. When discussing a unit on homes and domiciles, an enriching experience would be the study of the development of homes in America, including that of the variety of Native homes, settlers' homes, homes in the south after western technology was learned by such tribes as the Cherokees, homes in the north and northwest before white contact and after. When discussing local or state history, a unit should certainly be devoted to the story of the Native in that community, or that state. This is not currently being done. The Native history is spliced in here and there, fragmented in such a way that no real understanding occurs.

In the junior and upper high school levels, certainly more complex subjects should be offered to the students. The study of anthropology, the newest developments of that science, should be made available to the student. The uses of anthropology in the scientific study of man's history should be the emphasis, instead of the pot-hunter's dream of "excavating" bones and fragments. It is forgotten by many anthropologists (though certainly not all) that the Native American is still here, alive, remembering his ancestry, and that it is certainly in poor taste to put him under a "pin" like a butterfly, for the sordid curiosity and exotic edification of those who delight in the unique for its own sake, without scientific emphasis in the acquisition of knowledge.

The educational system is currently floundering in a sea of conferences, workshops, seminars, and "studies," about education. Nowhere else is there seen such lack of a sense of direction. In no other area

can one see the same errors committed again and again, in these very
researches, workshops and studies. One study, for example, (to be exact,
the Missouri Human Rights Commission study), has produced a serious
evaluation of the minorities in textbooks. Frankly, the emphasis is entirely upon the Negro in the textbooks. The American Indian appears
only in one sentence and in connection with one book. Too, the Indian
in the textbooks is treated through a reprint of an article appearing in
THE INDIAN HISTORIAN titled "Our Inaccurate Textbooks." We
are glad to note that this is being recognized, but the Missouri Commission on Human Rights should have been able to do some independent
work in this connection. At the same time, this commission has included
in its own evaluations, as part of a criteria, this section: On page 6
of the study, the criteria in American history is given. Number One
of the criteria is — IMMIGRATION. Other criteria are: slavery, resistance to slavery, reconstruction, segregation, Black self-awareness
and protest. Where is the understanding of the BEGINNINGS, and
the ORIGINS of this nation! The same errors, but in a different way,
are made by the Blacks as have been made by others. Despite the good
intentions and the lack of self-interest on the part of this group, they
have fallen prey to the usual ignorance, the usual dominant ideology,
and what is the difference, anyhow, between dominant white and dominant black ideology? The Indian has never attempted to exert a dom-
ineering position in any field of this nation's growth. A scholar would
take the same point of departure.

The Minnesota studies are by far the most fabulous in all the nation.
Thousands of pages of reports have been produced, in connection
with every phase of education, minorities, Blacks, Indians, and so on.
Concrete action for the correction of admittedly inequitable conditions
are still in the planning stages. But, under the pressure of a group of
Minnesota Indian people, the Human Rights Committee has come
forward and removed a most degrading book from school use.

At some point in the current investigative process, a decision as to
emphasis must be made. There is no course other than to decide how
to change content, how to change curriculum; and how to introduce
new and more historically truthful materials into content and curriculum. The social studies particularly suffer from an absolute lack
of relevance to the world of today. The problems of society, as handled
in the textbooks today, are treated with velvet gloves, as though fearful
of injuring the sensibilities of the young student. This is the same
young student who has grown accustomed, not only to space exploration
in all its many scientific aspects as seen on television, in cartoons, and

in the newspapers; but has also been subjected to television and radio programs dealing with rape and incest, murder and criminality. There is nothing to fear, so far as our youth is concerned. They will separate the good from the bad, the decent from the indecent, the valuable from the worthless. We have today the most progressive, alive, creative and intelligent youth this country has ever known. We are short-changing them in education, with our flaccid content and our unimaginative curriculum. If, for example, we tell them the truth about the gold rush, they will get the point, never fear.

—II—

THE BUREAU OF INDIAN AFFAIRS SCHOOLS

The only federally-controlled educational system in this nation is that directed by the Bureau of Indian Affairs, the so-called Indian schools, both boarding and day schools, from elementary to high school levels. The question as to how this fits into the democratic concept of education has been raised by the American Indian Historical Society already, and has been answered: It does not fit. Nevertheless, to change these schools, a proposal has been to put them under the direction of the tribal governing bodies and the Indian communities, under boards of education controlled by the people themselves. The situation at present is that the BIA controls the schools, the curriculum, the choice of textbooks, and the students themselves. According to a report by Dr. Charles Zellers, who is the current head of the BIA Education Division, these steps have been taken to institute new programs to help remedy the admittedly intolerable situation in Indian education: The Rough Rock residential school, at Chinle, Arizona, which has about 200 children from beginners through fourth grade living in dormitories during the school year. To alleviate homesickness, Indian adults are invited to tell them stories and to speak to them. (This is small comfort to the youngster who longs to go home.) Second, five residential schools near Tuba City in Arizona have set up homemaking centers to teach upper elementary students such things as sewing, nutrition, child care, sanitation, grooming, and other useful but non-academic subjects. (How this will solve the vast wasteland of educational failure is not stated.)

Third: The Sequoyah residential high school at Tahlequah, Oklahoma, is housing its 400 students in small residential units to try to eliminate the impersonality of living in a large dormitory. (We assume

this will help social studies, (but it won't help the youth to learn.)
Fourth, the Wingate residential high school for 1,000 students at Fort
Wingate, New Mexico is allowing the students more independence and
freedom to study. (How did they study before?) Fifth, Pima Central
school at Sacaton, Arizona, an elementary day school, has begun a
"widespread campaign" among its 300 pupils to improve their education through seeing and doing. They are taking "journeys to nearby
canyons," preceded by intensive study about the rocks and rock layers
to be seen there. This is the sort of "innovative" programming being
discussed with such weighty scholarship by the Education division of
the Bureau of Indian Affairs.

Late in 1968, the BIA Education Division started a new program
to improve curriculum and education generally, in the Bureau-directed
schools. Then began the biggest farce in BIA history, full of choice
scholarly verbiage, programs such as "Project Necessities," meetings and
conferences, groups of Indians brought in to "consult" about education.
Many of these people were Indian scholars with so much more expertise
and scholarship than those they were listening to, that the whole situation was ludicrous. The BIA has never recognized the development
of Indian scholars and scholarship. It has never given leadership and
permitted initiative to those Indians who are scholars. They are usually
called in as "consultants" while the whites hold the reins of power,
name the salaried people, have the final decision-making powers, and
are in fact, touted as the "experts" on Indian history, culture and current affairs. When, early in 1969, a group of outspoken Indian scholars
arrived at a conference called by the Education Divison, and spoke their
minds, demanding that the CONTENT of education be discussed, they
were met by stony silence. The question was, at this conference: Do
we continue to teach the children in the BIA schools that their grand-
fathers were savages, primitive people, unwashed and brutish? Do
we continue to teach them that Columbus discovered America? Do we
continue to avoid the truth about such things as the massacre of Indian
people at Fallen Timbers, or Wounded Knee, or the gold rush? Those
who raised such questions also submitted counter proposals to those
of the Bureau experts. The Indian scholars present rejected the BIA
proposals of Project Necessities, and submitted an excellent workable
program of their own. This was immediately scuttled by the Bureau
officialdom in the education division. Those who were responsible
for raising the question of truth in the textbooks, presenting a concrete program in education for Indian children, soon received a "Dear
John" letter from Commander Charles Zellers, whose official title is

Deputy Commissioner for Education of the BIA. This is the reaction to Indian "participation and leadership" so far as the Bureau-directed Indian schools are concerned.

Books used in the Indian schools by the Bureau are generally the same as those used in public schools. Here the similarity ends. In the public school system, there is a Curriculum Commission which approves books, discusses and evaluates them. There are Boards of Education which do the same. In the BIA schools, the agent or superintendent makes these choices, and he need not ask ANYONE. The chances are that this individual is not even an educated man. Those in the BIA schools who are Indian scholars, have little or no power. There is now another group of Indian "consultants" who have been roped in to lend an aura of Indianness to the playful exercises of the Bureau's education division.

A most enlightening document was issued by the BIA education division, in January, 1969. It had to do with curriculum development, and was penned by Thomas R. Hopkins, Chief, Division of Curriculum Development, BIA. Mr. Hopkins had these choice pronunciamentos in his paper: He defines curriculum "in the sense used by the Bureau of Indian Affairs Office of Education," as the "planned experiences which are designed to produce the specific outcomes or goals of a school." What, then, are the specific goals or outcomes of Bureau-directed schools? Mr. Hopkins is silent on this point, and one has the right to conjecture that it is no different than it has been in the past —to try to make good little white boys and girls of the Indian children. The Bureau has commissioned Dr. John Bryde, eminent churchman and scholar, to produce a textbook titled "MODERN INDIAN PSYCHOLOGY." This experimental book is reviewed herein. But the emphasis still is upon experiment with Indian children, not with hard-core education, the best education, the most skillful teachers, the highest quality books and most enlightened curricula.

And so, this is the Bureau's understanding of curriculum, in the words of Hopkins. All other scholars understand curriculum to be a simple course of STUDY, in a school or department of a school, necessarily with the objective to impart knowledge. Further examination of the ideas and philosophy of Mr. Hopkins, who heads up the division which presumably will improve curriculum, are these: Discussing the fact that students at a BIA school must have a certain minimum of blood quantum in order to be admitted, he states: "This means that it can be reasonably anticipated that the concepts of a child in a Bureau school will differ markedly from the middle-class child of urban America regarding their respective world-views. This establishes a cross-cultural function in all curriculum areas." Why is the middle-class child of urban America taken ᵜas a cross cultural function? And what is the meaning of this gobbledegook? Discussing achievement tests, Mr. Hopkins reveals the fact that "the curricula to which the Indian child has been exposed has not bridged the differences between the Indian child and his middle-class counterpart." Quite obviously, the BIA goal is to press the Indian child into the mold of the American white middle-class child.

Discussing I. Q. studies, those chosen and treated by Mr. Hopkins have been long discredited and outdated, but he insists that ". . . serious work needs to be done in order to assist American Indian children to think in such a manner that the results will be effective in the non-Indian American society." Quite the contrary, the Indian child needs to be effective in ALL society, to have a world-view which gives him the advantages of knowledge, and education. He will decide, soon enough, what society he wishes to be a part of—the Indian society which is his by right, or the American urban middle-class society, into which the BIA is attempting to push him. Insult is added to injury when treating cross cultural function, and after examining the Indian child under a psychological microscopic slide, Mr. Hopkins states, "The above mentioned characteristics of the Indian child and youth cast a definite negative profile as far as the Indian child and school success are concerned. It can be interpreted as a basic estrangement between the school and the Indian child which has never been resolved by the development of an effective curriculum. It is this challenge that makes the Curriculum Division's responsibilities take a positive turn." Besides being pure verbosity, this concept relegates the Indian child to the continuing posture of a "negative profile," which must be overcome by the BIA Curriculum department, and Mr. Hopkins.

Mr. Hopkins' discussion of art and the American Indian, art and the educational process, and the uses of art in culture and education, is so much a mixture of sheer hogwash and complete lack of knowledge that it bears consideration here as an example of the Bureau's stupidity in the direction of education: "Since art," opines Hopkins, "is a general strength, and a universal human characteristic that can transcend cultural differences, it can be used immediately for the improvement of Indian education curricula practices." This concept of art is general and mundane enough to pass it by, but the following statement clears up the Hopkins ideas in this direction: "Art lends itself to immediate use because it is less structured scientifically and its content is easier to communicate to the senses of the human." This statement is at first blush quite innocuous also. But upon examination, it does not bear the scrutiny of scholarship. In the first place, art is one of the most differentiated of characteristics. It is what makes a people unique, different, such as the Eskimo as compared with the Pueblo. In the second statement, he relegates art to the senses alone, as if to say, Well, these people are stupid, they can only "feel" instead of think. Let's reach them through the senses. Hopkins does not recognize, or forgets, or fails to understand, that art for the Indian was and is a philosophy of life, a way of looking at life, his religion shown in ritual through music, chant and sings. It was and is a highly complex part of the culture, the finest contribution the Indian has made to the world, which is still unrecognized in all its facets and nuances. It is further not understood, whether these people are talking about art in a developmental sense, or in a cultural sense, which is not necessarily a bridge to cross-cultural understanding.

It is certainly true, that the proper uses of the arts of the Native American can improve the entire educational process. Such uses involve the instruction of a superb master of the arts, and a knowledge of the various arts themselves. The philosophy understood and implicit in the arts of the Indian can be brought into the educational process only by an Indian master of his art. This, however, will certainly not "bridge the gap" between the Indian child and the urban middle-class American white child. If anything, it will broaden the gap, because the arts of the Indian depend upon his philosophy and lifeways, his thought and the meaning of his race; and this has nothing to do with middle-class America, child or adult.

The report, plans, "position papers" of the Bureau of Indian Affairs education division are so filled with mere verbiage, that one sees immediately that here is no scholarship at work, but just another bureaucracy spouting unintelligible phrases and actually doing nothing to change the educational situation.

The fact remains, that the Bureau-directed schools have the worst and most outdated textbooks and instructional materials. They permit Indian students to be subjected to the most outrageous research programs and psychological surveys. Only the innovations and leadership of the Indian people themselves can change the situation, by setting an example and showing that when left alone the Native Americans can again have the superb educational institutions once owned by the Cherokees, the Choctaws and the Delawares, before their schools and governments were destroyed by federal order.

–III–

NATIVE AMERICAN STUDIES

An encouraging development in the colleges and universities is the student youth movement which has introduced Native American Studies programs in these institutions of learning. It is currently estimated that there are more than 70 such departments in schools of higher learning in the nation. Usually, these are part of the Schools of Ethnic Studies, organized as the result of Black and Mexican-American demands.

These programs generally have been set up with four to six courses in anthropology, Indian history and current affairs, Native American arts, and related subjects. Because of the requirements that there be sufficient student enrollment to permit the hiring of an instructor for any course of study, many colleges have offered the same courses available in such departments as anthropology, history and sociology, to the Native American Studies departments. Thus, the instructor splits his time between his "home" department and the new course in the ethnic studies school. Wherever possible, a director is named to administer the Native American Studies program and often this director splits his time administratively and scholastically. The program is still in its experimental stage, and changes will undoubtedly be made to improve and enlarge the courses as well as the departments. Classes in these departments are as a rule more free as to student participation than those in the usual colleges and universities, the students raising question and opening discussion at will. Academic freedom is the desire of students who enroll in these classes, but the courses are still not structured in such a way as to encourage academic achievement.

One feature of the new "Studies" departments is that there is no consideration given to the scholastic and academic goals of the courses. Very soon, the student begins to wonder "what am I going to do with this credit when I graduate? Will graduate schools accept these credits? Will I be able to qualify in the normal professions following graduation? Will my qualifications be accepted in teaching, business, or engineering?" These are very important questions for the student who is not in school to exercise his "rights," or to gain a well-rounded education for the sake of education itself. The student knows that sooner or later the school days will be over, and he will be confronted with the need to qualify for a job. Thus far, to our knowledge, no comprehensive survey has been made as to the areas in which graduates of ethnic studies schools will be able to make a place for themselves in the everyday, mundane world of business or the professions. However, it is a certainty that this old world is changing, that new fields are opening up, and it is not inconceivable that some of these new fields may require the services of one skilled in the knowledge of anthropology, Indian history and culture, and Indian arts. At the same time, it should be recognized if it is not already, that some exact science is necessary for any profession and for every field. If the schools of ethnic studies fail to provide courses in such fields, they are doomed to failure.

More than a year has passed since the first Native American Studies departments were formed. It is now known that there are just not enough instructors or directors available to fill the posts required by so many rapidly growing new departments in so many colleges and universities. This, in itself, may be a source of professional activity, particularly for the Native American people themselves, once they graduate and qualify as instructors and professors. Just the same, if one considers the absolute maximum of such jobs available in the foreseeable future, it would be not more than 500 openings of this type. Thousands, however, are now enrolling in the new courses. The problem will have to be faced soon.

Far more important, however, than the question of the future of the student enrolled in these courses, is the matter of improvement in the field of curriculum and course content. Largely, the new schools of ethnic studies have left intact the entire educational system, with all of its weaknesses and white-dominated philosophy. In the departments of anthropology, history, social sciences, all the humanities, there has not been a single important change to our knowledge. The same books are being used; the same methodology is in full sway; and the same professors are spouting the same tired old platitudes as they have in the past. The same situation existing hertofore, exists today, in which the professor does a minimum of teaching, the teaching assistants taking over the burden of the actual daily grind of student preparation and instruction. The professors are usually busy preparing to publish, for it is said, the modern professor must "publish or perish." There are quite a few professors who have learned to exploit the students, who are set to work in research, typing, and as errand boys for the professor in his publishing program. The emphasis, which should be on help to the student, instruction of the student, preparing the student for his chosen work, is everywhere else but where it should be.

This is the system that should be challenged. It is not happening. Consequently, the time is fast approaching when the oldtime instructors and professors will see that the new schools of ethnic studies, and the new Native American Studies departments are after all not so bad, and may be even a Godsend. As to the American Indian in these departments, and the need to change radically the academic thought and content of education in this field, they have us caught in a bag. We are, by our own efforts, stuck in a nice little cupboard, isolated from the rest of the educational community, in our own cosy little ethnic studies courses, and will be (if this continues) no trouble whatsoever to the other departments. It will take a little while for the militant students to come to grips with this phase of the situation. It will take a little longer for them to proceed with any program in that direction. But, what will be realized, is that it is not so easy to change the ages-old system of inadequate education, poor and slanted textbooks, preoccupied professors, and irrelevant curriculum. The most essential task is to develop some method of inter-communication between all these new programs, course structures, and curriculum development. As it is now, nobody knows what everybody else is doing, or learning, or experiencing.

The students, sensing this condition, usually organize more conferences, meetings, seminars. It does not help. Someone has got to sit down and work, utilizing the maximum of his abilities to think about it, prepare proposals, make experiences available, and stimulate concrete discussion instead of slogan-shouting. Who will do it, that is the question! Here and there, academicians and teachers are working in this direction. Largely, they are working alone, without funds — because funds are going to the loudest shouters, the noise-makers. There is little or no recognition of scholarship, thought, the desire to effect permanent change.

These are the practical problems organizationally. There are other problems: such as the improvement in the courses being offered in Native American Studies departments, the development of a whole body of new literature, the training of superior instructors, the development of innovative, creative courses of study utilizing the whole body of oral literature and knowledge of the Indian people themselves. Of particular interest is the growth of schools such as the new junior college in Navajo country, and the Rough Rock demonstration school in Arizona, also by Navajo people. The experiences of these two institutions will be valuable to the educational community as a whole, and the Native American Studies departments in particular.

Bibliography

The bibliography presented here is intended as a mere sampling of the vast literature. Titles do not indicate that other materials of equal importance should not be used. The choices, however, do represent the direction taken by the editors of this Study. It should be stated that while the literature is indeed monumental, an equal amount of work must be done to provide materials for the use of the teachers and for classroom instruction. It is not possible at this time to list approved textbooks for classroom use. There are none to our knowledge which we could recommend without the most serious of reservations. Some children's books exist that could be utilized, but these are so few that a listing would be meager. What is presented here is a bibliography including books that can be used by the teacher, the interested scholar, the upper grade student, or the individual, as preparation for the development of an understanding of the American Indian in the culture and history of this nation.

BASIC SOURCES

FREDERICK WEBB HODGE, Ed.   Handbook of Indians North of Mexico, Bulletin 30, Bureau of American Ethnology, Smithsonian Institution, Washington, D.C. It appeared in 1907 in two volumes. Arranged alphabetically by subject, it is a marvel of condensation. For its time, it was very nearly exhaustive; while it did not go into extensive detail, its articles and notes are concise and clear. References to primary source materials are one of its principal advantages. Scholarship and scientific research has traveled a long way since 1907, and this must be remembered. A new edition of this work is under preparation by the staff of Smithsonian Institution. It will be years before it is ready.

JOHN SWANTON. Indian Tribes of North America. Bulletin 145, Bureau of American Ethnology, Smithsonian Institution, Washington, D.C., 1952. Includes the aborigines of Mexico and South to Central America and the West Indies.

FELIX COHEN. Handbook of Federal Indian Law, published by the U.S. Printing Office, Washington, D.C., 1945. A reprint is now available. Extremely important source book on Indian-Federal relationships. Contains discussion of developmental process of treaty-making, Indian land ownership, cases in litigation and court decisions, and a comprehensive bibliography on the subject.

CHARLES J. KAPPLER. Laws and Treaties. Volume 2 (Treaties). U.S. Govt. Printing Office, Washington, D.C., 1904. Kappler was clerk to the Senate Committee on Indian Affairs when he compiled and edited this work. Available in libraries. Beginning with the first treaty with the Delawares in 1778, contains all the treaties and agreements with the Indian tribes, verbatim.

GENERAL AND CURRENT

The above four works are a very small part of the literature which can be drawn upon as sources, and as learning materials. Below are recommended works in general history, archaeology and anthropology, and works on modern affairs.

HAROLD E. DRIVER. Indians of North America, University of Chicago Press, 1961. Recently reprinted with revisions bringing the book up to date. Such subjects as horticulture, subsistence, techniques, education, language, achievements and contributions. An important subject-classification book.

EDWARD H. SPICER. A Short History of Indians of the United States. Van Nostrand Reinhold Co., 1967. Printed in paper back edition, 1969. Chronological handling of American Indian history, up to modern times, Valuable objective treatment.

PAUL S. MARTIN, GEORGE I. QUIMBY, DONALD COLLIER. Indians Before Columbus (Twenty Thousand Years of North American History Revealed by Archaeology). The University of Chicago Press, 1947. Written for laymen and students. Gives a good overview of archaeological findings up to the date of publication. Deals with arts and industries, early arrivals, and various sections of the country as developed by early man. Valuable for archaeological survey and general information in this field.

ROGER G. OWEN, JAMES J. F. DEETZ, ANTHONY D. FISHER. The North American Indians, a Sourcebook. The Macmillan Co., 1967. Written for college and university courses. Contains articles now out of print or hard to obtain. Articles by Wissler, Willey, Hoijer, Swadesh, Underhill, Eggan and Kluckhohn, to name a few. Treatment by areas as well as important introduction.

HAROLD E. FEY AND D'ARCY McNICKLE. Indians and Other Americans. (Two Ways of Life Meet.) Harper & Bros., 1959. A brief history of Indians in the grip of contact with the white society, including social and economic conflict as well as the struggle in litigation and through Congress. Necessary for an understanding of the current situation.

WILLIAM BRANDON. American Heritage Book of Indians. Dell Paperback, 1961 reprint. Good overview of the native Americans. Well written, can be used in high school classes.

EDWARD H. SPICER. Cycles of Conquest. University of Arizona Press, 1962. The impact of Spain, Mexico, and the United States on the Indians of the Southwest, 1533-1960. A scholarly treatment and very readable.

GEORGE CATLIN. Illustrations of Manners, Customs and Conditions of the North American Indians, 2 vols. New York, 1841. An excellent, classic description of the Indian people and tribes met by Catlin in a journey across the United States. His paintings and drawings are of great historical interest, depicting authentic attire and general appearance of various Indian personages, tribes, customs, and domiciles.

PETER FARB. Man's Rise to Civilization as Shown by the Indians of North America. Dutton & Co., 1968. A great deal of information laced with opinion squeezed into a relatively small book for such a subject. Lacks the depth of scholarship which must be expected in such a work, but is a good introduction.

CARL ORTWIN SAUER. Land and Life. A selection from the writings of a distinguished scholar. University of California Press, 1965. Geography and anthropology meet in the works of this eminent author. Without an understanding of the Native's relationship to the land, there is little possibility for understanding the history of the white-Indian contact and conflict. Of special importance are the two articles in this collection: "American Agricultural Origins," and "Plant and Animal Destruction in Economic History." Dr. Sauer is a highly provocative scholar.

WILCOMB E. WASHBURN. The Indian and the White Man. Doubleday & Co., paperback edition, 1964. While this book should have been titled The White Man and the Indian, it is a useful source of information as to what the white men thought the Indian thought, and what in turn they believed of him. This is a collection of articles, excerpts, and descriptions from the Europeans and New Englanders, as well as such men as Benjamin Franklin who stated their thoughts about the Indian "problem." Fiction too is included, and this allows a good overall view of the literature as it developed on the subject of the American Indian at certain points in the history of the nation.

LESLEY BYRD SIMPSON. The Encomienda in New Spain. University of California Publications in History, vol. 29. University of California Press, 1929. Deals with forced Native labor in the Spanish colonies. 1492-155.

CLINTON R. EDWARDS. Aboriginal Watercraft on the Pacific Coast of South America. Ibero-Americana: 47. University of California Press, 1965. A very important and scholarly investigation into the subject, which opens up many new areas for further investigation. Of particular interest is this author's statement on page 115, that "... we cannot dogmatically restrict our most ancient travelers between continents to shank's mare."

D'ARCY McNICKLE. The Indian Tribes of the United States. Ethnic and Cultural Survival. Oxford University Press, 1962. Important for an understanding of action and reaction in white-Indian relations.

STAN STEINER. The New Indians. Harper & Row, 1968. Approach is from the Indian point of view. Deals with the new movement among young Indian people who are demanding speedy action in finding solutions to the Indian situation, and demanding leadership. Considerable information of value for an understanding of the Indian in the world of today.

HELEN HUNT JACKSON. A Century of Dishonor. (A Sketch of the United States Government's Dealings with Some of the Indian Tribes.) Roberts Bros., 1887, now reprinted in paperback. This extremely popular and explosive work did much to awaken the nation to the conditions of the tribes at that time. This work is a classic and ought not to be forgotten. Mrs. Jackson told it "the way it was."

HAROLD E. DRIVER, WILHELMINE DRIVER. Indian Farmers of North America. Rand McNally & Co., 1967. An excellent description of Indian food uses, farming and plants. This small book (64 pages) is available as a classroom resource book.

EDITH VAN ALLEN MURPHEY. Indian Uses of Native Plants. Mendocino County Historical Society, 1959. While this study is largely confined to plants of the west and part of the southwest, it provides considerable information as to the uses of food and medicinal plants.

GEORGE E. SIMPSON & MILTON YINGER, Editors. The American Indian and American Life. Compilation of articles by McNickle, Haas, Underhill, Havighurst, Dozier, and Adair, among others. Articles include background, administration of Indian affairs, institutional aspects of contemporary Indian life, and integration. Published in the Annals of the American Academy of Political and Social Science, May, 1957.

PAUL RADIN. Primitive Man as Philosopher. Dover Publications, 1957. Well known work by a distinguished scholar. Reprint.

ARCHER E. HULBERT. Indian Thoroughfares (Volume 2 of 16 vols.). Arthur H. Clark, 1902. Indian paths and trails.

ALLAN A. MACFARLAN. Book of American Indian Games. Association Press, 1958.

VIRGIL J. VOGEL. The Indian in American History. Integrated Education Associates, Chicago, 1968. Brief summary of the subject, contains bibliography by subject.

REGIONAL, TRIBAL

Of particular interest in revealing certain aspects of Indian culture and history are these regional and tribal works in history and anthropology. They touch upon cultures which are peculiar to the region or tribe; but applicability is found and understanding better developed by comparison with other Indian cultures. No attempt is made to offer a comprehensive bibliography in this sphere, either. Only a small sampling is given to show the variety of works available.

DAVID PRESCOTT BARROWS. The Ethno-Botany of the Coahuilla Indians of Southern California. Published as dissertation, out of print. Now reprinted by the Malki Museum, Banning, Ca. This book is a classic in ethnography and gives an excellent explanation of the material culture, uses of native foods and plants, by one group of Indians in one area of the country.

EDWARD P. DOZIER. Hano, a Tewa Indian Community in Arizona. Holt, Rinehart & Winston, 1966. Part of a series of case studies in anthropology. Written by one who knows the language, is one of the people, and is a distinguished scholar in his own right. The traditional history, society, religion, and contact with the white society.

S. F. COOK. The Conflict Between the California Indian and White Civilization. Ibero-Americana, 1943. University of California Press. An important contribution to Indian-white relationships, containing information, data, and specific examples. This work is in four volumes of Ibero-Americana (21-24) : The Indians and the Spanish Mission; The Physical and Demographic Reaction of the Non-Mission Indians in Colonial and Provincial California; The American Invasion, including military casualities, social homicide, disease, food and nutrition, labor, sex and family relations; and Trends in Marriage and Divorce in 1850.

WILLIAM DUNCAN STRONG. Aboriginal Society in Southern California. University of California Publications in American Archaeology and Ethnology, 1929. This classic is available now only in libraries.

A. L. KROEBER. Handbook of California Indians. Bureau of American Ethnology #78, Smithsonian Institution, Washington, D.C., 1925. Divided into sixty chapters, a comprehensive work about the Indians of the California region. Includes numerous maps showing past and present (1925) locations of various tribes, linguistic groupings, and ritual cults. There are also 17 tables of cultural traits, religious elements and material culture. Re-issued by photo-offset process by California Book Company, Berkeley, Ca.

ANGIE DEBO. Rise and Fall of the Choctaw Republic, University of Oklahoma Press, 1934. An excellent source book of Choctaw history.

JOHN W. DEFOREST. History of the Indians of Connecticut. First published in 1851, it has now been reprinted (1964) by Archon Books. An extremely interesting work on the Indians of northeastern America.

GRANT FOREMAN. Indian Removal. University of Oklahoma Press, 1932, reprinted 1953. Description and documented information concerning the removal of the Five Civilized Tribes from the southeast.

ALVIN JOSEPHY, JR. The Nez Perce Indians and Opening of the Northwest. Yale University Press, 1968. An exhaustive treatment of this tribe and its conflict with white civilization.

PHILIP DRUCKER & ROBERT F. HEIZER. To Make My Name Good. University of California Press, 1967. A re-examination of the Southern Kwakiutl Potlatch.

LEWIS HENRY MORGAN. League of the Iroquois. Corinth Books, 1962 reprint. Introduction by William N. Fenton. An attorney and politician turned ethnologist, Morgan was the first to develop a comprehensive description of a tribe's kinship system. Having given the world its "first scientific account of an Indian tribe," as Major Powell stated, Morgan continued his work until his death. We know much more now than we did then, but the work of Morgan remains of first consequence and important enough to have as part of any library on the American Indian.

EDGAR S. CAHN, Editor. Our Brother's Keeper: The American Indian in White America. Citizens' Advocate Center. World Publishing Co., New York, 1969. A critique of the Native American situation, relationship with the federal government and its various agencies and the failures of both.

ALFONSO ORTIZ. The Tewa World: Space, Time, Being and Becoming in a Pueblo Society. University of Chicago Press, 1969, 197 pages. Newly published at the time of this printing, Doctor Ortiz is already well known as a distinguished scholar in anthropology.

WILLIAM PERKINS' JOURNAL OF LIFE AT SONORA, 1849-1852. University of California Press, 1964. An account of the days of the Gold Rush, with information concerning treatment and condition of the Indians during those days of attempted genocide.

VINE DELORIA, JR. Custer Died for Your Sins, An Indian Mansifesto. The Macmillan Co., 1969. A moving and often humorous recital of the Native American situation today, from the inside. Mr. Deloria is an Indian, a leader in his own right, one who has had an opportunity to see and experience such phenomena as the onslaught of the anthropologists upon Indian country, the usurpation of Indian initiative and leadership by well-meaning missionaries, federal officials and nonIndian enthusiasts. With a rare talent for writing, Mr. Deloria has expressed the views of many Indian people, and has done it well.

JACK D. FORBES. Native Americans of California and Nevada. Naturegraph Publications, 1969. Written by the author following many conferences and participation in the organization of the California Indian Education Association. A valuable source book for teachers.

ARTS & LITERATURE

The arts and literature of the American Indian must be studied and understood if any deep appreciation of the Native contribution to society in America and the world at large is to be developed. Some of the most subtle nuances of the culture and personality of Indian peoples is to be learned from this source, and a true feeling of Indian life may be acquired from these materials. Here again, is a mere sampling of the literature.

N. SCOTT MOMADAY. House Made of Dawn. Fiction. Harper & Row, 1968. This book was a Pulitzer prize winner in 1969. It is a beautiful book.

— The Way to Rainy Mountain. University of New Mexico Press, 1969. It is said that this Indian author and professor of comparative English literature at University of California has the true gift of the epic in literature.

JOHN STANDS IN TIMBER. Cheyenne Memories. Yale University Press, 1967. An autobiography of an Honored Indian Historian (elected member by the American Indian Historical Society). This book is filled with stories and accurate information about the Northern Cheyenne, and is truly a joy to read. The work was done with Margot Liberty, assisted by Robert M. Utley, but to John Stands in Timber himself belongs the credit for collecting, recording, and making available the wealth of information contained in this book.

EMERSON BLACKHORSE MITCHELL. Miracle Hill, the Story of a Navaho Boy, University of Oklahoma Press, 1967. This book was written by a Navaho boy, with the help of his teacher, Mrs. T. D. Allen, who has most felicitously left the original manuscript untouched. It is a revealing and touching story of a young Navaho and his life in two worlds—his own, and that of western European culture.

NATALIE CURTIS. The Indians Book. Dover Publications, 1969. This old-time classic has been out of print for many years. Now reprinted by Dover in paperback, it can at last be made available in classrooms and for interested individuals and teachers. A source book of Indian music, songs, and related history.

JOHN ADAIR. Navajo and Pueblo Silversmiths. University of Oklahoma Press, 1944. Very good treatment of an ancient art.

DOROTHY DUNN. American Indian Painting of the Southwest and Plains Areas. The University of New Mexico Press, Albuquerque, 1969. Beautifully illustrated, this is the first comprehensive treatment of the subject, written by a former teacher at the Institute of American Indian Arts, Santa Fe.

DAREN DANIELS PETERSEN. Howling Wolf, A Cheyenne Warrior's Graphic Interpretation of His People. American West Publishing Co., 1968. Illustrations are from original drawings of Cheyenne prisoner of war. One of the truly beautiful books, the introduction by John C. Ewers is particularly valuable, "The History and Development of an American Art Form."

LOUIS W. BALLARD, The Gods Will Hear. A choral cantata for soloists, mixed chorus, piano and percussion. Bourne Co., 136 W. 52 St., New York. Music departments in junior high school, high school, college and junior college will find this extremely valuable for an understanding of Native American contemporary music. Should be utilized in courses such as choral music and sight-singing.

CAMPBELL GRANT. The Rock Paintings of the Chumash. (A Study of a California Indian Culture.) University of California Press, 1965. One of the most highly developed cultures of the Indian west, the Chumash people left rock paintings of superb beauty, many of which illustrate this book. Introduction by Robert F. Heiser is interesting. Valuable as source material and for teacher preparation.

BIBLIOGRAPHIES

A short listing of the bibliographies, which are as much a part of the literature as the materials listed above, include these:

FREDERICK J. DOCKSTADER. The American Indian in Graduate Studies. Museum of the American Indian publications, New York, 1957 (Heye Foundation). This scholarly work is necessary, both for the researcher and the serious student.

WILLIAM C. STURTEVANT. Bibliography on American Indian Medicine and Health. Smithsonian Institution, 1962.

GEORGE P. MURDOCK. Ethnographic Bibliography of North America. Human Relations Area File, New Haven, 1953.

BREWTON BERRY. The Education of American Indians. (A Survey of the Literature.) Research Foundation, The Ohio State University, Columbus, Ohio, 1968. Reprinted for the Special Subcommittee on Indian Education of the Committee on Labor and Public Welfare, United States Senate, U.S. Government Printing Office, 1969. An exhaustive and extremely valuable survey of the literature on Indian education, the best done on this subject to date.

DORIS OSTRANDER DAWDY, Annotated Bibliography of American Indian Painting. Museum of the American Indian, Heye Foundation, 1968, 27 pp.

Index